The Possibilities of Order

The Possibilities of Order: *Cleanth Brooks and His Work*

Edited by LEWIS P. SIMPSON

Louisiana State University Press
BATON ROUGE

ISBN 0–8071–0165–6
Library of Congress Catalog Card Number 75–18046
Copyright © 1976 by Louisiana State University Press
All rights reserved
Manufactured in the United States of America

René Wellek, "Cleanth Brooks, Critic of Critics,"
first appeared in the *Southern Review*, n.s., X
(Winter, 1974), 125–52.

Published with the assistance of the Council
on Research, Louisiana State University.

For the students of Cleanth Brooks

disorders . . . eloquent of the possibilities of order

—Cleanth Brooks,
William Faulkner: The Yoknapatawpha Country

Contents

Acknowledgments

THE EDITOR of this volume wishes to express his deep gratitude to its contributors not only for their individual offerings but for their patient and cooperative help during the process of preparation and publication. I am also indebted to Charles E. East, immediate past director of the Louisiana State University Press, and to Leslie E. Phillabaum, the present director, for their encouragement and advice; and for the same reason to Louis D. Rubin, Jr., man of many good works in the field of southern literature and of American literature generally. I am additionally obligated to Marie Carmichael, an editor of the LSU Press, for her indispensable labor in getting the manuscript ready for the printer. Indeed, I am obligated to all the members of the LSU Press staff for their very considerable aid.

This book, it will be noted, is dedicated to the students of Cleanth Brooks. The gesture is not limited to those who may have sat in one of his classes or seminars. It embraces all those who have responded—in agreement or disagreement—to his effort to represent the community of free and responsible critical discourse in the twentieth century.

L. P. S.

Introduction

SOME time ago I approached Robert Penn Warren with the idea of a collaborative endeavor which not only would constitute a recognition of the career of Cleanth Brooks as a man of letters but would also afford an examination of important facets of his work by some contemporaries familiar with Brooks and responsive to both the man and his writings. Warren replied that he lacked the detachment to write either a memoir or a critical essay dealing with his friend and literary partner. Instead, he proposed to conduct an "interview" with him. As our discussion developed I surmised that what Warren really hoped to do was to put on the record a wide-ranging literary conversation with Brooks, one touching on issues of mutual interest to them and offering a commentary on the twentieth-century American literary enterprise as he and Brooks have participated in it. I surmised also that Warren hoped, although perhaps not with an altogether conscious intention, to establish an emblem of a remarkable—and in American and modern letters generally, a singular—literary association. I encouraged him to make the interview as long as he and Brooks had the inclination and time to pursue it. The result would seem to fulfill what I divined of Warren's intentions; and it is herein put on the record both as document and symbol, its purpose and character granting us the dramatic license to present it as one long conversation, although it obviously did not take place at a single session.

If space permitted, it would be appropriate to survey in detail the history of the literary collaboration of Brooks and Warren— to discuss its fruits and at the same time to indicate its significant circumscription by the unqualified independence of each mind. This independence has always asserted itself; it is, to be sure, as the conversation reveals, a chief element in the collaboration. What underlies the power of such a text as *Understanding Poetry* is not a sweet unity of doctrine but the tension of agreement based on the reconciliation of often opposing ideas and emotions about poetry. This is why such works as *Understanding Poetry, An Approach to Literature* (first published in 1936 and made available in 1975 by Prentice-Hall in still another edition), *Understanding Fiction*, and *Modern Rhetoric*, far from being expendable classroom texts (nothing being more expendable than the average literary text), are books that not only have affected the quality of American literary life in this century but have enhanced the literary quality of American life. But it may well be that any attempt to detail the common literary work of Brooks and Warren would be superfluous in the luminous light of the conversation, which so completely calls our attention to a relationship that is fundamental to the career of each writer (but not more than fundamental, being not more than a solid aspect of the life and work of each). The essays that follow the conversation, varied in intention and character, frequently refer to subjects in the conversation. In them the reader notes resemblances, disagreements, and possibly some contradictions with respect to Brooks. The essays by Allen Tate and Robert B. Heilman, if largely accounts of two friendships besides Warren's that bear specifically on Brooks's career as writer and teacher, suggest interpretations of Brooks both as a person and as a critic. The third essay, by Father Walter J. Ong, focuses on an interpretation of a major issue in Brooks's work, the New Criticism. Taking a broad approach to the import of the New Criticism in terms of Western literary and cultural history, Father Ong's essay, in describing a crucial difference between the New Criticism and the rhetorical tradition, leads us back to parts of the conversation and forward to the remaining essays: Thomas D. Young's on the critical theories of John Crowe Ransom and Brooks, René Wellek's on Brooks as a critic of critics, and Monroe K. Spears's on Brooks's conception of the responsibilities of the literary critic. All deal in one way or another with Brooks and the New Criticism but at the same time elaborate the complex variety of his critical motives and interests.

Just such an elaboration is the intention of this book. The aim is to suggest that in the range and depth, not to mention the bulk, of his work, Brooks has his province among the major American critics of his time. In his role of the American man of letters as critic, his achievement is comparable to that of Van Wyck Brooks, Edmund Wilson, Malcolm Cowley, or Lionel Trilling—or, if we think of them in their role as critics, of John Crowe Ransom, Robert Penn Warren, Allen Tate, or Donald Davidson. In the perspective of literary history, it will be seen that (with the possible exception of Donald Davidson, a special case) all of these critics, like the expatriate editor of the cosmopolitan *Criterion*, T. S. Eliot, can be said to have identified their work with the Western polity of letters and to have expressed an allegiance, if not always overtly, to the literary vocation handed down in the tradition of the "clerks." W. H. Auden once remarked that "every European poet . . . still instinctively thinks of himself as a 'clerk,' a member of a professional brotherhood, with a certain social status irrespective of the

number of his readers . . . [and assumes] his place in an
unbroken historical succession." In America, Auden observed,
the situation is different. Here poets "have never had or im-
agined they had such a status, and it is up to each individual
poet to justify his existence by offering a unique product." Yet,
however true this may be, and its truth is unquestionably de-
monstrable, the aspiration to belong to the Republic of Letters
has never been lost in America. If this aspiration found a false
and sterile fulfillment in the "genteel tradition," the rejection of
this falsity by twentieth-century American men of letters was
not merely owing to the passion for a national literature.

After the First World War the whole of American literary,
artistic, and intellectual life became more self-consciously and
more genuinely cosmopolitan than it had been at any time since
the eighteenth century, and, paradoxically, nowhere did this
happen with more intensity than in a small group of writers in
the South. Because they lived in a culture that carried within
it the living memory of a world put to the sword, they experi-
enced the mortality of Western civilization, which was so terri-
bly and convincingly evinced by the First World War, in the
ambience of something approaching a world historical vision.
They had a vision of what it means to lose a world order, a
civilizational community (in contrast, we might say, to the more
narrowly focused, though highly poignant, vision of a Heming-
way, with its emphasis on the existential individual who must
behave well in the general chaos by disciplining himself not to
think about it). I refer of course to the Vanderbilt group of the
1920s. After combining for a time in a small community of poets
known as the Fugitives, they unexpectedly in another combina-
tion became a southern clerisy and—albeit with a zeal that was
never truly consolidated into a cohesive commitment—set out
to do something about the state of civilization both in the South
and in the nation. Their most notable venture, the publication in

1930 of *I'll Take My Stand*, with its message that you cannot have the world and consume it too, was a renewal of the American quest for a civilized community based on an agrarian economy. Agrarianism had no political or economic success; but as a literary action, as a critique by men of letters of the failure of science, industrialism, and technology to provide a basis of community, it bore on the essential drama of Western history since the inception of the modern age—this is to say, the drama of the quest for a symbolism of community, for the restoration of a symbolism of order, in the wake of the lapse of Christendom. The Agrarian movement, in brief, established a large context, a historical rationale, for the critical mind to work in. It fostered the growth of the modern literary intelligence in the South and made welcome the figure of the literary intellectual or man of letters. It was the inspiriting environment of Cleanth Brooks's development. Thus, although Brooks did not participate in the making of *I'll Take My Stand* (being slightly younger than Warren and several years younger than Tate) and although he had come to Vanderbilt too late to enter fully the company of the Agrarians, the self-conscious, highly literate Vanderbilt clerisy was an integral influence on Brooks, and he in effect became a member of this circle by the time he graduated in 1928 and went on to spend three years at Oxford as a Rhodes Scholar.

How much Brooks was influenced by the Vanderbilt writers was to be revealed in various ways during the decade of the 1930s, though not fully until 1939 when he published *Modern Poetry and the Tradition*. These essays in literary and cultural definition immediately placed Brooks as an important post-Agrarian critic. His was a literary mind which had developed out of the Agrarian context. He would pursue the literary implications of the movement without being burdened by an authorial identification with *I'll Take My Stand*, a burden only Donald Davidson willingly carried after the Agrarian moment. Although the underlying motive of *Modern Poetry and the Tradition* is not easily discernible, it emerges finally out of Brooks's thesis (to some degree, as Brooks says, adapted from I. A. Richards) of a "poetry of exclusion" and a "poetry of inclusion." And it is nothing less than the quest for civilizational community. In a poetry of exclusion, as in that of the Victorian age, Brooks states, an effort is made to minimize or reject the forms and subjects of the past in favor of novel patterns and, supposedly, new subjects of the present. In a poetry of inclusion, as embodied in the work of John Donne, its great exemplification, and other metaphysical poets of the seventeenth century, the controlling center is a synthesis, a community, of past and present, achieved not through a departure from but through a reinvigoration of the poetic tradition. Such a renewal of the tradition is available to modern poets writing in the English language. But American poets have tended to conceive that they have no choice between the "raw, unqualified present" and the "dead past." They have no choice because they think they have none; they "have broken with history," and this leaves them bereft of imagination. "Indeed," Brooks says, "every past is dead which is unconnected with the present—the past of the literary vacuum. Conversely, a present which is nothing but the immediate present of sensation—the present unrelated to history—is not even the present. It is apt to be merely a collection of sensations, or at best, unrelated images." Brooks finds particularly important for modern American poetry the rediscovery of the school of Donne, not only by the expatriate Eliot but by the Nashville poets, Ransom, Warren, and Tate. These southern poets are models of the necessity of "sincerity and integrity" in the attempt to "hold onto a tradition"—a southern tradition—through the "technique of inclusion." Neither sentimentalists nor local colorists (limited to "objective descriptions of the local color of the present"), they know that they "must of necessity mediate" their accounts of "the Old South through a consciousness of the present"; and yet, knowing this, they are aware that "the Old South cannot exist in the mind of the modern Southerner apart from its nonexistence in the present." They possess an honest, ironic sense of history, realizing that "modern man has a tremendous historical consciousness" but that this is being frustrated by his compulsion to scientific naturalism, which cuts him off from a living connection with the past. But, although the southern poets are discovered by Brooks to have the ironical sense of past and present and to have experienced the need for a transcendent myth—for a symbolism of order in history or an encompassing story of the community of man in history—he does not find this need fulfilled in them. His example of the need fulfilled is Yeats, and he explicates Yeats's *A Vision* at considerable length in *Modern Poetry and the Tradition*. Brooks's reading of *A Vision* (no doubt the most sympathetic and convincing given by an American critic up to that time) leads him to conclude that, although Yeats's myth is "not scientifically true"—it is a "fiction . . . a symbolical representation" which "intermeshes with reality"—it is "imaginatively true," a "world-view or a philosophy having for its object imaginative contemplation."

In *Modern Poetry and the Tradition*, Brooks established what I consider to be the central theme of his criticism over the years: the contemplation of the drama of the quest, among the disorders of history, for the true order of the human community; as this quest reveals itself, that is, in works of the literary imagination. He has constantly kept the works of Yeats before him as an exemplary text for contemplation. He has had before him as well the writings of Eliot and Auden and, more than we might suppose, of James Joyce. Always too he has had those of his southern colleagues. But above all others for the past twenty years or so he has had in his vision the work of a southerner who, scornful of the Vanderbilt clerisy, living in self-imposed isolation from the literary life about him in the South or elsewhere, created the largest and most complex world in American fiction to date—Yoknapatawpha County. It is the "sole owner and proprietor" of this mythical dominion to whose achievement Brooks has devoted his most sustained and thorough attention, an attention which became imperative once Brooks comprehended that in William Faulkner the "nonexistence of the Old South" stands existent, that, in fact, the whole South stands existent in Yoknapatawpha County—transfigured by the truth of the imagination of the literary artist and open, like the world of Yeats, to the imaginative contemplation of the skilled and patient reader. In *William Faulkner: The Yoknapatawpha Country*, Brooks comments:

> Taken together, the Yoknapatawpha novels and stories create for us an amazingly rich and intricate world, and one that embodies its own principles of order. The human society there depicted shows the influence of the physical land and the climate. Even the town dwellers of Jefferson have not broken their ties with the land. Moreover, the society of Jefferson and Yoknapatawpha has its location in time as well as space. It bears a special and significant relation to history. It has a sort of collective memory. Because it does, it can see itself in a dramatic role. It embodies a style of life. Most of all, this society is bound together by unspoken assumptions—that is to say, it is a true community. Its members are related to each other not merely by function but by common loves, hates, and fears. The fact that it is provincial does not prevent its serving as an excellent mirror of the perennial triumphs and defeats of the human spirit. Nor does that fact insulate it from the great world outside. The special problems of modern man, on occasion, make their appearance within it, and their modernity is more sharply defined by being set against the concrete particularity of its old-fashioned order.

Far from being antihistorical, as has been said, Brooks's criticism in its full scope is an expression of a deep conviction of our existence in history. Because of this conviction, Brooks is always aware of how the secularity of modern history threatens to blind us to the condition of our life on earth. He feels the tension between form and the formless subjectivity of modern consciousness, which has resulted from the Cartesian transference of man and nature into the mind, and the tension which has resulted from, it is hardly too much to say, the internalization of history.

The secularizing of history, it appears, resulted not from the objectification of consciousness through the scientific emphasis on the materiality of existence, but from the subjectivization of consciousness that occurred in the effort to apprehend the nature of things, once it was discovered that the senses are not reliable guides for the mind. The Cartesian internalization of reality in the activities of the mind has meant a slow erosion of the sense of great deeds and great words in the drama of human community. As the internalization of history has proceeded, the mind—thought and consciousness—has begun to assume its historicity, rendering the mythic mode, and thus the religious mode, of transcending history antiquarian and the philosophical mode of transcending history (the "life of reason" as set forth in Plato and Aristotle) obsolescent. In a world divested of custom and tradition by the historicity of consciousness, not only the myths of heroes and the mighty deeds embodied in epics, but the simple drama—the rituals and ceremonials of the days and seasons which make the community actual and present to us—seem less and less relevant to any discernible reality; for, as Hannah Arendt strikingly argues, the sole action, the entire actuality, may become what goes on in the processes of the mind. The poet, however, mediates meaning through form, form which is both the object and the consequence of contemplation. To restore order, the contemplative sense of the literary craftsman must be restored. The hands and tongue of the literary artist fashion or make poems—stories or dramas. But the power of metaphor—the power to fashion, to make—derives from the capacity to wonder, to let the busy hands drop while the vision is directed to the contemplation of man's history in the nature of things. This is a history man cannot know, save through his symbolizing of the community he struggles to make in the midst of the mystery. Form and structure in the literary work, its dramatistic quality, reflect the structuring of community, which is the imperative of history. Whether or not we look at the criticism of Brooks in quite such an austere way, we are aware that he constantly reminds us that we must keep the storytelling going, since the storyteller, the poet, is the first to envision the struggle of man to realize his nature in community, the first to know man both as subject and object, the first to experience the deliberate detachment that comes with the responsibility of telling what has happened so that it will be remembered. The storyteller is after all the scribe, the keeper of the scroll. If he is absorbed by what Hannah Arendt calls the "process character" of the modern effort to understand and to dominate nature and man, the mystery of history will not disappear but the awareness of it may. The poet may depart from us. In reminding us of this stark possibility, Brooks recalls to us too—especially because he has not attempted to combine the roles—that the poet and critic are not disparate figures. They are both aspects of the maker and of the making of literature. Criticism may be in a sense no more than a way of describing the techniques of telling a story, but criticism may be conceived, and has been in Western civilization, as a poetics and, in its own way, as an integral part of the telling of the story.

If he is quite wary, and it must be observed that he is, of any attempt to portray the critic as the keeper of the scroll (or, for that matter, to portray the storyteller as the author of the human community); and if he is consistently fearful of the modern literary ego and its inclination to assume a religious aura—if he never wishes to attribute to the man of letters, either as critic or storyteller, a priestly character or to confer on the writer any special degree of status or authority—still Brooks writes with the authority of one who has had a vital experience of the possibilities of order which open up to the contemplative critic. In its deeper meaning, the body of criticism that Cleanth Brooks has created (and continues to create as he writes, among other things, a second volume on Faulkner) is a response to literature as the most effective mediation between the modern historicity of consciousness and the transcendent mystery of consciousness, which remains forever a mystery, despite all the power and control man assumes he has acquired by his transference of himself and the world into the processes of mind. The openness of the soul to the mystery is, as Brooks indicates over and over, not ultimately to be sustained by poetry. But literature affords a knowledge, a kind of special knowledge, as he says, which helps to keep open the possibility of the transcendent knowledge of order and meaning that belongs to religion.

Brooks's devotion to literary criticism is not directed toward getting anyone to experience religious faith. His intention is to understand poetry, approaching it both through the forms it has assumed in its long experience as the integral expression of the drama of human community and through an investigation both of its depletion in modernity and the chances of its restoration. In sum, Brooks holds that the storyteller is the keeper of the mystery of history but not inherent in the mystery. The story he makes is apposite to the mystery, and the critic may make a useful interpretation of the character of the apposition. But, within the frame of our temporal quest for community, the poet has the last word. The vision of the story is fundamentally his, and beyond all doubting Brooks will give the privilege of saying

the last word to the poet. He might well give it to his friend
Robert Penn Warren in his role as poet:

Tell me a story.

In this century, and moment of mania,
Tell me a story.

Make it a story of great distances, and starlight.

The name of the story will be Time,
But you must not pronounce its name.

Tell me a story of deep delight.

The Possibilities of Order

Robert Penn Warren   # A Conversation
with Cleanth Brooks

MY FIRST *conversation with Cleanth
Brooks occurred when we were both students at Vanderbilt University
in the winter of 1924–1925, and numberless others, at many different
times and in many different places, have delighted and instructed me
over the subsequent years. In that half century, Cleanth Brooks has
been one of the few people to whom I have turned with the scribbled first
version of a poem or a half-baked or half-formulated notion; in such
moments I cannot be sure what I most sought, the comfort of his
generosity of mind or the rigor of his logic. And, no doubt, he often had
to suffer the tension between his natural kindliness and a natural love of
truth. Both the comfort and the truth have been, over the years,
significant to this participant in the conversations, for, though we
share enough to provide a firm basis for friendship, there are between us
vast differences in temperament, character, and sense of the world. So
every agreement has, in the end, to be regarded in the dramatic context
of such differences, and every difference, in the context of sometimes
hard-won agreement. Now, after the half century, I have tried to
recapture for myself, and evoke for others, something of the quality of
those conversations—or of the one long conversation, for what is printed
here is the record of a conversation, not a series of formal discussions.*

1

Naturally, certain elements, the merely personal, the anecdotal, and the humorous and ironical, have been drained away. I trust, however, that there remains something of the structure of a mind, the flavor of a personality, and the weight of experience. As for method, we began with merely casual conversation. Later, I would sometimes scribble notes for topics and give them to my friend as a reminder (to me as well as to him) of what might be explored. But we still trusted most to the ranging suggestions that may arise in conversation and sought to retain the flavor of conversation. The process of editing has been mainly aimed at avoiding repetitions, purging irrelevancies, and clarifying formulations. Looking back on the series of conversations that went into the making of the long conversation printed here—and, in fact, on this note itself—I must confess that a stranger, not an old friend, might have better served as interviewer or interlocutor. Perhaps the friend may make unconscious assumptions that a stranger would probe or bring to light. It is too late, however, to change our procedure, and certainly time will take care of whatever defects result. And meanwhile I have been gratified by another "conversation."

R. P. W.

Fairfield, Connecticut
May, 1975

WHAT LITERATURE IS
AND WHAT LITERATURE DOES

WARREN: Cleanth, how early would you say your interest in literature began and what pushed you in the direction of making it your profession?

BROOKS: Well, any child who is read to is interested in literature, literally from the cradle. The first book I remember is the *Iliad*, read to me by my father—in some simple translation, I suppose—when I was about four or five years old. My early schooling did nothing much to kindle my interest, but

I can see now that my prep school years at the McTyeire School at McKenzie, Tennessee, gave me a pretty fair background to support the literary interest that developed almost at once in my freshman year at Vanderbilt. McTyeire was a little classical academy, very much like, I should think, the more famous Webb School at Bell Buckle, of which it was a kind of offshoot. The headmaster was a Webb graduate. There were no electives, no sciences, no laboratories—just four years of Latin, three of Greek, four of English, four of mathematics, one of history.

WARREN: Would you say that your boyhood training in Latin and Greek was of real relevance in turning you toward an interest in English literature?

BROOKS: Well, fairly early at Vanderbilt, I found that English literature was what I was going to be interested in. In my freshman year my instructor, a graduate student, read an interpretative essay written by Donald Davidson on one of Kipling's stories, and this opened a new world to me. It revealed that you could look inside a story and see how it was put together, and could make sensible observations about it. Davidson's account was fairly simple, but it showed me that the inner workings of a poem or a story were important. I'm sure that my prep school discipline in reading Latin and Greek—discussing the meaning of passages and parsing them—had prepared me rather directly for this new discipline of literary exploration.

WARREN: As I remember, I had the same sort of experience with John Crowe Ransom in talking about some poems when I was a freshman at Vanderbilt. The same sense of the inwardness of the poem being the meaning of the poem. That was a day of revelation.

BROOKS: Of course the thing that I got most out of Vanderbilt was to discover suddenly that literature was not a dead thing to be looked at through the glass of a museum case, but was very much alive. Walking around on the campus were people who were actually writing poems, who were talking about the making of poems, who were getting them published.

WARREN: This was dramatized for me when I was told that John Crowe Ransom, my freshman English teacher, was a poet and had published a book of poems. I bought the book, and the book of poems was about a world that I knew perfectly well, the world of backcountry Tennessee and Kentucky.

BROOKS: Was the book *Poems About God*?

WARREN: Yes, *Poems About God*. But this double connection was very important for me. On one hand, the sense of technique, the structure of a thing as related to the life of the poem, and then the life behind the poem—landscapes and people. And tied together, somehow related to each other. Was that your experience too?

BROOKS: Yes, though I think it's something a good many people never learn, including some people who teach English literature. It's very important to learn it early.

WARREN: I don't see how you can do without the two things. On one hand, the relation to the physical life, the world behind the reader of the poem. And then, the peculiar life of the poem itself. The revelation of these things seems to have come almost simultaneously for me.

BROOKS: I think that you're recapitulating precisely what happened to me at Vanderbilt. This was the great discovery, and from then on I got intensely interested in literature. This carried over to my first year of graduate work at Tulane, where I was appalled at the fact that so much of the conventional graduate study seemed to have nothing to do with the interior life of the poem. What was provided was solid stuff, and I profited from it, but the question of whether a given poem was good or bad was either waived or never asked. You consulted a book to find out whether somebody had said it was a good poem. If you couldn't find anybody who had passed judgment on it, you were at sea. You had no equipment to make an aesthetic judgment. I remember a pleasant, big, blonde girl who sometimes, when she had searched the library for some judgment on a poem, would bring it to me. If I said, "This is God-awful stuff," she would write down in her paper the academic equivalent of that. But otherwise, she didn't know, honestly didn't know. No one had ever taken the trouble to raise the question for her—how you thought about these things. Graduate training at that time didn't pay much attention to it. It was all purely historical and biographical.

WARREN: Well, the obvious question is, of course, what the poem performs for you.

BROOKS: By the time you and I met again, at Oxford in the autumn of 1929, I was very much interested in this, though I was still thrashing about. I think this was the time when you called to my attention I. A. Richards' *Principles of Literary Criticism* and his *Practical Criticism*. I started reading it at once, not liking it and yet fascinated by it, learning a great deal from it because I was on a good many points actively resisting it. I didn't like Richards' terminology. But what he was doing was nevertheless exciting and revealing.

WARREN: It was vastly exciting for me when I first read the *Principles* by Richards—one of the great events for me in my interest in poetry.

Let's jump far ahead. Let me read you a quotation in your last book—that's quite a sight ahead from 1929—in the book you call *A Shaping Joy*. I think that is a wonderful passage from Yeats that you draw the title from. Let me read that: "This joy, because it must always be making, mastering, remains in the hands and in the tongue of the artist, but with his eyes he enters upon a submissive, sorrowful contemplation of the great irremediable things. . . . That shaping joy has kept the sorrow pure, as it had kept it were the emotion love or hate, for the nobleness of the arts is in the mingling of contraries, the extremity of sorrow, the extremity of joy." It's quite a wonderful passage. Very germinal. What I was going to ask you is this: In your last book you refer to an underlying unity in your various books and essays. I presume that you're referring to your work over a long time, but principally to the essays in this volume. Let's pursue this topic with the quotation from Yeats in the background. In fact, if things work out that way, I'd like to hold this joy question in mind as the idea behind much of our conversation, no matter how much we wander from it along the way. Here is the question: the underlying unity of your own critical writing.

BROOKS: I'm glad to try to talk about that. Before I get off into that, however, let me mention one, or several, things that this Yeats passage holds for me. One, the idea that poetry is finally contemplation. It's not social engineering; it's not propaganda. You're dealing with some things that lie beyond or outside the practical world. Yeats speaks of the poet's "submissive, sorrowful contemplation of the great irremediable things." Two, the theme of detachment. The poet is terrifically involved, and yet he's standing away from his own involvement—has an impersonal view of art, to go on to what Eliot would be saying later. There's a tensional view of art too. A work of art involves oppositions which are somehow reconciled. But enough for the moment of this very brilliant, thick, massive passage. Let me go back to the underlying unity of the passage. As I look back over my first fumblings at criticism, on down to my present fumblings, I see probably one constant trait: I've been obsessed for a long time with trying to define what literature is. Because our age is dominated by science and technology, the question demands an answer. What is literature? How can you distinguish it from philosophy or religion or social essays, and so on? What are its constituent principles? Is it simply a message, a doctrine, a philosophical or historical truth, fancied up, put in some kind of pleasant or attractive or persuasive form? Or is the unity of a piece of literature more intimate that that? Do form and content really come together? If so, in what sense? Another question, a related one, is: If you can come up with a definition of literature itself and not of another thing, what then about its relation to other things? One wants to grant literature its autonomy, but one certainly doesn't want to cut it loose from the rest of the world, which in a thousand different ways it is constantly reflecting. What is the relation of literature to other things, the other things that men make and the other things that men do and think?

WARREN: You have clearly, don't you, on one hand the irremediable things, the contemplation of irremediable things, which by definition you can't do anything about. The human fate of man as animal: he dies. And other irremediable facts in individual life. Contemplation of the irremediable things is the province of religion too, isn't it?

BROOKS: Yes.

WARREN: We're dealing with the attempt to be disciplined, developed or disciplined, to make it possible to look with joy upon the irremediable things.

BROOKS: Yes.

WARREN: Now, I'm sure you're going to come to this. You've expressed it many times in your previous writing. But, if both these things are—if this is true of both religion and literature—then where's the distinction? We'll come back to that later, but they do touch on the same thing.

BROOKS: Yes, they do touch on the same thing, and for Yeats, of course, they are close to being the same thing.

WARREN: They are close to being the same thing for so many people.

BROOKS: Particularly for many contemporary artists.

WARREN: But, on the other hand, there are many remediable things that religion touches on that fall in the province of social engineering. And I think—I've been trying to say, myself—that the poem does involve a potential action. It modifies our being in some way. Our being is a seamless garment and I don't see a sharp line, but I see an important distinction. I'm not going to speak for you, however. I'm saying that remediable and irremediable things both have some overlap with religion or with social engineering. *Some* overlap. The distinction remains crucially important.

BROOKS: Yes. And my way of getting at the distinction would have to be, at least at this moment, through a metaphor. Suppose you have a society that's sick, or suppose that there are things in the society that need to be remedied. It seems to me that the prime function of literature is not that of recommending a specific remedy but of making a diagnosis. If the society is sick, the poet may well be the one who tells us the nature of the illness. He gives a useful diagnosis of the malady. Of course this act has a very real connection with remedying the situation, for a good diagnosis may facilitate finding a proper remedy. I think, however, that, when the poet or the novelist actually goes out upon the hustings to argue for a specific remedy, it is very likely that he will move out of literary art into some kind of practical rhetoric. There is another consideration too. Several different remedies can be proposed for a particular disease, and one may be more effective than another. The politician or the social engineer may prove better at remedies than the literary artist. But few are better than the artist at making the all-important diagnosis.

WARREN: Because he is concerned with what the disease "feels" like.

BROOKS: History provides certain proofs of this point. As has often been remarked, it is the sensitive literary spirit who detects something wrong, a generation or so before anyone else in the civilization does.

WARREN: You mean people like Kafka. He gives us a nightmare picture of the world we've been moving into—bureaucracy and dehumanized relationships, the sense of isolation in the relation of man in the technological bureaucratic society. Or people like Eliot. And Conrad. Or Dostoevski.

BROOKS: Or even like Edgar Allan Poe, on this side of the Atlantic, who in some sense gives us intimations of the American nightmare to come—what Henry Miller was later to call the "American air-conditioned nightmare."

WARREN: Now this is by imaginative projection, but imagination in action, isn't it? So that we feel them and feel into them. Let me ask you another question while we're on this—it stems off this—before I forget it. You're talking about the distinction between the diagnosis and the remedial action, or the action accepted as the remedial. Now you're not implying, are you, that the actual poet or novelist, say, or the dramatist, should eschew personally that world?

BROOKS: Oh, no. As a citizen he is subject to all the responsibilities that any other citizen has. It's even conceivable that the literary artist might be a person of real political genius. Here I am simply trying to make a distinction between the poet *qua* poet and the poet *qua* citizen—and to distinguish between what equips a man to be a first-rate poet and what equips him to be a first-rate political scientist or social engineer. I'm not denying that one particular individual may not have both, though I think that is rare. In any case, the artist has his duties and responsibilities as a citizen.

WARREN: We ought to be sure to get that point clarified. We are using the word *artist* or *poet* as though he might be cut off from the world of action in his physical role, his role as citizen, and all the rest.

BROOKS: No. I don't suggest that the artist hold aloof from the world of action, except in the special sense indicated in the Yeats passage we quoted before—his need for a certain kind of detachment. But the detachment does not have to be permanent. It's not a complete severance from the world of things and actions outside him.

Let me develop one subsidiary point a little further. In talking about the artist's special role with regard to the sickness of his culture, I used a metaphor in saying that his special role was that of diagnostician. Mine has all the inexactitudes of any other metaphor picked up almost casually. Let me try to get at his special role in another way. The poet, it seems to me, is constantly relating the human predicament of his time to the universal qualities of human nature through all the ages. His view of a situation, however sharp and immediate, is nevertheless always part of a long view. The great novel or drama or poem for this reason is always much more than a topical comment or a piece of propaganda for a particular cause. But I concede that there are what look like exceptions. Take the case of Jonathan Swift's *Modest Proposal*, a work that presumably reflects a very practical and immediate concern, the grinding poverty of the Irish in the early eighteenth century. Yet *A Modest Proposal* manages to touch upon issues far beyond those that prompted Swift to write it. It turns out to be such

a fine piece of satire that we treasure it as a piece of litera-
ture. Or, to put it in another way, the general issues with
which it deals so brilliantly are not all dead: human torpor,
blindness to the sufferings of others, and a self-serving
caution against inspecting too carefully what our own
well-being may be costing others continue to flourish.
Mind you, I'm not trying to prevent the writer from
whatever propaganda he feels impelled to produce. To
provide it may speak well for his capacity for moral indig-
nation.

WARREN: Is it that the passionate realization may lift mere practi-
cal protest to the level of imaginative rendering—passion
being the key?

BROOKS: Yes, but my concern here is simply to try to establish
the fact that, if a work has real literary merit, it isn't finished
off as literature by its success in achieving its political objec-
tives, or rather the converse: that its success in extirpating
the evil it means to extirpate guarantees nothing about its
success as literature. The example of *Uncle Tom's Cabin* is
pertinent here. If that book has any literary merit, and I
think it does have a modest literary merit, it has won it
through dealing with issues which in some sense are never
dead. Otherwise, the ending of black chattel slavery would
constitute the end of *Uncle Tom's Cabin*; we could simply
put it on the library shelf as a document of a past age which
has little or nothing to do with us.

WARREN: Let me nag at this question a little bit more, Cleanth. If
your house in on fire, you grab the baby or the family silver
or the fire insurance policy and get out. You don't stop to
write a poem or to knock off a little sonata on the piano.
There is a time and a place for such things. If I understand
you, you are simply asking us to keep the distinction clear,
whatever the circumstances.

BROOKS: Yes.

WARREN: We are not to confuse the nature of the act of writing a poem—even in a time of crisis.

BROOKS: That's right, Red. I think we have a very interesting instance of that from the late Marianne Moore. During the Second World War she wrote a poem which is perfectly fine in its sentiments but not really much of a poem. Now that the heat of the war is over, everybody can pretty well see it isn't. A few years ago the poet herself said as much. To paraphrase her, she wrote: "I was all worked up at the time, but as I look at it now, I can't be proud of the poem. I'm not ashamed of doing what I thought I was doing for the war effort. I thought it was a just war and we ought to throw ourselves into it. But 'In Distrust of Merits' is not much of a poem."

I'd like to nag at another aspect of this problem, one we haven't really brought out thus far. It has to do with the deleterious effects of mixing the modes. Auden has a very interesting piece in one of his essays in which he asks us to imagine a scene in a hospital. The poet is there at the bedside of a civilization which is in trouble. The patient asks the poet: "Sing me a song that tells me I'm getting well. Tell me I'm happy." The patient is actually turning blue in the face; he's desperate for someone to tell him, "You're just fine." The poet, Auden says, must resist that. The poet must not tell lies. He's got to tell the truth as he sees it. But, Auden goes on to say, if the nurse asks the poet to do something practical and useful, such as taking out a bedpan, this he should cheerfully do. It's a job within his capacity as a citizen and as a well-wisher to someone in trouble. But the poet must not allow either his human sympathy for the patient's plight or the offer of an extra ration card or the threat of harassment to make him deviate from the standard of truth or the standards of his art.

WARREN: There's always a kind of double vision involved here, isn't there? That the artist is involved in more than one way almost all the time?

BROOKS: Yes.

WARREN: And to understand this about himself maybe is the beginning of his integrity. Now, let me ask you a question here, Cleanth. Men have political passions or political theories that involve, consciously or unconsciously, two things: appeals to issues far beyond the issue involved in the problem of a remedy for a present social abuse or evil. They also bring different kinds of passion to bear on such a political or social question. Men are deeply stirred by these temporary concerns, and usually when they are stirred deeply enough, they make poetry.

BROOKS: Quite right. Provided, of course, that they are men who have the gift for creating poetry. I'm just spelling out here what was your unspoken assumption.

WARREN: How does this apply or relate to what you have been saying about this division of man as poet and man as politician or citizen, a being concerned with politics and social arrangements?

BROOKS: Well, the poet certainly writes out of his interests and passions. Even if he isn't consciously involved, there may well be hauntingly obsessive themes which usually are the residue of deep passions he once felt. Allen Tate once remarked that the subject matter of literature is constituted of concrete moral acts. I think he's right, and one could broaden his statement a little to include, as one would have to, political and social attitudes and commitments. Such are the things about which, and out of which, the literary artist writes. Nevertheless, we properly distinguish between a poem of merely topical excitement, one produced to promote some partisan course, and a poem which, whatever its local and temporal setting, reaches on toward timeless themes and universal issues.

WARREN: Let's take one as an example, now. I know a poem you admire very much and I admire it very much too. This is Marvell's poem on the return of Cromwell. What's the exact title?

BROOKS: "An Horatian Ode upon Cromwell's Return from Ireland." It is a very fine poem, though some readers see blemishes in it, places in which they believe Marvell could not rise above partisan spleen and vindictiveness. I remember a friend of yours, a fine young Irish poet, who pointed out as such an instance the line that reads, "And now the Irish are ashamed"—ashamed presumably because they had tried to thwart the purposes of this great man. Perhaps the criticism is just, but the poem is much more than an expression of an Englishman's blind hero worship. In an essay that I wrote many years ago, I attempted to point out some of the tensions within this poem, arguing that at the time he wrote the poem Marvell was still a Royalist, that he regarded Cromwell as a usurper and a dictator and yet recognized that historical necessity had hardly allowed Cromwell to act other than as he did. Marvell was genuinely stirred by Cromwell's dedication to the state and praised his great accomplishments for the state.

WARREN: At the same time, Marvell has a great tribute to Charles the First on the scaffold.

BROOKS: Right. Therefore, in trying to interpret the poem I tried—whether or not my attempt was successful is not the question here—I tried to see whether even the reference to the Irish wasn't also related to Marvell's very complicated attitude toward Cromwell. In any case, a poem that praises (though with carefully articulated reservations) a man who represents for the author a treasonous usurpation and lawless dictatorship is in its attitude very complicated indeed. The "Horatian Ode" is truly a poem characterized by a great deal of inner tension and, on the part of Marvell as commentator on the events depicted, great detachment. Thus I saw even the bold statement that "now the Irish are ashamed" as possibly representing more than an ardent Cromwell supporter's vindictive nonsense. At all events, I prefer my reading to the alternate procedure, which is to say: Well, let's find out what Marvell the man, along with a good many other Englishmen, was probably thinking at this time; and if Marvell, the typical Englishman, was vindictive toward the Irish, as he seems to be in this poem, then we'll read the poem at this level. To do this might leave us with a fine poem, but a poem with some notable blemishes in it. I can't, of course, prove that the blemishes are not there; but I think we have to read poetry with the fullest appreciation and assume that it is fully coherent and fully significant until it proves itself otherwise. If this is a variant of the ancient adage that we assume a man innocent until proved guilty, I concede as much. But I think that we must try for the richest and most complex reading of a poem. We must at least not judge against it before we attempt such a reading. In this instance, one must see whether Marvell, even in this topical poem, has not possibly transcended the local and special passions of the moment.

WARREN: Would some statement such as this be appropriate even if not as total as what you were saying—at least as another way of saying it: Marvell is trying in his "Horatian Ode" to see the tragic inner tensions of human history. Cromwell can be both admirable and wicked; a great man in certain situations can be seen as both the bulwark of public order and yet subversive of it. In fact, can't we say that the very central concept of the tragic mode springs from exactly this sort of tension?

BROOKS: Right.

WARREN: To return to Marvell's poem: Cromwell is enacting a force of history and doing it superbly; yet his antithesis, King Charles, is enacting his opposite role superbly too.

BROOKS: Yes, precisely.

WARREN: The poem ends, one remembers, with Marvell's admonition to Cromwell: "Still keep the sword erect." That is, since you are not in power as the "legitimate" king, but exercise power because you embody the force of history and depend on the mere sanctions of history—

BROOKS: And of power.

WARREN: And of power—you'd best keep your sword unsheathed, for you have appealed to the sword as the arbiter of history.

BROOKS: With an ominous little underplay, perhaps, of the biblical observation that those who live by the sword may also perish by it. Marvell's last admonition to his hero is a kind of grim reminder. If the poem is a celebration of the hero, it is also a warning to him. That is: "Remember that you do not have the divine right of kings as your sanction, but simply that of naked power. We've seen the legitimate sanction trampled upon by you."

WARREN: And Cromwell's sword takes over.

BROOKS: I would add to this illustration from Marvell an instance from more recent literature. Ernest Hemingway refuses to make villains of all the Fascists in *For Whom the Bell Tolls* or to make all the Loyalists good and decent people. In fact, one of the most brilliant episodes is his account of the Communist partisans brutally murdering the right-wing landholders of the village.

WARREN: That's right. The massacre there is a massacre of the enemy by our side—our side in quotes. Or take another instance from the same novel. Remember the nice young Fascist Francisco who, as the novel ends, comes into the gunsight of the dying Jordan's machine gun. Hemingway might have made the last person whom Jordan killed a Fascist monster, or at least some nonentity on the other side. He refuses to do that. The dying Loyalist hero will cut down the pleasant and fair-minded Francisco. It's all cross-hatched sympathies in that book.

BROOKS: And I think that probably the greatest political poems and novels will prove to be of this kind. I grant the case—I think we were mentioning it a little earlier—of an impassioned indictment, even a kind of incitement to action like Milton's great sonnet "Avenge, O Lord, thy slaughtered saints whose bones." But the real reason why we revere that fine poem is that it gets at far larger issues than the particular incident that prompted Milton to write it. The poem dramatizes what it feels like to learn of any such brutal act—genocide, for example. The modern reader can lift the poem out of its narrow local context and place it in the larger context of universal human affairs.

WARREN: Isn't there another, more general, issue involved in this sonnet of Milton's? History does not go according to justice and decency; and sometimes, in our outrage, we can appeal only to the justice of God. Or to justice, for we don't even stop to consider whether we are ourselves godless people.

BROOKS: There's another issue, too, one that relates to this general matter of tension we were talking about a little earlier. In this sonnet, we find a man who evidently believes passionately in his God. Yet, though he prays, "Avenge, O Lord," in doing so he raises the whole question of God's power and his providence over man's affairs. Why is it that God has permitted his "saints" to be slaughtered by evil men? I don't mean, of course, that

Milton was naïve, that we would have felt any great difficulty in reconciling God's omnipotence with the fact that good men often find no justice in this world. But, in his prayer, the fact that injustice flourishes is the very basis for the poem.

Considerations such as these make it plain—to me, at least—that poems and novels cannot be created as if they were newspaper reports, editorials on current events, or even philosophical essays. They have their own kind of truth and their own mode of utterance. Consequently, if we want to know what a literary work "says," we may have to go far beyond ordinary prose logic. If we are really interested in literature, not interested just in expressions of the poet's personal ideas at the moment or in reflections of a period of history, we do have to respect the mode of art, the particular way in which ideas and emotions are presented.

WARREN: Let's cut back now and perhaps come again to this topic. Everything has a history. Have you a clear idea—though it's very hard to have a clear idea about one's own history, of course—about how you came to focus on the question that led to your first book *Modern Poetry and the Tradition*?

BROOKS: Yes, I remember very vividly. I came to write the book because my new conception of poetry as alive naturally led to an interest in contemporary poetry. But I so often ran into friends with old-fashioned tastes who didn't know the new poetry and couldn't see it as poetry at all. I found myself constantly arguing with them, defending the new poetry, trying to win them to an interest in it. All of this came to a head at Oxford, where my closest friends were not reading English literature, but subjects like anthropology, mathematics, and law. Some of this talk with them was partly a talking out loud to myself, because I was secretly having my own difficulties in relating this startlingly new poetry to the poetry that I had always been taught was "good" poetry. Anyway, I conceived that book initially for one of these Oxford friends. I found it useful to write with a particular person in mind. I could assume that he was basically ignorant of many important issues. Therefore, I must try to inform him of this and explain this to him and, in general, help him discover the poetry that seemed to me so valuable.

In the meantime, however, as I worked the book out, a great many other things demanded to be included. One of them was my interest in I. A. Richards; another was my interest in John Ransom and Allen Tate and the Fugitives. Still another was my reading of the poetry and criticism of T. S. Eliot. I was particularly stimulated by two paragraphs in one of his essays on the metaphysical poets. In this brief passage, he suggested that the metaphysical poets were not to be regarded as a rather peculiar offshoot of the main course of English poetry, but that they had a deep, hidden connection with its central line of development. This, to me, new way of looking at the tradition of English poetry was another thing I tried to get into my book.

WARREN: Am I right in remembering that, somewhere along the way in that period between Oxford and the publication of *Modern Poetry and the Tradition*, you were saying that you were trying to find a common ground, at least a fruitful relationship, between what Eliot stood for and what Richards stood for, and one of your concerns in the background of that book—

BROOKS: Yes, very much so. I found much to link what Eliot was saying to what Richards seemed to me to be saying. I remember in this period also writing long letters to Allen

Tate and to John Crowe Ransom, in which I tried to ac-
commodate Richards to Eliot and to positions taken in their
own criticism. I remember arguing that really they were
being too hard on Richards. In spite of his terminology, I
suggested that they look at what he was really saying. I put
such questions as this: Look at it in his full context. Does it
really differ so much from what you and I believe? Isn't this
point basically that which Eliot makes here, and here?

If those letters are still extant, I'm sure that I'd find them
awkward and jejeune. But I mention them because they
indicate the passionate interest of my thinking of the
period. I thought that some important relationships be-
tween the two men were there, though I was to discover
only many years later that Richards and Eliot had actually
maintained a close personal relationship from a very early
period—from, I would say, at least 1925 or 1926. And this
is, I think, all the more interesting since they differed sub-
stantively on so many big issues. One of them had become
committed to positivism; the other was just going into the
church. Yet they maintained a genuine respect and warm
friendliness until the end of Eliot's life. Richards, in a
memoir of Eliot, tells of their early association and of what
attracted him in Eliot's poetry. So I felt later on that I had
not been doing anything wildly anomalous in trying to
reconcile the ideas of these two people, both of whom had
influenced my own thinking so much.

WARREN: Did you ever hear Eliot make reference to this relation-
ship? Is there anything on the record?

BROOKS: I had very few meetings with Eliot and I can't remember
any comments by him on Richards. One recorded com-
ment that I do recall is in "The Use of Poetry," where he
criticizes Richards' "ritual for heightening sincerity."
Richards had suggested such exercises as sitting "by the

fire (with eyes shut and fingers pressed firmly on the eyeballs) and considering with as full 'realization' as possible [man's] loneliness (the isolation of the human situation)." After criticizing the five rituals point by point, Eliot concluded that Richards was here unwittingly engaging "in a rearguard religious action" in the spirit of "religion without revelation." In fairness to both Eliot and Richards, one ought to read the passage in its entirety. But whatever judgment one makes as to the cogency of Eliot's argument, the two friends here obviously differed sharply on a fundamental point, for Eliot believed that you cannot have a serious religion without revelation.

WARREN: We're at a key collision here, all right.

BROOKS: Yes, we are.

WARREN: Well, shall we talk about this matter later on, and turn now to a question that bears directly on criticism and not on religion and literature as background? What about the kinds of criticism as you see them? There's more than one kind. And the second question is: What are their interrelations?

BROOKS: Well, here I must invoke the names of several people. I do so to make clear the development of my own thinking. I suppose that from my college days and certainly later, under the influence of Eliot, I had come to be concerned with isolating the nature of a specifically *literary* criticism. I never doubted, of course, that there were other and ancillary kinds. Later still, here at Yale, that concern deepened with my acquaintance with René Wellek and Bill Wimsatt. Conversations with them and my reading of their books have done a great deal to clarify my notion of a specifically literary criticism and its relation to some of the other kinds.

WARREN: Now you were saying earlier—am I right?—that the question of the locus of the poem or the locus of the novel in one sense involves the structure of what is signified by the verbal structure. Those two kinds of structure are both part of the thing as it exists.

BROOKS: Yes. Yet any insistence on structure can easily be misunderstood by people who say, "Oh well, all you're interested in is just words, empty tokens, and counters, and the structure you talk about is only a formal arabesque, a verbal arrangement." Nobody in his right mind, of course, is really interested in empty formality. Words open out into the whole world of emotions, ideas, actions. So that the "arrangement of words" about which I am talking is a kind of special reflection of manifold humanity itself. Words are not mere phonetic improvisations; they are meaningful.

WARREN: Words, Santayana says, inevitably throw a net of theory over things. In one sense, they can never—or only in a special kind of discourse—be used abstractly, not even by Gertrude Stein at her most radical nuttiness. What makes us read her at all is, in one sense, the fact of the tension between her effort and what actually happens on her page and in our heads. But I want to go beyond that notion. Words *are* a medium—yes. But once you put a few together you have created a rhythm. So even in the most minimal dimension, part of the medium of language is not *mere* medium but an experience in itself. Let me put the matter in this way: If people accuse you of indulging in an empty formality in talking about a poem or novel as a verbal structure, would you reply that you are not using verbal structure in a constricted and narrow sense? Let me also ask whether there is a significant difference in this regard between a poem and a novel. What I have in mind here is that in fiction the stylistic elements are less prominent than they are in a poem. In reading fiction, for example, we go faster and we tend to hurry over local verbal effects in our concern with the narrative. Style is more obviously recessive in a novel. That doesn't mean, of course, that style is not important in a novel—it may be crucial. But it is more recessive. It invites less attention to itself. In fact, if it seems to flaunt itself it can seem distracting, because in fiction we are concerned with another structure which is equally part of a novel *qua* novel—the structure of, say, the narrative. A novel has a narrative architecture too. Now this narrative architecture is distinguishable from what may be called verbal architecture, for you can more readily translate a novel than a poem.

BROOKS: Well, you've asked two questions, though they interlock. My answer to the first is that I'm not using verbal structure in a narrow but in the richest and widest sense. My answer to the second question is that I see the difference between the structures of poetry and fiction as one of degree rather than of principle. That is, Marvell's "Horatian Ode" or even Milton's sonnet—not to mention his *Paradise Lost*—has an architecture of narrative, a tonal structure, often a structure of symbols, and so on. In poetry, because it has a condensed and concentrated form, certain stylistic features, such as the interplay of metaphor or the formalization of rhythm, are prominent. But the difference between poetry and fiction is not absolute. In fiction, too, rhythm may be very important, and so may be shifts in tone. Consider the short stories in *Dubliners* or a novel such as *Ulysses*.

In talking about verbal structures, I was really focusing on words because it is through words that we come to apprehend the narrative, tonal, symbolic, and all the other structures in literature, whether in poetry, fiction, or drama. In talking about the poem as a verbal artifact, I do not mean to exclude the various structures that become available to the reader through the author's use of language. A novel has an obvious narrative structure, but, though less obviously, so does a poem.

WARREN: I'd like to talk for a bit about emotional structures— this much "down feel," this much "up feel"—about emotional tensions that can be distinguished from, though they are related to, the narrative of the novel or the implied narrative or the implied dramatic situation or the temper of imagery in, say, a poem. But you're not proposing a poem that speaks in a monotone. In an authentic poem, the reader is going up and down. This rise and fall is equally a part, isn't it, of the structure of the artifact. What I am getting at here is, of course, a potential structure of rhythm beyond the rhythm of words as sound.

BROOKS: Quite. For the artifact of which we are speaking is not static. It is dynamic or, at least when realized by a human being, it unfolds as a dynamic experience. As an analogy, consider the musical score for Beethoven's Seventh Symphony. The notes written on the page don't literally move us but, as realized by the orchestra, they do move us.

WARREN: Let me interrupt, please. They "move us," you say. And doesn't this imply an actual physical experience—the resonance, the enactment, in the whole human organism, from tongue to toes? Body and nervous system, shall we say, as a participating sound box? If so, what then?

BROOKS: "Verbal artifact" is not a very satisfactory term—at least it is easily misunderstood, but then most critical terms are. But let me repeat, criticism begins with the words of a text, the words as heard in the ear or read from the printed page. For me, a very important kind of criticism—perhaps the primary *literary* criticism—is the kind that takes the literary work as we encounter it on the page and tries to determine what it means and how it means. But there are other kinds of criticism, and very important kinds they are. One kind undertakes to tell us, for example, how the poem or novel came about: its growth, its development, the matrix from which it issued. We could call that a genetic criticism. Another kind of criticism records the impact of the literary work on different kinds of human beings or on people of different age levels or on people of different epochs. This could be called an affective criticism.

WARREN: Here's another question: Is it fair to say that what you have been suggesting in connection with the structure of the artifact—such things as the emotional structure, its emotional composition, even its narrative composition— all imply a relation both to the human being creating the work, the maker, and to the person reading it, responding to it, because the emotions don't exist in a vacuum? The narrative doesn't exist in a vacuum. It depends on human theories, dispositions. Can't we distinguish among them without chopping them apart?

BROOKS: Yes, and of course it would be foolish to think that we could chop them apart. We can, however, distinguish to our profit, for we need to know what we are talking about at this point or that. But before I speak about the value of making some distinctions, let me say this by way of summary: the imagined world, which is the world created by a particular poem or play or novel, is instinct with humanity and with all of humanity's potentialities. This has to be so, for our words were created by human beings and in some sense played their own part in creating humanity. Anyway, language is the product of society and, like society, has its own history. The words of a literary work constantly point back to the human being who chose and patterned them, but they also point forward to the human beings who read them, understanding or misunderstanding them, accepting or resisting them. The "verbal artifact" can't be purged of human meanings. Even Gertrude Stein in her various experiments never succeeded in doing that. Only by making up what were truly nonsense "words" could she have done that.

Yet, to try to see what a poem or novel "means" rather than what the author tried to say (or thought he was saying) in, say, *Antony and Cleopatra,* or rather than what an eighteenth-century rationalist or a Victorian member of the Oxford Movement thought *Antony and Cleopatra* said to *him,* seems very much worth doing. Here are where the distinctions among genetic, affective, and formal or structural criticism seem to me to make sense. One of the special advantages of stressing the work as such is that such criticism has some hope of remaining *literary* criticism. If we try to investigate that very interesting matter of the genesis of the work, we begin to move away from the work, and we may very well end up with attempting some kind of psychoanalysis of the author or an account of the climate of ideas that influenced him. If we stress the effects of the work on various readers, we may move off into a study of reader psychology or perhaps the sociology of the Restoration period or the taste of the *fin-de-siècle* reading public.

WARREN: What is the problem? Isn't it to maintain a focus on the relation between literature and the other interesting perspectives—concerns—contexts?

BROOKS: We want to know about such things. But such studies do move us away from the strictly literary concerns. So also, if we pursue the matter of origins, we are sure eventually to get into psychology and sociology. In short, granted that human experience is ultimately a seamless garment and granted that poems don't get here by way of a metaphysical stork, granted further that the words on the page are simply the *potential* poem, they have to be *realized* by some actual flesh-and-blood reader.

WARREN: Are you now suggesting that the locus of a poem is the mind, body, being, of the literal reader, Mr. X?

BROOKS: No—

WARREN: Let's push this a little. Can we say, instead, that the poem is a structure, maybe an organism, of potentialities? Where would this take us?

BROOKS: Let's postpone this and come back later. I was saying that, granted all the interaction and the continuity that the nature of literature demands, nevertheless I maintain that we gain a great deal in distinguishing a specifically literary criticism (founded on the meaning of the work of art as such) from a genetic or an affective criticism. To say this doesn't, it seems to me, demand any unnatural isolation of the work. The isolation is provisional; it can be abrogated at any moment—that is, whenever common or uncommon sense urges that it be terminated.

WARREN: Give me an example.

BROOKS: Suppose that I'm interested in trying to understand Marvell's "Horatian Ode." Unless I'm a nitwit, I'll certainly try to find out a little about the political circumstances of the day; for one thing, I have to know something about Cromwell. That is, I've got to learn the meanings of the proper as well as of the common nouns in this poem. I need to know something about Cromwell's political career and about his relation to Charles I. I must have at my disposal such information as this in order to grasp the ode as an aesthetic entity, for the proper nouns in this poem are very important and entail our knowing (or else being willing to learn) a certain amount of biography and history. The poem even as an aesthetic object is not merely formal and empty. I refuse to be backed into that particular corner simply because I insist that a poem may legitimately be treated as primarily an aesthetic object and not as, say, a political document, the importance of which derives from its political effects, or, say, a biographical document, the importance of which depends on the evidence it provides for the understanding of Marvell's personality.

On the other hand, I concede that it is perfectly legitimate for us, in the interest of other concerns, to stress the genesis of Marvell's ode or its effects. Why not, if we like, try to see how much, if anything, the ode can tell us about the very interesting human being who created it? In my published account of the poem, an account which put its stress on the poem as artifact, I had to insist—because the text of the poem itself seems to insist—that when Marvell wrote the ode he was still a Royalist, not a committed partisan of Cromwell, as I think most readers up to that time had supposed. (When I began to read the poem I too had supposed so; many readers still do.) But the value of the ode does not rest on what it can tell us about the history of Marvell's changing attitude toward Cromwell. Its primary value resides in that complex of qualities that we associate with any rich and significant poem.

WARREN: To cut back to your remarks about the genesis of a work as distinguished from the work in itself. Is the issue something like this: that all the information we can get, even that which seems oriented toward, say, a genetic criticism of a poem, is valuable, provided that we do not make it reductive?

BROOKS: Right.

WARREN: That is, we must not confuse the thing that is made with the material out of which it is made. Is that right?

BROOKS: Yes. One welcomes all the information he can get. But it must not be used reductively; for example, to conclude that the ode is outdated because the political issues with which it deals are irrelevant to modern man or that Marvell displays a kind of nationalism which is injurious and so contaminates the poem. Speaking of what is irrelevant, we must never forget that the biographical and historical facts that we may dredge up about a piece of literature very frequently prove to be irrelevant to an understanding of that particular work. Thus, though we must not dismiss offhand background information about a poem or novel, it can in certain circumstances distract us from what is important in the work—and that distraction can be almost as damaging as reduction.

WARREN: You haven't explained your views about affective criticism, the criticism that has to do with the effect of a work on an audience, on the individual or on a society—the various kinds of political or moral effects in terms of which a work may be valued or rejected.

BROOKS: No. I've only mentioned those briefly in passing. I've suggested earlier that a genetic criticism, which tries to find the origins of the work in history or geography or a climate of ideas, tends to move us away from the literary work itself to more general cultural matters; but an affective criticism, the study of the work's impact on various kinds of audience, probably moves us still further away. If we emphasize the impact of the work on its reader or hearer, we move rapidly off into reader psychology, the sociology of literary taste, and the changing cultural climate. On the one hand, one version of affective criticism is the appreciation of art as "an adventure among masterpieces." In such criticism the reader's own sensibility becomes the important thing; another version of affective criticism is the study of the growth of sentimentality in the eighteenth century, say, or of Victorian prudery.

One of the most interesting developments of affective criticism of recent years was the effort of F. W. Bateson to make the reactions of a particular audience the locus of the literary work. What he said, in effect, was this: "Look, we've all agreed that we can't define the true meaning of a poem as the meaning *intended* by the author. Authors write from the unconscious as well as the conscious mind. Besides, it's often impossible to get, except through the work itself, an account of what the author intended. So I'm going to say that the real meaning of the poem is that which a particular audience would have got from the poem." Bateson was well aware that different audiences get different meanings from the same work. Thus, Bateson chose a particular audience to be the standard for each cultural period. I won't go into how he determined just what the ideal audience was for a particular literary work except to say that it was a special class of society of the epoch in which the poem appeared.

WARREN: Why that particular class? And, if the poem in question is Marvell's "Horatian Ode," why should the authenticating readers be taken from even the seventeenth century? Why not the eighteenth or the nineteenth century? What about you and me? Why not our friends and relations?

BROOKS: Precisely. Besides, it's almost as hard to find out what the poem must have meant to Bateson's ideal reader of the past as to find out what was the "real" intention of the author. Certainly what the ideal readers of the past made of the ode seems to me even harder to determine than what Marvell intended to do before he got the poem down on paper. Both are abstractions.

WARREN: The notion of the common reader, to take Dr. Johnson's phrase, as somehow an ideal audience, valid over the ages—what about that? Certainly there's no definable common reader, is there?

BROOKS: No. What I as a reader must try to do, with all the help that I can get from history and elsewhere, is to become that ideal reader myself. I obviously can't count on succeeding. You, and every other reader, must do the same. But in any case you are in better position to judge the poem for yourself—to try to see it in the perspective of history and also *sub specie aeternitatis*—than to tailor your reading of the poem to that of Bateson's hypothetical ideal reader of the seventeenth century. It might be even harder to figure out what the "Horatian Ode" meant to him than to try to figure it out for yourself.

To take another writer as an example. What do we have to do when we read Shakespeare? We have to explore the *potentialities* of his work. We can, it is true, note what readers in other periods of history have seen in the text of his plays. But we need not confine ourselves in doctrinaire fashion to what we can prove *earlier* readers found in the plays—if we can prove even that. At any rate, we must be cautious in supposing that we, or any other readers, have exhausted his work. We certainly can't predict that the men of the twenty-first century won't find something additional, or perhaps quite new in it.

WARREN: Eliot's comment is a metaphorical way of putting matters, I suppose. He says that the work changes, but what actually happens is that it comes to be thought of in other terms. Thus, we know more about *Hamlet* than Coleridge did because, among other things, we know what Coleridge knew about *Hamlet*.

BROOKS: Right.

WARREN: This knowledge itself becomes a conditioning factor, a view with which we agree or disagree, a concept that we absorb consciously or unconsciously when we read *Hamlet*. There's bound to be a change in audience and, in that sense, a change in the work.

BROOKS: Yes.

WARREN: But the question of the locus of the work too is a problem that requires a very arbitrary definition, doesn't it?

BROOKS: Perhaps so. It is a real problem, all right. I've already implied that I don't think that you can locate the poem (or novel or play) in the author's intention. It does less than justice to the intricacies and what one may call even the mysteries of the creative process. Authors discover what they really mean in the process of getting it into words on the page, and a wise author may answer the question, "What were you trying to say here?" by pointing to the finished work and replying, "Read this. I've said it most fully and accurately in this text." Wimsatt and Beardsley and Wellek have been decisive on this point.

I'm attracted to René Wellek's effort to solve this sticky problem of the locus of a literary work by regarding the poem as a "structure of norms." But I'd better pick up his text to be sure that I quote it correctly. Yes, here it is: "a structure of norms, realized only partially in the actual experience of its many readers"—*e.g.*, you and I don't experience *King Lear* in precisely the same way, and probably neither you nor I will realize it twice in exactly the same way. René goes on to say, "Every single experience (reading, reciting, and so forth) is only an attempt—more or less successful and complete—to grasp this set of norms or standards." I confess that I have my problems with the terminology used here. My mind is too doggedly concrete to accept without some resistance abstract concepts of the sort presented here. But I can see some of the merits of this definition. It avoids sheer relativism: the norms *are* standards, and even if no reader can realize the norms of a poem fully, there yet remains what Wellek calls "a certain 'structure of determination.'" One reading can be shown to be "better" than another. Again, the poem—Wellek says this specifically—is an "object of knowledge."

WARREN: I might prefer to say a structure of potentialities. Perhaps, just as a starter, we may think of a poem as an acorn. Only an oak can grow out of an acorn, but the particular oak grows into a unique world of contingencies —not quite like the world any other oak grows into.

Since literature is a realm of potentialities, we have some very strange things, discoveries, late in the day, of a whole style or of an individual writer—Donne being the most famous example, in this century, of rediscovery; Skelton, a less sensational one. And well, after all, Henry James was rediscovered in a sense, too. So has Mark Twain been rediscovered. These writers mean more to us than they meant to a generation immediately after their work was finished.

BROOKS: Yes, and I'm happy to see our conversation taking this turn, because it provides an occasion for me to point to some of the more admirable traits in modern criticism. On the whole, it has not been reductive; it tends to see the work in question as a nexus of rich potentialities.

WARREN: Yes, that's what I've been driving at. But I think there are in our immediate time certain forms of criticism that are reductive. These tend to use literature merely for something else or see it really in terms of materials or its origins. Those impulses are still with us.

BROOKS: Oh, they are with us, all right, and they keep coming on like the hydra-headed monster. Lop off one head, and you find two or three new ones growing in its place.

WARREN: Myth criticism has a big element of that in it, it seems to me.

BROOKS: I think so too. Though when myth criticism is used by a resourceful man—Northrop Frye would obviously be the person to come to mind—it may prove very exciting and interesting.

WARREN: And relevant, too.

BROOKS: *Very* relevant. On the other hand, if you try to reduce—I think *reduce* is the proper word here—every literary work ever written to some phase of the seasonal myth, what you've really done is something very close to the old game that I remember was being played fifty years ago. Somebody had proved to his own satisfaction that there were just thirty-eight possible plots for fiction. Any story had to fall into one of those thirty-eight slots. If you take the view that all literature is expressing some aspect of the late spring phase or of the early autumnal phase, you may possibly turn up some fresh and exciting things to say about the work. But unless you can do much more than that—Frye, as an alert and resourceful critic, often does do more—you've simply offered a classification, and classification, left to itself, is always reductive.

WARREN: The trouble is that, if you put, say, ten works into the same slot, the differences among those works is obscured. The great work and the slight work begin to look alike.

BROOKS: That's right. Frye, for example, in a remarkable piece of speculation, somewhere argues that Pope's *Rape of the Lock*, Shakespeare's *Winter's Tale*, and two other works, whose titles I have forgotten, are all examples of the Proserpine myth. Well, this is exciting and shocking. It may even have an element of truth in it, but the differences between *The Winter's Tale* and *The Rape of the Lock* are so great as to force one to conclude that the alleged common element just doesn't make any significant difference.

WARREN: The differences are still to be insisted on, anyway.

BROOKS: They've got to be insisted on.

WARREN: There is a parallel here to certain kinds of psychoanalytic criticism. For instance, concerning a recent book by Frederick Crews on Hawthorne, Henry Alexander Murray, the great psychologist, a retired professor of clinical psychology at Harvard and an authority on Melville, has remarked that Crews only says Oedipus, Oedipus, over and over. That's all he has to say about Hawthorne. But there are obviously many more things to say about the psychology of Hawthorne. Even if one could establish the Oedipal character of Hawthorne beyond the shadow of a doubt, a monotonous emphasis on it is reductive. *Oedipus* becomes the magic word that explains everything about Hawthorne. As Dr. Murray puts it, the Oedipus complex is not the only complex.

BROOKS: Well, anybody who has taught English and American literature as long as you and I have knows that reductionism is the ubiquitous monster in our profession. The harried teacher, in trying to make a poem plain to his students, classifies it, sticks a label on it, attempts to reduce it to something manageable.

WARREN: I've caught myself doing that a thousand times.

BROOKS: So have I. It's a tendency that has to be resisted, not only because it damages the work, but because it's so insidious. It's ready to jump out of the corner at any moment.

WARREN: Or out of your own mouth. Let me push you back again to the matter of affective criticism. Would you want to say something about the forms it takes? How does it appear?

BROOKS: Well, perhaps because I've been less interested in it, I may have to stop to think a little about it. But I can think at once of two or three ways in which it appears. One impulse

toward affective criticism is a concern to show what litera-
ture is good for by inspecting the effect it has on different
audiences.

WARREN: Well, the moralistic emphasis is certainly a clear in-
stance. Poetry makes people bad or it makes people good.
Plato says drive the poets out of the ideal state because they
tell lies and distract people from serious occupations.

BROOKS: Yes. Such seems to be the nub of Plato's criticism—at
least, as most men have interpreted it.

WARREN: Hitler and Stalin, granted their own special morals,
came to do the same thing. A certain part of America, too.
Look at American public opinion.

BROOKS: I think one of the saddest but also funniest instances of
affective criticism has to do with Herbert Hoover. During
the days of the depression he said, perhaps in desperation
of economic remedies that had not worked, that if some-
body would just write a really good poem, a hopeful poem,
it would restore our faith in ourselves and in our country.
Well, this sort of pronouncement is touching. How
mad—but also how worshipful of poetry—to think that the
right poet could have saved the economic fabric by writing
a really bang-ho poem on how great America's future was.

WARREN: Yes, affective criticism does take strange forms. I'm
not talking now about moralistic criticism or censorship of
that sort, when I say that Matthew Arnold had a big streak
of that in him. In fact, he tried to make poetry take the place
of religion, or at least serve its purposes. But nowadays we
tend to say that Arnold has been one of the great liberators
of critical thinking. Or I. A. Richards (I'm thinking of his
early phase). Richards emphasized what poetry can do for
the reader by way of organizing the reader's inner being.
Now, I think there's a truth in that but, as stated, it em-
phasized the utilitarian and the projective value of the

poem in a way that may be open to objection. I hasten to point out that I have merely said "emphasized" the utilitarian value—emphasized it too soon and too much—for I can't conceive of anything's having come to pass in human development that in one way or another did not have, or promise, a use.

BROOKS: Yes. This emphasis occurs particularly in the early Richards. Such terminology and emphases, mingled with other elements, have certainly had a liberating and stimulating effect on contemporary criticism. The liberating effect was to show us how poorly and how oddly people read poetry and what very different things various people made of poems. This was liberating—to make us see the importance of teaching how a poem is to be read, to reinspect how well or ill we were actually reading. But Richards is indeed the spiritual descendant of Matthew Arnold, and most obviously in his insistence on what the poem would do for one's psychic makeup. On the other hand, of course, Richards, at what I regard as his best, joins those thinkers who have been saying from the beginning of time that poetry was and ought to be a civilizing agency.

On this issue, he joins hands with his great friend, though in certain respects his great theoretical opponent, T. S. Eliot. Though Eliot clearly did not believe that poetry could be substituted for religion, he saw it as an enormous potential force for good: it helps keep the language supple, flexible, and accurate, and makes us more conscious of what we say and how we attend to what other people say. Moreover, because it is constantly demanding of us imaginative projections, the person steeped in literature not only knows something about human history and psychology; he gets into the habit of putting himself into the place of the man across the room or out on the street—the man who takes a different view from his own. Potentially, at least, literature broadens our sympathies with other men, not only of the present day, but of past epochs. It can make it possible for us to live in the past as well as the present. But I want to break with this line of thought for a moment to say something that I might otherwise forget. Affective criticism has a long history. Even Aristotle, who wrote the first great systematic piece of formal criticism that we have, gets into affective criticism at one point.

WARREN: Yes. In his notion of catharsis. Sure he did.

BROOKS: Yet, in spite of Aristotle's reference to catharsis, the purgation of pity and terror, his basic emphasis in the *Poetics* is on the structure of the play: a tragedy has such-and-such a structure; it typically involves a reversal of fortune and a recognition; the best tragedies connect this reversal of fortune with the hero's recognition of his true plight, and so on. Tragedy, therefore, through its special structure, provides us with a special sort of knowledge. Thus, I see Aristotle's brief excursion into affective criticism to be just that—an excursion, a temporary departure from a radically different kind of criticism. In any case, there seems to be no general agreement on just what Aristotle's catharsis meant or what it accomplished. But, though the *Poetics* is basically formal in structure, there is, of course, no question but that Aristotle was interested in politics and morals. The author of the *Nicomachean Ethics* and of the great commentary on *Politics* obviously did not inhabit an ivory tower. In any case, and however we interpret the term "catharsis," the Athenian drama, which furnished the concrete material for Aristotle's theories about tragic poetry, provided plenty of occasions and incentives for imaginative projection. The Athenian audience could participate vicariously in the feelings of the guilty man, in the hubris of the tyrant, in the terror of Orestes pursued by the Furies, and so on. The Greek drama provided for enlarged sympathies and imaginative projection.

WARREN: And of self-knowledge, too.

BROOKS: Yes, though Aristotle in the *Poetics* does not give a moralistic or even fundamentally affective account of poetry, the notion that literature has consequences is there by implication. Those of us who prefer not to define literature in affective terms are nevertheless quite aware that literature does have effects. Our friend John Crowe Ransom in his writings was much concerned with its effects and with the general relation of literature to the human economy. Surely it is a matter worth discussion.

WARREN: Not merely worth discussing, but inevitably to be discussed.

BROOKS: It's been unfortunate that critical emphasis on the structure of the work (though it was also Aristotle's emphasis) has been misinterpreted to mean that the so-called, and unfortunately named, New Critics have no concern for the effects of literature on the human psyche and on the good health of the culture. I see, for example, no final incompatibility between such a concern and my interest in the structure of particular poems and novels. I like to try to see how this poem or play works—to test its depth and richness and to try to ascertain its precise meaning. But this interest doesn't mean that one has no concern with the "usefulness" of literature in that special sense in which I think literature can be of use to a society. Most of us are good enough citizens and good enough moralists to care something about that.

WARREN: Would you go so far as to say that the "good"—the fulfilled—poem is inevitably, in its nature, morally valuable? What I mean is this: a good poem, even in its most technical aspects, represents subtleties of distinction and organization of impulses and delicate responses to various situations and values, and moral concerns, if past the matter of crude labels, always involve just such distinctions and responses.

BROOKS: This started out as a question. But I'd say—

WARREN: I'm certain we'll come back to that topic again. But I'm going to pull us back for a moment to something a little nearer to the nature of the poem as a structure. Aristotle's discussion of catharsis, as you have said earlier, was a kind of excursion from his primary interest in the structure of the tragedy. Yet it is interesting to observe that, in this very first discussion of these matters in the culture of the West, Aristotle deals with both the verbal structure and what you might call its psychological and even social effects. Criticism begins by touching on both these things and raises, at least by implication, their relation to each other.

BROOKS: Yes, and the relation, though I think mainly implied, is important. Aristotle clearly indicates that you can't just put any slapstick farce on the Athenian stage or tell any cock-and-bull story and make a serious impact on the audience. Catharsis isn't effected by a character's simply committing a senseless murder or falling off a ladder and breaking his neck. The makeup of tragedy is obviously all-important.

WARREN: In our talking about the various kinds of criticism (and I remember that you refer to them in the preface to your last book), you say that you believe in free trade among them—no tariff walls. You acknowledge, I take it, their interpenetration and the mutual relations among the various kinds of criticism. Would you agree that one kind of criticism may lend enlightenment to another kind?

BROOKS: Yes. Occasionally in the classroom I draw three panels on a blackboard, describing these three kinds of emphasis, though conceding that these three categories do not exhaust the types and varieties of criticism. In the classroom I have used the words *tariff walls* when I pointed to the chalk lines that mark off the panel, observing that the lines are not meant to seal the areas of emphasis off from each other. I do want free trade among them. But I also want geographical boundaries. If there's some crucial event, say a murder, it may be necessary to know in what country the murder was committed and what court has jurisdiction. In short, we need to know what we are talking about—with what aspects of the problem we are concerned. To give a very brief illustration: if I decide that the prime evidence of the value of a novel is the size of the reading public that it attracts, if I say in effect that forty million Frenchmen can't be wrong, then I'm relying on affective criticism in my determination of literary value. If so, I at the least ought to realize what I'm doing. Is any best seller automatically proved great? Or must it have been a best seller over a period of centuries? Or must it have won the suffrages, not of just anybody, but of serious and disciplined readers? And by what criterion do I determine that they are the best readers and judges? If, on the other hand, I say a work is valuable because I know its author wrote it with passionate sincerity, I'm using a kind of genetic test. How do I know that he was passionately sincere? Because he says so in a notebook or a series of letters? Because a posse of friends and associates can be assembled to testify to his sincerity? If the latter, is my criticism now genetic or is it formal and structural? These crude examples may suggest—I hope they do—that it is important to know on what basis your judgment rests. They may point out, furthermore, that the affective and genetic modes of criticism have certain limitations and in certain situations have to be used with caution.

WARREN: Now, let me raise the question about the general function of literature. Assuming that you are right about these perspectives on the object you call different modes of criticism. Each is a kind of perspective directed toward the work of literature. Assuming that they are all interrelated and that they all have a bearing on the work of literature, what service do they perform for the reader with regard to the literary document before his eyes? Do they simply complicate things for the reader? Do they simply get in the way of the reader who says, "I know what I like—I like a good story," or, "As for this poem, I just like it." Are all these critical distinctions simply a pedantic embarrassment to him? Or is there some value, not for the specialist merely, but for the intelligent reader as well?

BROOKS: Well, it's a good question. The man in the street is extremely distrustful of criticism as needless pedantry— and not merely the man in the street. I expect that plenty of reviewers for the newspapers, and I'm sure very many people who teach in English departments, share this distrust. Maybe the best way to approach this problem is through a simple analogy. Who, let me ask, is the man who really loves automobiles? The boy of fifteen or sixteen who stays half-covered with grease and is constantly taking his car to pieces and putting it back together, experimenting with a new carburetor, putting in a new manifold; or the lady who gets into her car and says, "Home, James," and has no idea what really makes her sedan go? I think most of us would say that it is the boy in the backyard taking his automobile to pieces, seeing how it works, trying this or that rearrangement of parts. He's the man who really loves automobiles, not the lady in her Rolls-Royce. People who love fishing rods are always working with them; people who love guns know the different models and are always comparing them, handling them, cleaning them. Or take still another example, one that I think makes an additional point. The good driver, the man who enjoys driving, is the man who has an intimate acquaintance with his car. He drives effortlessly; the machine has become a kind of extension of himself. But let something go wrong and he picks the trouble up right away; he can "hear" the motor; he knows what the motor's doing. He is all-analytical then. But his analytical ability, far from making him resemble the centipede that couldn't walk because he had to think out which one of his hundred legs to move next, makes him precisely the man for whom a good drive becomes an almost instinctive, streamlined performance. I would claim the same thing for the man who truly loves literature.

No English teacher yearns to turn out a lot of little niggling pedants who write cold-blooded "analyses" for the sake of the activity of analysis. What the instructor hopes is that he can help his students to read—that conscious "analysis" will become so unconscious, so much a habit of mind, that his students will become able to read fully, appreciatively, but unpedantically, and even, one could say, "innocently." But, if the reader achieves such ability, it will be a new kind of innocence, not awkward and tongue-tied.

WARREN: An earned innocence.

BROOKS: Yes, an earned innocence.

WARREN: Or you could use the word *love*. A man doesn't love his wife until he's taken the trouble to know what she's really like as a human being. If she's just some sort of useful object, a figure of convenience, that's one thing. If he loves her, he must make some effort to understand her, her whole nature.

BROOKS: Yes, that's a fine analogy, because the poem is a much more human thing than any machine. In fact, we keep talking about poems as having an *organic* structure. Some-

times a rich and massive poem seems to possess a life of its
own, not merely a life breathed into it by the person who
reads it. At all events, the man who really loves poetry is
the man who at some level has come to understand it, not
the man who is temporarily infatuated by it or who at a
glance dismisses it by saying, "I know what I like and I
don't like this."

WARREN: I don't want to get too far afield here, but you used the
word *innocence*. I'd like to explore its meaning in relation to
a poem. When Milton says that a poem is "simple, sensu-
ous, and passionate," it sounds as if he's making an argu-
ment for Sara Teasdale's poetry or the *Love Song of India* or
something like that, instead of *Paradise Lost*, which doesn't
seem at all simple, sensuous, and passionate in the com-
mon implication of those words. Nor is *Samson Agonistes* or
any other of Milton's poems. But I suppose that by "sim-
ple" he means that it can be perceived.

BROOKS: Yes. It has unity; it can be perceived to be all of a piece.

WARREN: It's all of a piece. It can be perceived to have unity
through its sensuous quality. It has an immediate relation-
ship to this unity.

BROOKS: The words spoken make an impact on the ear.

WARREN: The images make an impact on your senses. It's all
good Aquinas, I guess. And Milton's phrasing touches on
the qualities of a work of art: its felt unity, its appeal to the
senses, its concern with the human passions. But he
doesn't mean that you go into a sexual swoon or a political
excitement—not passionate in that sense of the word. But
getting back to one thing here. The simplicity, sensuous-
ness, and quality of passion imply immediacy. But you
can't have an immediate relation to a poem that you don't
understand. We may have to pass to the immediate rela-
tionship by the aid, the mediation, of criticism. We may

even have to "work" at the poem before we can arrive at the unmediated relationship, which I say is the innocent relationship.

BROOKS: The point's well taken. Let me come at it with an illustration. T. E. Lawrence, in his book on the Arabian revolt, tells a story which is very hard for men of our Western tradition to believe, though I think Lawrence was telling the literal truth. He had secured a picture of one of the Arabs' great leaders, Auda. And he showed it to some of the Arab tribesmen. To his surprise, they could make nothing of it at all. They had never seen pictures or line drawings. They were not able to fuse the lines and shadings into one object. They knew Auda the man very well, but they couldn't see Auda in the picture. Or to take another and perhaps simpler instance. We are told that, when a British eighteenth-century sailing ship arrived at some island in the South Seas, the natives didn't know what this object was. It wasn't *an* object for them. It was not one thing, but a confusing mixture of spars, ropes, rigging, ladders, everything.

WARREN: There was no functional unity.

BROOKS: That's right. And, until they had learned what a ship was, they couldn't see the ship when they looked at it. There could not be an immediate relationship without a prior mediation, which obviously comes from acquaintance and explanation. Let me say further that I'm delighted by your invoking Milton's "simple, sensuous, and passionate." The point of most interest is that the most learned and careful poet in the English language should have used just this phrasing.

WARREN: Yes. He says that, and then writes *Paradise Lost*, which requires a great deal of mediation. Scholarship and criticism, if used properly, are moving toward innocence. They are a way toward innocence, in our final confrontation of the work.

BROOKS: A theological reference may not be out of place, in view of the fact that we are talking about *Paradise Lost*. The innocence in question is not like that of the innocence of the unfallen Adam. It's the innocence that has been regained by the redeemed Adam, who has learned much in the terrible and complicating experience through which he has gone. His final, once again unified view of reality is not precisely that of the unfallen Adam.

WARREN: He's not the Adam of the Garden of Eden.

BROOKS: No, not that of the Garden at all.

LITERATURE AS KNOWLEDGE

WARREN: It seems to me, Cleanth, that almost everything we've said thus far implies some notion of what literature is and what literature does. Now, granting that it's more than one thing, or that it can reasonably be thought of as more than one thing, and has more than one use, is it true that you specifically think of it as a form of knowledge? Is that the key to your thinking about the nature of literature, or am I reading something into you there?

BROOKS: I think I would accept that, though the term "knowledge" here needs a great deal of qualification. If literature is a form of knowledge, it's clearly not scientific knowledge, for example, though it may incidentally involve scientific knowledge. Nor is it historical knowledge. Still, for want of a better term, I think that I'd say it is knowledge—though of a special kind. And, if we can suggest what kind of knowledge it is, I think we have the best working basis for talking about literature.

WARREN: This is an old topic, isn't it? What does the poet know, says Plato. Or is it Socrates? Does he know how to drive a chariot or steer a boat or command an army? The poet writes about these things, but does he know about them? If we get knowledge of those things from him, what kind of knowledge can we get? Or Giambattista Vico, in his *Scienza Nuova*, offers the notion of a knowledge that he would distinguish from Descartes' mathematical knowledge—a knowledge based on empathy and imagination, the knowledge that we can get from history *because* we are men, for instance.

BROOKS: Yes, Socrates and his interlocutor, Ion, in the dialogue tussled over that point. The upshot of the discussion, I would say, is that it is only incidentally that one derives the technical (scientific or historical) knowledge from the poet. The knowledge that one finally gets from Homer or any other poet is of a rather different kind. I think we could describe it as a kind of dramatic knowledge, a knowledge of "what it is like" to go through a process, to fight a battle against foemen, or to fight an internal battle with oneself, to mourn, to be happy, to test one's courage, and so on. Allen Tate, in an essay published many years ago, asserted that poetry gives us complete knowledge, though I think few have accepted and fewer still comprehend what he meant. I'd interpret Tate's complete knowledge as concrete knowledge: it includes the value-structured world of the human being. Poetry—and Tate means literature generally—is not information or techniques; nor is it a compound of generalizations and abstractions. Physics or chemistry, by contrast, have to leave out the value-structured world— and, I hasten to add, necessarily and properly. In all its mathematical equations, physics finds no room for the human equation. Its kind of universality demands the elimination of that subjective factor.

WARREN: Would you say that literature is knowledge by enactment, imaginative enactment? Immediate knowledge by imaginative enactment? Again, Vico argues from the notion that you can only "know" what you can make or do. In other words, this would be knowledge by enactment? Or the possibility of enactment?

BROOKS: That's good phrasing and perhaps superior to "dramatic," which can be misleading because "dramatic" is so closely tied to drama and theater. Yes, knowledge by imaginative enactment. To get at the matter in still another way, one might invoke a theological term: thus literature is a kind of liturgy, a symbolic action.

WARREN: This would apply to the simple lyric poem as well as to the big novel or the big drama?

BROOKS: I would think so. This again is where Eliot was quite right in pointing out, or maybe he was merely rediscovering, that even the simplest lyric is dramatic. "Blow, blow, thou western wind, / Let the small fine rain down rain" is a little dramatic poem, an imaginative enactment of an action.

WARREN: That is, the lover longs for the absent beloved and cries out. Let me ask another question on this. It's a commonplace, voiced by people as different as Sir Philip Sidney and John Dewey, that art in some sense completes nature. Could this notion—it might be interpreted in various ways, I know—but could this notion have any application to what you are saying here about the kind of knowledge provided by poetry?

BROOKS: Yes. I think it might throw more light on Allen Tate's characterization of poetry as a complete knowledge. We may think of it as active, as a *completing* knowledge in that it brings to the matter described human values. The matter in question becomes known as a human being would know it, not merely as an interplay of abstract forces devoid of human reference.

WARREN: What about the naïve notion that poetry completes nature by giving us what nature won't give us—say, a daydream to take refuge in. Yet, I suppose that even a daydream is a naïve version of "humanized" and, in that sense, "completed" knowledge. Is that your notion? Or am I missing something here?

BROOKS: Well, I resist the notion that a dreamworld represents the kind of completion I have in mind. In any case, I'd be happier to illustrate by citing more serious and meaningful dreams. Freud's account of dreams, for example, certainly indicates that dreams may be serious enterprises and afford genuine knowledge. In such dreams the human psyche untangles its experiences, sorts them out, learns about itself, and perhaps even fulfills itself. At any rate, such dreams are not simply idle expressions of feelings or sentimental indulgences. Poetry as an indulgence we've always had with us, but I think everybody has agreed that no authentic poetry, let alone great poetry, amounts to nothing more than escapism.

WARREN: Are you saying, then, that in part at least the poet, the novelist, or the imaginative writer of any kind, in composing his work, comes to know himself, to create himself? Is the process of composition a kind of self-discovery?

BROOKS: Yes. But again, I think one has to be careful here. Several recent articles on American writers push such a view of composition too hard; they are intent on seeing the contemporary American writer as so disoriented and alienated in this world that he is forced to create not only his whole world but himself in the bargain. In some deep but special sense such a claim may be true but, if that is basically what American writers are up to, then I think their case is desperate indeed. But maybe we'll come back to the topic of the loss of a sense of community and the writer's attempt to do for himself what the community used to do for him.

WARREN: Would this situation be more true now than in the past, do you think, or not? Or do we have simply more of the same in a new context?

BROOKS: I think that probably, with our best writers at least, it's more of the same in a new context. In any case, there's a great temptation here for the writer to try to become his own psychoanalyst or his own priest or the prophet for the present day, and so on.

WARREN: If we pick Alexander Pope or Franz Kafka, we have a different set of cultural conditions, don't we? In relation to the self, that is. In Kafka, what is the view of the self in relation to a society?

BROOKS: Obviously a very great difference from what we find in Pope. The difference is so great that I think it might be interesting to try to see whether there is any likeness at all, to test the notion that Pope and Kafka are really doing much the same thing in spite of their differences. Pope clearly felt that his own identity would be pretty well defined by the basic values of a society of which he regarded himself as a member. Kafka obviously saw himself as cut off from and threatened by his society. Yet, it's interesting to look at modern scholarship on Pope. One scholar, for example, interprets Pope's *Dunciad* as a satiric (but quite serious) prophetic vision of his solid eighteenth-century world, in which science and letters had made so many advances, becoming a spiritual wasteland. Pope saw in his imagination the whole rational order made luminous by the force of reason now in peril and about to fall to the dunces, the pedants, and the cranks. So, in a sense, Pope himself perhaps was giving his reader a glimpse of what Kafka was to see writ large. But certainly the change in the community between Pope's culture and Kafka's has made a profound change in the poet's imagination. It's clearly reflected in Kafka's work.

WARREN: Of course, we did have mad poets in the eighteenth century in England, too.

BROOKS: We certainly did, and in fact someone has pointed out that one of the ways in which the poets of the mid and late eighteenth century were able to create any authentic poetry was by going mad or pretending to be mad or projecting themselves into a kind of mad persona.

WARREN: Let me add another digression here—I think I drew you from that line. We were talking about poetry or art as a fulfillment in knowledge.

BROOKS: In a sense, perhaps you did draw us away from the main line of our discussion, though all of these things are tightly tied together. But in that digression, if digression it was, we were still talking about the nature of the poet's experience and how that experience is transformed into knowledge—knowledge of a kind—in his work.

WARREN: It is so transformed if he is not thinking of himself—he should be thinking of his work, not of himself—yet the process of composition nevertheless serves as a way, consciously or unconsciously, of completing himself in knowledge of himself. Let's turn to the reader now. What about him? If we look at poems A, B, C or X, Y, Z by different authors, in what sense can a poem in general be said to constitute a "knowledge" for the reader?

BROOKS: Well, there's the very fact of imaginative engagement. The literary work draws him out of himself. If it's a centuries-old poem, it may draw him out of his own age and time. The reader can, of course, also get something of that sort simply by imaginatively engaging himself in biographies of people of earlier ages. But, quite apart from the historical transference, literature primarily and especially draws him down into a deeper self, a self that perhaps he hadn't quite realized that he had. One of the most brilliant things that Yeats ever wrote—he was talking about the writer, but it applies in full, I think, to the reader—was a letter to his fellow Irishman, the playwright Sean O'Casey. He admonished O'Casey not to write plays that ride particular issues and topics. Yeats goes on to ask O'Casey whether he thinks that Shakespeare taught Lear and Hamlet what they know. Far from it, Yeats answers. Lear and Hamlet taught Shakespeare what he knew and exposed sides of himself to Shakespeare that he'd never known existed. I think Yeats's observation is profoundly true and, if it is true for the creative artist, it is true for the reader as well, for the reader, by following the play of mind of Lear and Hamlet, discovers some of the potentialities of the human spirit, including his own potentialities, which otherwise would never have been explored or tested.

WARREN: Another way, maybe, of saying it, or something like it, would be that, if the poet's poem isn't any better than he intended, it's not any good.

BROOKS: I would agree heartily. The good poet writes not off the top of his head, but out of his innards, not just out of his consciousness, but out of his unconscious. But I think that matters go even further than that. The writer is making discoveries about himself as he makes discoveries about the poem or the novel that he is writing.

WARREN: That is, the composition is a mode of discovery, testing whether he can accept certain possible explanations of himself or of the world around him. And the process in-

volves a new and very special relation between the con-
scious and the unconscious dimensions of being.

BROOKS: Yes. And this again is a reason why it is so attractive to
regard poetry as a kind of knowledge. Our reference in the
last few sentences to poetry as a means of exploration and
discovery implies that poetry, and literature generally, is
indeed a mode of knowledge.

WARREN: Now, you've said in one of your essays that the
themes of literary works are not generalizations to be
affirmed, but situations to be explored.

BROOKS: Yes. What I was driving at was this: that, once the
writer has made up his mind about some generalizations or
has simply adopted from a sociologist or a psychologist or
political scientist a generalization about mankind, his task
is not to set this forth as exposition (however embellished
rhetorically); he must put it into a dramatic situation. Even
if he starts with a theme which he thinks can be stated as a
generalization, in enacting it imaginatively in terms of a
concrete situation, he is going to end up by testing the
generalization. And, just as he probably discovers things
about himself that he had not anticipated when he began
the work, he will also probably discover that the generaliza-
tion won't quite fit. In fact, he is moved beyond mere
generalization to a kind of dramatic application of it which
will reveal still other considerations, qualifications, am-
biguities, perhaps even inner contradictions.

WARREN: This is what leads, isn't it, to a kind of crosshatching of
sympathies, a contradiction among sympathies in a big
work, not cowboys versus Indians. We've touched on the
Hemingway thing, about his dramatizing the atrocities
committed by the anti-Fascists. But we have beautiful cases
even in *Paradise Lost*.

BROOKS: Yes. People of great sensitivity and intelligence persist in seeing Satan as the hero of *Paradise Lost*—and this in spite of Milton's own known sympathies as a man and known intellectual position as a man. In his dramatization of the issues, even the devil has to have his due.

WARREN: Milton's intellectual position is one thing and his dramatization is another.

BROOKS: I myself believe that Adam is the hero. I came to this view fairly late after a tussle with the idea that after all Satan may—

WARREN: Even if Satan is not *the* hero, he is heroic.

BROOKS: He is heroic. He is not simply the horrid devil of the Middle Ages with a tail and cloven hoof. He becomes a very attractive superman in whom we can clearly see ourselves and some of our most admirable traits.

WARREN: Well, in Dante's *Inferno* we constantly see great men, heroic people, all very touching, good people, suffering their torments: Paolo and Francesca, Ulysses, and many more. Many of them are men and women of great presence and great stature and appeal to our hearts in one way or another. We find there the same tension, the same cross-hatching of sympathies that we find in Milton. So Dante, in the *Inferno*, facing Paolo and Francesca, is so inwardly torn that he faints, falls down as a dead body falls, to paraphrase the line.

BROOKS: Or, to instance a contemporary writer, take one of Faulkner's novels. Thomas Sutpen wreaks death and destruction on all around him. He ruins himself and in the process ruins the lives of his children. On the other hand, he is not a contemptible figure. He has a certain kind of nobility: there is unwillingness to give up; there are the pressures that he puts on himself; there is his firmness in holding to a particular view. The presence of these traits produces a real tension in our feelings about him. We don't just dismiss him as we would some really simple villain.

WARREN: Isn't this touching at the very center of the tragic—of tragedy?

BROOKS: I think so. I'm thinking not only of Aristotle's famous "tension" passage—if it is a tension passage—that is, his remarks about pity and terror. I'm thinking of statements in the *Poetics* as simple as this: that you can't have a tragedy unless it be the tragedy of a good man. Now he doesn't mean by "good" a man who is entirely virtuous. But he does mean that he's not contemptible.

WARREN: He's a man of stature. He embodies some great values, or we take no interest in him. Otherwise the play becomes a police action. Call the cops to come over and get rid of him. Dr. Samuel Johnson apparently could not accept this tensional double view, if I remember correctly his distaste for the criminal king as tragic hero.

BROOKS: Which was that?

WARREN: I'm trying to remember the spot. He's talking of *Richard III*. And he sees the play as calling for a police action rather than as a tragedy—as a great many people do. They must have their sympathies simple and uncomplicated. But let me ask another question here.

BROOKS: Sure.

WARREN: Nietzsche says that art, poetry, enhances the sense of life. If you grant that this is true, how do you connect it with poetry as knowledge?

BROOKS: I don't remember the passage in question, but without rereading Nietzsche I can make a confident guess as to what he probably meant. Life is not static: it involves movement, action, and drama, and these are the very stuff of poetry and literary art in general. As we were saying earlier, literature is an imaginative enactment. It is drama, and authentic drama always involves tension and emotions wrought up to full pitch. The authentic poem or drama or novel seems not so much an account of life, but an embodiment; it may even seem to possess a life of its own.

WARREN: I would like to connect this sense of life that you have just spoken of to what I shall call an emphasis on spontaneity, the quality of spontaneity, in poetry or fiction, as being in itself a virtue. Now many poems, including some magnificent poems, are written with great spontaneity—they seem to pop right out. One can find examples from "Kubla Khan" to the poems of Robert Frost. Frost says his best poems always came easy. Nevertheless, there are kinds and kinds of spontaneity, aren't there?

BROOKS: Yes.

WARREN: And the poem that seems so spontaneous may or may not have been actually spontaneous. I'm thinking of Yeats's comparison of the poet to the beautiful woman. Beautiful women labor to be beautiful. The labor in itself may be immediate or it may be in the past. But the labor is there. Only labor makes genuine spontaneity possible.

BROOKS: We think of Keats as a warm, sensuous poet who, one evening, sat on his lawn and listened to a nightingale and then quickly wrote an ode. The facts of this account are essentially true, but what preparation lay behind this remarkable performance? In general, if we look at Keats's manuscripts, noting the cross outs, revisions, and rewritings, we see right away that this wonderful sense of spontaneity goes along with evidence of almost painfully hard work. I remember, for example, Ridley's book on Keats's revisions of "The Eve of St. Agnes." One sees at once what a hard-won spontaneity Keats's was.

WARREN: Or consider the manuscript of the ode "To Autumn."

BROOKS: Or take a look at the manuscripts of Faulkner's novels. There is still a view that Faulkner was a kind of genius who went into some kind of inspired blackout and later looked down at the paper on his desk and saw, on the page, a great piece of passionate rhetoric. It had just boiled out on the page, foaming with spontaneity. But now that we have had the opportunity to look at his manuscripts, we have discovered that he was a painfully careful artist, revising again and again.

WARREN: Is something of this sort not true even of a literal spontaneity that is effective, that gives you a beautiful poem? It comes almost like a dream—or does come as a dream. Yet the dream comes only, the spontaneity comes only, to the man who has labored. Fortune favors only the prepared spirit, Pasteur says.

BROOKS: Wordsworth saw that, as you once pointed out to me. This warm nature poet, who so often celebrates spontaneity, wrote—I believe you can quote the passage better than I—

WARREN: I don't even remember what it is, now.

BROOKS: I'm thinking of the passage in which Wordsworth tells us that it is only the man who has thought and meditated long on certain subjects—

WARREN: Yes, in the introduction to the second edition of *Lyrical Ballads*.

BROOKS: —who is able to write authentic poetry. Only for such a man is that which wells up spontaneously likely to be poetry.

WARREN: Well, I'm thinking now about the contemporary emphasis on the spontaneous which—well, I don't want to begin to make speeches here. I'll simply say that the misinterpretation of the nature of spontaneity is very current right now. Would you talk to that point or do you think saying it is enough?

BROOKS: I think that little needs to be said beyond this: when one looks very hard at some of these so-called spontaneous poems, they quickly appear very thin and spotty. If you've ever had the misfortune to hear, on the next morning, a tape recording of some of the brilliant, witty conversation that, after a few drinks, you managed so easily the evening before, you have been shocked. What has become of all that spontaneous wit and those brilliant quips that you so distinctly remembered you uttered?

WARREN: I'd rather not think about this. It's a painful topic.

BROOKS: It is.

COMMUNITY AND RELIGION

WARREN: Let's switch, Cleanth, to two more general topics; they're related, as a matter of fact. First, *community*, that word you often use, for instance, in your book on Faulkner; and, second, *religion*. Sometimes it appears that for you these constitute one topic. Is this getting too far away from literature? Both community and religion touch on the matter of the crisis of culture, which has been the great subject of literature in this century. And you say yourself, in an essay called "Poetry Since *The Waste Land*," (I am now quoting you): "I must confess my suspicion that the decisive issue lying beneath the kinds of modern poetry has to do with that cloudy and difficult topic, religion." I would take up community first. Let's start there.

BROOKS: All right. I think the problem of community affects us in every way—politically, sociologically, psychologically. But it has a very direct bearing on literature and most obviously on the writer himself. For whom is he writing? Does he have an audience out there with whom he is, in some sense, in touch? Or does he feel himself a complete alien to his audience? These are evident problems. I'm sure I'm not alone in stressing the importance of this matter.

A typical example is an article written a few years ago by Alan Pryce-Jones, former editor of the *Times Literary Supplement*. I'm not sure that Pryce-Jones ever uses the word *community* in that article, but his thesis is the American writer's loss of community. Pryce-Jones regards the typical American writer as baffled, alienated, bewildered, and unable really to understand the situation in which he finds himself. He so completely lacks a live tradition that he feels the need of reconstructing the whole moral life—to develop a sense of values *de novo*. In fact, Pryce-Jones asserts that the American writer, unlike the English writer, does not write for fame or money, but writes in a desperate effort to achieve some sense of reality.

WARREN: I think he's got us wrong there.

BROOKS: Well, I suppose any writer from Homer on writes to discover his own reality. That may always be a deep, though often unconscious, motive, a secret motive. But surely Pryce-Jones becomes absurd in denying that Americans write for fame or money. I think most of my friends like their royalty checks. Why shouldn't they? And, as for fame, who really believes that any American writer is so much an anchorite as to despise it? Pryce-Jones is also wrong, it seems to me, in implying that all American writers are neurotically seeking to discover through their writings who they are. But I must not, in deploring his exaggeration of the American situation, impugn my own witness. For I have invoked Pryce-Jones to support my contention that the writer needs a community and is deeply affected when all sense of community is lacking.

One of the most brilliant histories of English literature turns on such a loss of community. It is the sketch that William Butler Yeats took over from his friend John Eglinton but on which, as he developed it, he improved amazingly. Here is a paraphrase of Yeats's version. First, we have Chaucer's company of Canterbury pilgrims, moving toward a common goal, a common shrine. This company—it is a "community"—comprises all sorts of people: good, indifferent, and corrupt; people of high and low degree: knights and farmers, clergy and tradesmen, finicky ladies and hearty gossips. But they all have a deep relation to each other. They share a common goal: they are journeying to a common shrine. They share basic beliefs about life and about reality. In the next cultural stage, Yeats says, you can see this company breaking up, its members becoming individuals; and so you have the typical Shakespearean drama, with its much more intense focus on the inner life of particular individuals and, accordingly, with a larger measure of interest in personal psychology. The ties of community have loosened enough to allow the individual to stand free, capable of being inspected in the round, and to sense, at moments at least, his own isolation.

WARREN: Remember, Shakespeare too is writing about the nature of community, the pressure it exerts, actually making possible the harmony of human relations. That pressure is what makes it possible for men to live together.

BROOKS: Well said, and, though there is by Shakespeare's time a loosening of the bonds, the community is still very much present in the lives of men. This constant pressure makes possible the dramatic tension.

WARREN: Part of the issue being talked about, which Chaucer did not talk about.

BROOKS: Yes, for Chaucer felt he didn't need to talk about it—or maybe simply wasn't interested in talking about it. But there is a further stage in the breakup of the community. That next stage occurs, as Yeats sees it, in the era of Wordsworth and Coleridge.

WARREN: Well, let's think in terms—may I interrupt a second?

BROOKS: Yes, but let me first make one further comment. Yeats would presumably say that, by the end of the eighteenth century, the individual has so far broken out of the older community that he finds himself gazing into the pool of Narcissus. He becomes lost in the secret depths of himself. You have, for example, the visionary poet described by Coleridge in "Kubla Khan." Other people are fascinated by him. He's a kind of madman, an awesome figure, but obviously quite mad. Granted that he has drunk the milk of paradise and fed on honeydew, you'd better draw a circle around him, stand well back from him, and cross yourself. If he is blessed, he is also clearly cursed, the *poète maudit*. But I interrupted your interruption, so—

WARREN: Well, my interruption amounts simply to what you've said. I'll pick up with the romantic period and say that from that time onward the writer has been alienated. The history of the more recent Western literature, it seems to me—it's almost summed up in the alienation. The history of, say, British and American and French and some other literatures of the last 150 years becomes intelligible only in terms of the increasing alienation of the writer. Baudelaire deliberately stands outside his world, seeing it as a world that he can't inhabit, a world that treats the poet like, you remember, the albatross caught by the stupid sailors and spread out on the deck. All his poetry is about this problem, the fact of alienation. And Balzac is doing much the same thing in a very different way. He's anatomizing the bourgeois world and the other world around him; and the mere fact that he acknowledges his separation distinguishes him from the society which he is analyzing. He is outside it. By the time you get to Flaubert or Verlaine or Rimbaud, my God, you're a long, long, long way outside it. The attack on the bourgeois world becomes more and more

marked. Melville, looking at American society after the
Civil War, found little there that he could embrace or con-
done. And over and over again, by the time you get the
Dreisers, the Hemingways, the Faulkners—they're all of
them alienated men.

BROOKS: Poets like Eliot and Pound, and to some extent Yeats,
have a very special relation to this issue. The alienation
associated with the present cultural crisis becomes the
overt theme of *The Waste Land.* As for Pound's *Cantos,* here
too it is the great theme, though I speak with less than
confidence about the meaning—any one meaning—of
this marvelous jumble of a poem. The cultural crisis is also
the theme of nearly all of Yeats's big poems of the twenties
and thirties, and it comes up again and again for some-
times fascinating discussions in his essays and autobio-
graphical chapters. Confronting such a crisis in culture,
Eliot and Pound may be said to have attempted to create a
new mode of poetry as the only adequate way of coping
with it. What is in a sense more impressive is Yeats, in his
fifties, changing his whole style of poetry, not simply
under Pound's influence, but in order to deal with a cul-
tural situation now radically reenvisaged.

The theme of a crisis in culture is rich and pervasive. It
extends beyond the various dramatic situations to be found
in modern literature and involves the plight of the artist
himself—what he thinks about himself, what he thinks
about his fellows, what he thinks about the civilization. To
anticipate something we may be talking about later, I think
that it may be that one of the resources of the southern
writer in our time—I'm thinking not merely of Faulkner,
but of Katherine Anne Porter, Allen Tate, you, and many
another—is that, though the southern community doubt-
less is beginning to dissolve, there is enough left of it to
constitute a real resource for these writers.

WARREN: We don't want to try to rewrite the history of the world in the next ten minutes, but I do recall a passage from Alfred North Whitehead, which I read a long time ago, which argues to this effect: that man, before the industrial revolution, had never known change. He had known vicissitudes, famines, plagues, wars, and ups and downs of fortune, but the basic order of life had always been the same—for example, the same old plow for thousands of years. The man knew where his food came from, knew the graybeard on one side of the street and the babe on the other. He felt himself rooted, sometimes perhaps even painfully rooted, in relation to other men, in a society which had a structure that he could comprehend, whether he liked it or not. Well now, Whitehead said that in the moment of the industrial revolution man discovered change. He discovered a new relation to time and a very disastrous relation to time. He felt cut off on one hand from his place in nature and on the other hand from his relation to other men and, as Marx put it, alienated from his work. Whitehead was writing a long time—a half century—ago about what it was like before the great technological revolution of our own day, before, that is, the enormous acceleration of change that we have witnessed. Has there been something like this watershed event in the matter of the disintegration of the community? By the way, an interpretation of Faulkner's characteristic themes certainly has a relation to nature on one hand and to mankind on the other. These are the two prongs, as it were, of the problem. Is this view of Faulkner pertinent?

BROOKS: You put matters very well, and your reference to Whitehead is much to the point. I think that even in our day, fifty years later, we haven't fully absorbed the implications of what he said; and the case of Faulkner is thoroughly apropos. Faulkner still had a grasp on nature.

He knew and loved the wilderness. He was part of a traditional society. He also had a grasp on history—history had visibly shaped the community; it entered into the fabric of the family. One of the many things that held the community together was the heritage of service in the Civil War and the experience of common disasters as part of the outcome of the war.

WARREN: And responsibilities for it.

BROOKS: Yes, responsibilities for it. Moral problems thus were not abstractions. They were concrete and closely related to your own blood. You had to look them in the face.

A significant thing about modern industrial man in America is how little relation he has to either nature or history. Nature becomes more and more remote. Not only has nature become remote, but history as well, for when history is reduced to a kind of costume drama on TV or a movie—something to be dismissed when one has a serious problem to solve—then history has become an amusing dream or perhaps not even that: maybe no more than a means for congratulating ourselves on our own dazzling progress. There's a further point: when you feel that you have the means to remake the future to suit yourself, what has history got to tell you that is of any consequence? What modern man has suffered, therefore, is a double loss, not just the loss of nature but a loss of history itself, in the sense of human continuity.

I don't want again to talk too long on this big subject, one on which so many people with much more expertness have spoken. But I do want to make a fairly simple and obvious point: the enormous technological success of modern man, the overwhelming concern for means rather than ends. The problem for any society is to make a successful adjustment of means to ends. Means may well come to determine ends. I suppose this possibility goes back to the cavemen. Better stone axes tend to cause change in the whole cultural setup. But Whitehead is right: until the industrial revolution, the improvements in technology, though important, were not decisive. But now the realm of means has gotten so far ahead of the realm of ends—

WARREN: Is this what Shelley meant by saying that our calculation has outrun our conception?

BROOKS: It may very well be and, if that is what he meant, then three cheers for Shelley. Yes. This has occurred, and it has occurred in such devastating degree that man is indeed now living in the Promethean age. (In *Prometheus Unbound*, you remember, Shelley named the age to come, our present age, the Promethean.) Man is now Prometheus, and this means that his thinking is all forethought: everything is oriented toward the future. Most moderns are guilty of a real hubris in feeling that they can accomplish practically anything they want to, can remake the world to suit themselves. The real problem for modern man is to determine what ends he should aim to accomplish. Yet, when he addresses himself to that problem, instead of finding an array of ends certified as proper by an objective science, he is presented with choices that can be dismissed as hopelessly subjective. Their validation is no more impressive than the funded wisdom of illiterate tribes and perhaps no better than mere myths, whims, and prejudices. No wonder that he may have to stretch himself out on the analyst's couch in an attempt to find out what he really believes and what his real values are.

WARREN: Isn't B. F. Skinner's theory of what society should be an attempt to overleap such difficulties as these?

BROOKS: I think it is.

WARREN: And by arbitrary means, to establish a community.

BROOKS: But the community he would establish, with all respect
to Skinner, that most amiable man, seems to me entirely
too close to the "community" of the bees and the ants. If
you brainwash everyone or condition everybody, you get
what Eliot refers to in one of his poems as a society so
perfectly organized that nobody has to be *good*. But, if
nobody has to be good, then the human dimension, the
realm of choice and temptation, is gone. We are outside the
human realm altogether. We have become in a real sense
machines—automata.

WARREN: Because we have no possibility of selective experience,
is that right?

BROOKS: Right. Because if you are really the perfectly con-
ditioned white rat, who has learned the maze now and
can't possibly take a wrong turn, you will obviously stay
out of trouble. But what is goodness for the human being if
the possibility of evil is eliminated? Does goodness in that
case have any significance?

WARREN: Skinner's theory puts man in the premoral state; he
becomes a member of the primitive tribe, as it were.

BROOKS: Yes. But with this difference. Man does not return to
the unfallen Adam's Garden of Eden, living happily and
without effort on the bounty of nature. He goes into a kind
of sanitized dormitory attached to a scientific refectory. His
meals are chosen for him. His bed is made up for him. Any
wrong choice is eliminated, because if you allow him
choices you inevitably introduce the possibility of bad
choices.

WARREN: Well now, Skinner's argument is that societies have
always tried to condition people so that they would make
the right choices. According to his view, if I read him aright,
a society always tries to remove man from the necessity of
the moral choice so that he responds properly, without
pain.

BROOKS: I suspect that there is a large element of truth in what Skinner says about past societies. Though the great prophets, philosophers, and statesmen of the past have always seen the danger of what we today call brainwashing, shortsighted people (and most of us are) have doubtless, from the beginning of history, pushed toward a rigid conformity to the going rules. Yet, if Skinner is right, then all that one can say is thank God the societies of the past weren't *able* to eliminate moral choice, because, lacking such choice, the human being couldn't get into blessedness any more than he could get into sinfulness. In moral relationships he will be a eunuch. It may not be irrelevant that, as a kind of by-product of our inability to dodge the moral choice, the societies of the past achieved a great literature. Such a work as Dante's *Divine Comedy* would be impossible in Skinner's world.

WARREN: Skinner might reply that in heaven there will be no need for literature. There's to be no marriage or giving in marriage. He thinks he's creating another heaven.

BROOKS: His point about literature would be a shrewd one. We don't know what the songs of heaven—either Jehovah's heaven or Skinner's—will be, because in our human, fallen world the only significant poems we have deal at some level at least with the possibility of evil, failure, and unhappiness. Even the most lighthearted song of spring has behind it a reminiscence of winter. It's a mortal world about which our poets have written their great poetry, and not merely their great poetry. I would add "all their authentic poetry."

WARREN: Well now, are you saying by any chance that we should cling to our vision of a fallen world in order to get good poems?

BROOKS: No. My position is not a modern variation on "sin that grace may abound"—welcome sickness, poverty, and cruelty so that literature of a significant order can be written. Rather, I would put my position this way: Skinner's world is possible only at the price of dehumanizing man, and we don't want man dehumanized. It would be a great gain to conquer or at least mitigate the evils of this world, to make sure that nobody died of cancer, that all were well fed, that everybody was freed from drudgery. We have to work for that. But, even if Skinner's world were possible, which I certainly doubt, it would be humanly intolerable. To bring it about would demand too high a price—the giving up of the human dimension. The point has been made eloquently by Orwell in *1984* and by Huxley earlier in *Brave New World*. Such a world would be inhuman.

WARREN: Yes. And so would be Skinner's world. And Soviet Russia is a try for such a world.

BROOKS: I agree.

WARREN: Well, my point in bringing Skinner up is not—I'm glad we got off it. I wasn't really aiming at that. I was saying that man is so desperate for community. We find projects like Soviet Russia and its hideosities and things like Skinner's proposal to create, in an equally arbitrary way, a community which he does not find now existing among us.

BROOKS: Let me interrupt with a little quibble here, though I hope that it points toward an important distinction. Is Skinner really promising to found a "community"? Would his world actually constitute a community? Auden has a very interesting distinction that I think may be relevant here. He distinguishes a crowd from a society and a society from a community. People gather around the scene of an accident—that is a crowd, a purely random assemblage. A society is different; it is a group of people who are related by their economic and social functions—so many bakers, so many tinkers, so many tailors, so many candlestick makers, all related by function. A community is different still; it is a group of people who are related to each other by common loves and hates, by the values they share. Now, of course, a society can also be a community. But some societies are not communities, and one way to put the case against the state of human affairs in a highly industrialized world is to say that it has ceased to be a community. Skinner, it seems to me, is promising a society efficient, beautifully adjusted, and frictionless, but lacking the character of a truly human community. Can men really feel affection for each other as brothers if you have eliminated the possibility of their being able to quarrel with each other? You remember Allen Tate's criticism of modern society in his "The Last Days of Alice." In that society men are "blessed without sin," but the blessedness is arrived at by simply denying that sin is possible. But if you eliminate sin in those terms you have also eliminated blessedness.

WARREN: What we're probably seeing in our time, or may be seeing presently, is that, the community having failed, society begins to fail.

BROOKS: That's a very shrewd insight; it may very well be a true insight.

WARREN: We just don't know.

BROOKS: But surely if we look back at the past—if history and the great literature of the past mean anything—a society, however efficient, which failed to be also a community would be a spiritual desert, a social machine rather than a human community.

WARREN: And couldn't even exist except in Skinner's terms. I'm thinking of Baudelaire's poetry in this connection. He saw a world going to pieces around him, and he saw—as far as I can make out the meaning of his poetry—he saw this as a corollary of a failure of the religious sense.

BROOKS: Yes, I think you're right.

WARREN: And he saw the streets haunted by ghosts, by specters.
In poem after poem, he looked at the sky and found the sky
empty. It's the God-abandoned world that he saw around
him, the teeming, swarming world of people without pur-
pose. To remark this is to take our discussion back to
religion now. But this theme of the failure of the religious
sense goes back a long way—before Baudelaire, no doubt,
although he's the great dramatic moment for us, I guess.

BROOKS: I suppose he is. Eliot, in his poems about the city (and
all of his early poems are essentially "city" poems), was
frank to say that Baudelaire provided him with a knowl-
edge of what the business of the poet was. Like Baudelaire,
Eliot describes a world in which people move in circles.
They are not going anywhere, simply revolving. They are
without purpose and life has no meaning. Eliot eventually
came to see this meaninglessness as a failure in religion. A
major problem for Eliot is whether a civilization can get
along without a religion.

Let's go back for a moment to Yeats's condensed history
of English literature. Chaucer's world, obviously, was a
world steeped in religion. Yeats, of course, was well aware
that in Chaucer's world a good many awful things hap-
pened. In that world the ecclesiastics themselves could be
vicious people. On the highway to Canterbury rode the
worldly monk as well as the poor parson, and, worse still,
the cavalcade included the friar, the summoner, and the
pardoner. But the world of Chaucer did have cultural uni-
ty, and Yeats valued that. (Perhaps because of his own
situation as a modern, he may have overvalued it.) Besides
unity, this medieval world had a sense of purpose. This is
not to say that the general sense of purpose set every
member of the community moving on the right path. For all

its sense of religion, it was clearly not a world in which everybody had become good, in Christian terms, or even had become "good citizens." No religion can guarantee that it will discipline and regiment its members so that they will faithfully exemplify its doctrines and practices. Even such horribly misguided attempts as the Inquisition failed to do that. I'm inclined to think that believers and non-believers alike tend to ask too much of a religion. Yeats was on safer ground surely when he emphasized the role of religion in a culture as providing a ground of unity, based on some particular view of the nature of reality, that provided meaning for the lives of human beings. Such has been its primary role in the history of religion. The civilizations of the past usually have started with what looks like some kind of unifying impulse, based on a set of values which were regarded as transcendent.

WARREN: Even with the recognition that, in the very century (the thirteenth) that Henry Adams idealized, the century of Chartres, the world of faith was rent by heresies and schisms, not to mention human failings, and that, as Meyer Schapiro has pointed out, artists were more often concerned with aesthetics than with salvation. Even recognizing these things?

BROOKS: Yes, even so. Acceptance of these values holds the civilization together. The death of a civilization comes with the decay of religion. In the decline of the Roman Empire, one sees the old religion dying away. Nobody really now paid much attention to the cults of the Roman gods. And you got, perhaps to fill up a sense of emptiness, a growing interest in the mystery cults of the East, the worship of Mithras, temples dedicated to Isis, and so on. Without getting into the matter of cause and effect, whether the decay of religion "caused" the fall of Rome or the fall entailed the decay of the older religion, clearly the two events were related. With the breakup of the empire you got, for better or worse, the new religion of Christianity, and it provided the foundations for a new community.

WARREN: Now here is, to me, one of the key questions that we have to face. Many people, including many believing Christians, either take the fatalistic view that Christianity is dying or that, even if its life can be revived, a revived culture will have to wait for its resurgence. Or perhaps there must be some readaptation of it to new conditions or some new vision of it to redeem us. On the other hand, many people think that the problem is humanistic: that we must find some equivalent to Christianity, some sense of mission that rests upon a naturalistic and humanistic base. Unified by such a sense of mission, modern men might attain to community once more and be, not a mere society, but a functioning community. Now I know that you are a communicant and a believer. A person like me, who is not but who finds in Christianity the deepest and widest metaphor for life, might be described as a yearner, you might say, though I don't know that I yearn. I simply take what I have taken from the Christian tradition, but see that "something" only in humanistic, naturalistic terms. I regard religious value as something that I can "do" myself, rather than connecting myself with some organized church. But I may be wanting to have it both ways. I say this because my whole instinct is to try to find, I suppose, the Christian values in terms of humanistic action, or action based on humanistic means, even naturalistic means. Now this is putting it badly, and this may be a confession of a confusion of mind. But, clearly, you and I might go very different ways at this point. Well, probably not very different ways in action, though that is possible. I'm not even sure that we would go such different ways in our thinking.

BROOKS: The difficulty of my position is, of course, obvious. It's hard for the believer not to put himself in a false position: how can he affirm the Christian claim to absolute truth without seeming arrogant, and yet how show a proper tolerance for other claims without appearing wishy-washy? I hope that, talking with an old friend, I can avoid being punctured by one or the other horns of this dilemma. So much for my little preamble.

In the first place, Christianity by its very nature actually seems to invite the kind of problem you put a moment ago—the translation of the supernatural into merely humanistic terms. By having a man-God, through its doctrine of the Incarnation, it came very close to humanizing at some level the whole nature of religion. John Crowe Ransom had some very interesting things to say on this subject years ago in his *God Without Thunder*. Certainly Christianity has argued, rightly or wrongly, that men can act out God's will and must try to do so. The Christian prays, "Thy kingdom come, Thy will be done, on earth as it is in heaven."

On the other hand, Christianity has retained—that is, if it's orthodox Christianity—a transcendental element. Ultimate truth and value do not depend on the success of the human enterprise. The church has always insisted that, even if the human enterprise collapsed altogether, if the world simply burned to a cinder, the truth would still be true and the realm of virtue would still be intact. This latter claim has from time to time been interpreted as being simply a promise of pie in the sky, the promise of a never-never land in which all hopes will someday be fulfilled. Undoubtedly certain Christian heresies have tended to show such a view. We have had a kind of quietism which has said, "Oh, well, the situation on earth is hopeless. We can't do anything about it. The good man will have to find his true reward in the afterlife." That notion is, of course, a heresy.

What might be regarded as a contrary heresy is millennialism. Modern-day millennialism puts all its eggs in the secular basket and assumes that with our powerful technology men can indeed become as gods and produce a heaven here on earth, whether in Skinner's terms or in some more fully human terms. But I state these fairly obvious matters merely to clear the air. As far as the immediate future is concerned, I think that all of us, Christians, humanists, and naturalists, are in the same boat. It is a boat that has sprung a pretty serious leak. Whatever we think the ultimate future can be, we shall all for a while have to bail like hell. We must take short views and do the best we can to avert disaster, whether out of an enlightened selfishness or out of disinterested concern for our fellowmen.

If one takes a somewhat longer view and believes that one can establish a community again, a truly human community, but do it without reference to some kind of transcendental faith, I have my grave doubts that he is right. These, however, are simply my doubts, and I am in no position to sneer at people who don't agree with me. To take a somewhat longer view myself, let me say that I don't look for any immediate revival of Christianity. I don't, for example, think that a powerful dose of the old-time religion or the application of certain revivalistic techniques will serve. They will certainly not work for the emancipated man of our day. On the other hand, I see no future for the church if it simply commits itself to a program of good works. Important as that is, it does not provide a *raison d'être*. Secular humanistic organizations can do this and have an excellent record in such work. If this is all that religion amounts to, then I think the church should transfer what goodwill it has left to such organizations and simply go out of business as a special institution.

WARREN: We see all about us people groping for some kind of community—all kinds, from hippies to serious philosophers—some sense of anguish and a failure in the sense of a human bond in our society, or in what passes for society today. Almost an anguish. But to turn back a moment: there are people who say that we are entering a new dark age and that they have to sit it out, retire to some small cubbyhole and wait for the return of the faith. Or there are people like Yeats, who said that the dream of his early manhood for a modern nation to return to unity of culture was false and who decided that in his time such unity could be achieved only by some small circle of men and women. The rest of us would have to wait, he decided, for the moon to bring around its century. Like Eliot, he sees the select circle pulling away from the world outside and waiting for the turn of the moon to bring its century or for God to offer a revelation.

BROOKS: Well, I have certain sympathies with Yeats because I really think he had a profound sense of history, more profound than I once credited him with. On the other hand, Yeats was a determinist, if I understand him correctly; he didn't claim to be a Christian, except in a very vague and general sense. At any rate, I can't accept that view. I don't think that our future is tied to the courses of the stars or that we are simply the victims of blind forces of history about which we can do nothing. I would differ from Yeats in another regard. I think that history is ultimately unpredictable.

WARREN: Eliot talks the same way—in the same tone of voice, rather.

BROOKS: Well, I think that Eliot's may prove to be a rather accurate prediction of what probably lies immediately ahead. On the other hand, I would interpret rather differently the spirit of his remarks on this subject. In one essay he mentions a "Christianity of despair" and indicates that what he hopes for is something very different from that. I don't think Eliot ever counsels us to retire from a hopeless world and let the devil take everybody else. But, if men go awhoring after false gods, what do you do? Your concern for truth forbids you to join them. You may even view your retreat from the world not as a retreat, but as a rearguard action, and your true concern, a resolve to save from the wreck something truly precious, not just your own precious skin. Consider what happened at the onset of the Dark Ages fifteen hundred years ago. Communities of people who were like-minded did band together to grow their crops and to preserve the manuscripts of the ancient world, to transmit the old tradition, to worship what they believed to be the true god, and to minister to wayfarers, the sick, and the hungry. They clearly didn't feel that they could do anything more, and today it's hard to see how they could have effected any immediate change in the course of history. (They did, of course, in the long run change the civilization, for the better or for the worse. I put it this way, for many intellectuals today would say it was for the worse.)

But to come back to the place where your question really pinches. No sincere believer could make his retreat from the world either with an air of nonchalance or with a prim self-righteousness. Nevertheless, one can imagine circumstances in which he might feel that he was forced to go underground to maintain his truth—not to exclude other people but to keep alive something valuable for mankind.

In fact, though I'm only moderately sympathetic with the hippies, I would agree with what you said a few minutes ago about them. It's possible to interpret their communes as attempts to do something like this.

WARREN: They are trying to form communities.

BROOKS: What they are saying is that the contemporary world has no room for something that they regard as all-important. I doubt that they are trying to exclude any like-minded people. They simply want to cultivate their own little garden. They would be happy for you to cultivate yours too.

WARREN: As I observe some hippy communes in Vermont, what is wrong with their plan is rooted in their own ignorance. They don't know the nature of their predicament. They don't know how to make it real in terms of what nature provides—or what nature does not provide.

BROOKS: In other words, part of their trouble is that they don't know how to cultivate a literal garden, how to grow beans and tomatoes. But, before we drop this matter of whether Christianity has any vitality left in it or whether we are not fixed irrecoverably in a post-Christian era, let me make two points, the first of them by way of reiteration. I repeat that any recovery Christianity ever makes will probably be slow and not achieved through spectacular evangelical methods such as crusades for Christ, conventions of Jesus freaks, and such-like procedures. If Christianity is to be recovered at all in our day, its method will have to be that of—to use an old-fashioned term—witness. That is, the professed Christians will have to lead such lives as to convince other people that they are in possession of something important. Though witness has always been the most effective kind of evangelization, it is, God knows, the hardest on the would-be evangelizers. Human nature being what it is, it's always hard to live up to your professed standards. But that's a failing not peculiar to the Christians. Even politicians find it hard to *be* the image that their speech writers and PR men devise for them. The political events of the last two years will furnish striking, even lurid, examples.

The other point I want to make is that whatever "religion" —whatever set of established values—supersedes Christianity will, like Christianity, finally have to be accepted as a matter of faith. For example, we both know people who believe passionately in the equality of all men. I think this is a noble thing to go to the stake for, but I don't think that one can ever found that belief on scientific evidence. One can certainly show that it is a "reasonable" belief. One can also point out the sorrow and distress that's been caused when people believed otherwise. One can show that the most admirable societies we've had in the past, at least the ones that we men of the twentieth century regard as most admirable, shared this faith at some level or tried to move toward it. But application of physical, chemical, and biological measures will continue to show all sorts of inequalities among human beings.

WARREN: You've said that the admirable societies of the past accepted the equality of men. Well, the Greeks didn't accept it, not unless the helot was not to be regarded as a "man." Nor did the Romans.

BROOKS: No. And this brings in another matter. Certain great civilizations have, of course, to be regarded as seriously defective.

WARREN: Well, even though the Greeks didn't accept man's innate equality and the Romans didn't, can we have a community today that refuses to accept it? We have learned more, perhaps. We've experienced more. I don't mean learned from scientific sources, though there's evidence there too. But, waiving the evidence, it's a very different thing to say that, since the Greeks did not accept a notion of the equality of men, we needn't accept it either. Their nonacceptance is no evidence to justify our nonacceptance.

BROOKS: No, no evidence for us. My point is simply that the "evidence" for men's equality is not finally naturalistic evidence—that is, evidence attested by the natural sciences.

WARREN: I'm sorry. Actually, you're right.

BROOKS: I wonder how far can you have what we would call a true humanism without bringing in certain transcendental beliefs, faiths, and the like.

WARREN: Well, transcendental beliefs and acts of faith are not necessarily the same thing, are they? They are ultimately acts of faith, but it seems to me that we perform every day of our lives acts of faith that are quite different from transcendental beliefs.

BROOKS: Maybe so. I suppose it's possible to say that there have been certain religions which have had no transcendental elements in them. I suppose it can be claimed that Buddhism, if properly understood, contains no transcendental element at all.

WARREN: And Marxism has its religious aspect.

BROOKS: Marxism, in its religious aspect, I think involves a contradiction. Why should people wear out their lives and give up their own well-being for the future well-being of other people? They make a sacrifice for which they get no naturalistic reward at all. The reward they get is by some kind of imaginative projection. I don't think that dialectical materialism actually allows for such satisfactions in its system, though in practice it has obviously produced what I would have to call Communist saints and martyrs.

WARREN: They were indeed: people who had a faith in some value that was not provided for by any natural base. But this kind of thing is not uncommon.

BROOKS: Not uncommon. And speaking of nonmaterialistic re-
wards, consider the ancient Jewish religion. So far as we
know, it did not have a belief in an afterlife. Yet it surely
produced a true community, and it was a transcendental
religion. That is, the Jews believed in a god who was in
some profound sense outside the universe he had created.

WARREN: They held a transcendental belief, all right. But the
Marxists do not. Yet the Jewish faith and Marxist dialectical
materialism have worked to create true communities. Or
maybe you'd say that the Marxist state is not a community
but only a society. Yet, when you have saints and martyrs,
you have the makings of a community.

BROOKS: I would add that, if you are going to have a real
community, the values affirmed must be accepted by sub-
stantially the whole group.

WARREN: Well, I accept that.

BROOKS: To get back to what was defective in Greek and Roman
civilization—the denial of the equality of men—how much
of our modern faith that all men are equal derives from
Christianity?

WARREN: Well, let me ask, how can you have a belief in the
equality of men in a pretechnological period? To reverse
things, to have a civilization at all you have to have
machines, and, if literal machines aren't available, then
certain poor bastards get made into machines—slaves, and
so forth. All I'm saying is that we can't talk about equality
outside history and, sure, we can't avoid our Christian
history in this part of the Western world. We can't avoid it
and we are living on benefits from it. That is true indeed,
and I know that I live on benefits which I am not willing to
pay the price of in one sense of the word. I've said that
before. But does one have to accept Christian theology as a
whole and as an article of faith simply because he acknowl-
edges a certain historical indebtedness to Christianity?

BROOKS: Though Eliot presumably believed that a true and enduring community has to be underpropped by a religion, he concedes that the relation of religion to the individual man is a special case. For example, he frankly says that, if a man can't believe in religion, he'll just have to do without. You can't, for example, make a religion out of poetry.

WARREN: That's another point, now.

BROOKS: He goes on in the same context to make a further point that there are decent, able, fully humane people who are frank to say that they have no religious faith whatsoever. As an instance, he mentions York Powell, one of the people that Yeats talks about so much. Here was a man who was as happy, untroubled, and serene in his unbelief as the most devoted Christian was in his faith. I think Eliot is clearly right here. There are individuals who do seem to get along happily without any religious faith at all.

WARREN: Well, here again is the question of a religious sense equating with Christianity. That's the problem. That problem arises too with a particular man such as Powell.

BROOKS: York Powell obviously, when he gave up Christianity, gave up religion altogether. We don't find him—

WARREN: Well, did he? That's the talking point at this stage. There are many people whose religious sense is so absorbed in their lives that it's not visible to the naked eye, but yet the behavior of such people may be totally that of a religious man. Such a person recognizes values that can only be arrived at by faith—cosmic values, shall we say.

BROOKS: Eliot's most interesting point on this particular subject (and perhaps his soundest point) is this: that individuals can live on the spiritual capital of their ancestors and lead virtuous lives.

WARREN: Well, virtuous or not, I feel myself to be living on the spiritual capital of history.

BROOKS: Well, all of us are.

WARREN: In the same way, on the literary capital as well.

BROOKS: What Eliot worried about was whether a society, a community, as a whole, could maintain itself without a religion. He described a series of dilutions that he regarded as typical: orthodox Christianity first becomes a kind of very liberalized Christianity; in the next generation this becomes Unitarianism, probably, which then in a succeeding generation becomes humanism, and, ultimately, naturalism.

WARREN: Well, that is a matter of public record about the course of society in the modern world, the modern world of the last several centuries. We can trace it in America, play by play, stage by stage. In this pattern of degeneration of orthodox Christianity that Eliot remarks on, that you have remarked on, do you see a historical necessity in it? Is it determined, an unavoidable thing? Or do you see some human options in it? Historical options, social options in it? Options that haven't been taken? How do you regard it?

BROOKS: Well, I regard it this way: I think that the person of our world who holds to the Christian doctrine finds himself committed to a double vision. He certainly is enjoined against locking himself into some kind of historical determinism, which may issue into ethical defeatism. On the other hand, if he has any acquaintance with history, he is bound to recognize the great difficulties in changing its course and he is also bound to recognize the stubborn cantankerousness of the human mind. A recognition of those circumstances, let me repeat, does not commit one to defeatism about improving the human condition. It may, however, induce a little caution against accepting the promise of new elements that have come into the modern world, things like "science" or "education" or "planning" that many people hope will provide a breakthrough into a new world. Maybe they will—let's hope so—but anybody who's been engaged for most of a lifetime in education—people like you and me—is bound to have his confidence in education shaken just a bit. We know how many crimes have been committed in the name of education. In fact, caution about whether we can improve the human lot and by what means and how rapidly is in our times a sign of health, for a very present danger in our society is what I have referred to earlier as millennialism, an overweening confidence that the road to utopia is broad and easy.

WARREN: Well, this is a very marked belief in America—has been from our very beginnings—that the City of God or the City of Man as perfected by man could be just around the corner, that it could be prepared for even by force of arms.

BROOKS: This is a dream that has dominated our history.

WARREN: Vietnam's the last example of it.

BROOKS: Of course millennialism has in it some good elements as well as bad. From my perspective it is a Christian heresy. I mean by heresy a part of the truth taken to be the whole truth. It is specifically a Christian heresy because it is rooted historically in the notion of the New Jerusalem or in Saint Augustine's terms, the City of God, the heavenly city of eternity as distinguished from the secular city. In the course of time, the notion of the heavenly city was gradually secularized and brought down to earth. American religion today is basically a kind of millennialism, and even institutional Christianity has been heavily influenced by millennialism.

WARREN: Progress is a common name for it.

BROOKS: Yes. That is, all problems are held to be soluble and, granted good intentions, sharpness of intelligence, and enough money spent in the technological laboratory, whether the social or the physical—

WARREN: Or enough rockets—

BROOKS: Or, to mention the better side of it, enough expenditures on various kinds of aid, so that we can take a primitive people and provide them with supermarkets and up-to-date hospitals—

WARREN: And democracy—

BROOKS: And democracy—or take an unsophisticated people and provide them with arable fields and pastures, the heavenly city will appear on earth.

WARREN: Well, isn't democracy caught in the same paradoxical situation as religion?

BROOKS: I think it is—the same kind of paradox. History tells us that a democracy without proper leadership does not work. On the other hand, the leadership has to maintain some sense of the *respublica*, some reverence for the common good. That means, among other things, that they must have respect for the people at large. If the leaders develop an arrogant elitism, there is danger, and worse danger if they aspire to some kind of dictatorship.

WARREN: Or Skinner's utopia again.

BROOKS: That's right: a "perfect" state arrived at by brainwashing the populace. The citizens are so conditioned that they can't run off the rails onto which their wheels are properly grooved.

WARREN: They can't run off the tracks even into evil. There's another aspect of this paradox in democracy, one recognized by Jefferson and Washington. On the one hand, they trusted democracy. They were willing to risk their necks and their treasure and their sacred honor for it. But they were aware of adverse forces afoot in history, such as the tumultuous citizenry of the great cities. They worried about the possibility of the electorate of the great cities degenerating into a mob, for a democracy could fail through the corruption of the electorate as well as through the corruption of the leadership. Our history, as we look back on it, shows, on the one hand, a movement toward democracy but, on the other hand, disintegration of the democratic spirit into mob spirit, corruption, pressure groups, and self-interest—and contempt for community. Can you have democracy without a sense of community?

BROOKS: No, I don't believe you can. There has to be some spirit of community if there is to be a democracy. The people must share common values, including some standards of justice and a genuine concern for the commonweal. Otherwise it can be expected eventually to break up into warring groups at odds with each other.

WARREN: In his autobiography, Yeats declares that he believes abstraction to be the enemy of cultural unity, by which he says he means not the distinction but the isolation of occupation or craft or faculty. In a way, Santayana was in substantial agreement with this, saying that the old springs of poetry may dry up because of the constant presence of abstraction in the thought of the modern world. And others have said this; all the romantic poets have said this in one form or another.

BROOKS: I'm familiar with the Yeats passage you've cited and I've given it a lot of thought. In some of his comments there is, of course, a good deal of folderol: for example, his assertion that in the great days of the past, the Venetian ladies, or maybe it was the ladies of one of the other north Italian cities, ended their balls on the sidewalk at dawn so that the common folk could take part in the dancing. I wonder whether this literally ever happened. But I see what Yeats was driving at, that if you isolate the classes from each other, if you break them so far apart from each other that you have no common meeting ground, then the culture is in trouble. Factions form and harden and the civilization begins to break up.

WARREN: You've got not only Yeats, Eliot, and Faulkner and people of that stripe and kidney who complain of this loss of the sense of community in our time. Long ago, Bertrand Russell remarked the same thing in the world of his time. He was saying that in the great modern state it's very hard for the individual to make contact with the society. Its ramifications and exfoliations make up a complex structure. The sense of power becomes abstract and removed from the individual. He feels lost in it and lost in facing it. Russell suggested that in the modern world perhaps the only community in which a man could take refuge was some small organization—a labor union, a club, some small group—that could give him a sense of relation to an on-going project of any kind, that would give him some human warmth, and that would be comprehensible to him as a structure.

BROOKS: I'm glad to have this citation of Russell's observations on community in the modern world, for comments of this sort made by literary men are too often dismissed as inconsequential. Besides, Eliot and Yeats are often regarded not only as impractical but as reactionary, opposed on principle to the modern world. But Bertrand Russell was a philosopher and a great mathematician, a liberal and one of the architects of modernity. His testimony ought to count heavily in certain quarters. Now that you've mentioned Russell, I recall his distinction between what he called "power knowledge," the knowledge given by modern science, and "love knowledge," which he regarded as an important knowledge too, but knowledge of a very different order.

WARREN: Yes. Russell's distinction points to the very core of the matter we are discussing. And in *The Scientific Outlook* —that's the book you refer to, isn't it?—Russell wound up with his version of the nightmare of a "brave new world"—this before Huxley, I think. Just before.

BROOKS: To return to the isolation of the classes as a factor in the loss of community, let me say that one of the most interesting things about American history in the eighteenth and nineteenth centuries was the comparative flexibility of the classes. This was an important element in the strength of the early republic. There was little isolation of individual from individual, of individual from community, of class from class, of occupation from occupation. Even the wealthy merchant, for example, probably had farming ancestors. He might himself have begun his life as a farm boy.

WARREN: The fluidity, up and down, in America has been enormous. It's been our salvation, I suppose. It's been a dynamic of our achievement.

And now, back to this matter of abstraction as a force calculated to corrode cultural unity. We often have heard it said that the difference between the northern mind and the southern mind, if one is allowed to use these big, sweeping myths and metaphors, has to do with the sense of abstraction; that is to say, it has been argued that a certain concreteness marked southern thinking, whereas northern thinking manifested a more sophisticated handling of abstract ideas. The northern mind was, in a sense, the more thoroughly trained in science. The difference would often show itself in treating problems of race in the civil rights movement during the fifties and sixties and in subsequent movements involving race. Ralph Ellison speculates on this point in some of his interviews and essays. He sees the concreteness versus abstraction as distinguishing the two sections in their thinking about race. This is only one example and perhaps even a debatable example.

BROOKS: I don't think so, for surely it is only one of many such examples that could be adduced. This quality of concreteness I find very definitely in my own experience; it's also very easy to point to in southern literature. I hasten to concede that the southern concreteness sometimes causes difficulty. It does not constitute the best way to handle certain problems. One sometimes sees problems only in terms of their density and their immediacy when a somewhat cooler and more detached view would be more useful.

WARREN: The real point may be in this whole question of abstraction—as discussed by Santayana and all the rest who have talked about it—the need for a double vision. We haven't been able to achieve it yet, to keep a sense of the immediacy and the concreteness—in Ransom's phrase, "the world's body"—in contrast to the abstract formulations which deny experience as experience.

BROOKS: Yes. And, with the rise of a highly complicated technological civilization, the stress has been on means rather than on ends, on techniques rather than on values. Modern civilization has a penchant for abstractions and tends to disparage concreteness.

WARREN: I'm sure you don't want to set back the clock at this late hour. I'm sure you recognize as fully as anyone that abstraction is a necessary sophistication of mind.

BROOKS: Yes. One certainly doesn't want to set back the clock. We do want the best of both worlds, that of the future as well as that of the past. But I must make the observation that sometimes history itself sets back the clock. I'm not predicting anything so awesome for us as the downfall of civilization, but surely a citizen of Rome in the fourth or fifth century must have regarded the invasion of the barbarians as setting the clock back by centuries. Civilization had pretty much to start over again. There was a reversion to near primitive conditions before a high civilization could once more be developed. I'm not a prophet of doom. All I'm saying is that unless the civilization can be restored to some kind of good health, history itself will see to stagnation or regression.

WARREN: One difference now is this: our barbarians are inside our gates. Barbarism is of our own making.

BROOKS: Yes. Who was it—the Spanish philosopher who wrote a very interesting book called *The Revolt of the Masses*?

WARREN: Ortega y Gasset.

BROOKS: Yes. And, although that book has rather gone out of fashion, I think the problem he was talking about is still with us. The new barbarians are inside the fabric all right, coming right up through the floor of the civilization, between the cracks. They say, "We don't want discipline; we despise it; we hate the establishment; we want everything to be radically new." Some of them have an admirable barbaric vigor. Some present a true bill against the establishment, in many of its particulars, at least. But many are barbarians nonetheless.

WARREN: Well, Ortega y Gasset is no patch on some of the nightmare possibilities envisaged by, for example, Zbigniew Brzezinski in his "America in the Technetronic Age." For instance, he envisages a cybernetic world with a massive population without occupation or purpose, supported in comfort, even luxury, and constantly lulled by diversions to prevent psychic explosion of some sort. Here is the new kind of barbarism—womb culture. But right now our society, the West, harbors, creates, its own kind of barbarism. Senator Proxmire has lately answered such dire predictions by saying that Americans all like to feel proud of their occupations, of achieving something. I pray to God he is right, but I am thinking of some places and people I know. And I'm not talking of the working man. I'm thinking right now of the managing man, right at the top of certain organizations, who makes certain expensive products that are sold to me and aren't worth a damn. But back to the other barbarians. Our society contains forces that loathe all the arts in all their manifestations except the most obvious popular arts. Such forces are working from the top down as well as from the bottom up. Both ways.

BROOKS: I agree. The best case for some of the youthful barbarians is that they're fighting another and perhaps worse barbarism, the barbarism of the elderly. Yet the presence of those two barbarisms is depressing. I expect that the best hope for our civilization is to maintain some kind of fruitful tension between these barbarisms. You want vitality; you don't want inertia. You want flexibility, not petrification; it would be intolerable to have to choose between the affirmation of a debased status quo and a protest that dismisses the past as completely meaningless.

WARREN: Well, if you look at the modern world, you see that there has been for a long time a great tension, a conflict, between the establishment and the intellectuals and the artists. And some historians or sociologists have remarked that capitalism as a system has recognized that you must not be repressive toward your intellectuals and your artists. Don't repress them. Choke them with butter. Repression would lead in the end to the destruction of free enterprise, capitalism's prime sacred cow. Now my fear here is that as long as the arts weren't even necessarily recognized by governmental powers, except by an occasional little gesture of censorship or official praise of a Longfellow, the result was harmless. In a way, the recognition of the arts officially carries a real danger—the control of the arts. Capitalism thus tries to defang the arts, to defang the intellectuals by taking them in and drowning them in butter, not just choking them with butter. I have a real fear that the arts may be killed with kindness of this specious sort.

Let's look back at this matter of the structuring of society in another perspective. There is the role of the artist, of the writer, of the creative scholar. Ever since the industrial revolution or, if you want to put it differently, ever since the romantic movement, as I remarked earlier, the artist and intellectual types that I have mentioned have been in the position of alienation, if not protest, vis-à-vis the big, Western, capitalistic, bourgeois, industrial society. Now sometimes the artist will find himself lining up against the values of the industrial or the capitalistic order. What do you make of this?

BROOKS: Well, that fact is highly significant if we are looking for signs of the disintegration of—or, if that term is too drastic, the maladjustments of—Western culture. Wordsworth in his day, for example, was terribly troubled about the status of poetry. He had to ask himself whether it had any real importance. In a world that was just coming out of the Age of Reason, did the poet really have anything to say? What was his "truth"? How did it measure up against what the Royal Society had delivered as the truth? Or consider Shelley, who wanted to assign a great function to poetry. One remembers that he called the poets the unacknowledged legislators of mankind. He was eager to have a revolution, to stir up Ireland, to defend the Manchester Chartists, and so on. Such has been one role of the literary artist as he comments explicitly or implicitly on the world about him. But ever since the romantic movement there has been a countertendency, a turning inward, as the writer explores the depths of his own psyche. One aspect of this tendency reveals itself in the vast amount of what is called confessional literature. This turning inward of the modern writer, especially of the contemporary American writer, was the theme song of the Pryce-Jones article that I mentioned earlier in our talk. He tells us that the typical American writer who lives among the concrete cliffs of the skyscrapers, "far from the flash of dogwood blossoms or trout streams"—I'm quoting him here—feels himself alienated, helpless, frustrated, driven back into himself, either railing at the establishment or else exploring some interior anguish. His reference to those "concrete cliffs" tells us to what special latitude he has calculated his findings. American writers closer to the dogwood blossoms and the trout streams may show less frustration. Nevertheless, he points to a cultural crisis that is real. Alienation and cultural crisis: these are the salient features of the American literary life as seen by many observers both at home and abroad.

WARREN: Most Europeans, it's my observation, tend to diagnose the American scene as simply American and thus fail to see that the same thing is happening all over the Western world. What's happening to us is implicit in, maybe necessarily implicit in, the whole notion of the technological society, the industrial order. Or, to take another angle, I would consider Sartre as one of the most "alienated"—to use the dirty word—writers ever. "Alienated" always raises the question of alienated from what? Consider the billboards along Italy's highways. If you look at them or

those of any country of the West, you'll see the telltale
symptoms of what is too often thought to be an "Ameri-
can" disease. All the countries of the West reveal the same
disintegration of values that we have. It's not quite as
marked in the European countries, perhaps, but it's
there—or is it *more* marked?

BROOKS: Yes, in certain regards the disease is more devastating
there. I was given an interesting comment by a young
Greek here at Yale a few years ago. He told me that
American-style advertising was far more damaging in his
country than here. Because it had had its start in America,
the American people had built up some kind of antibodies
against it. But the Greek peasant was defenseless; he took it
as truth. There it is before his eyes on the TV screen.
Presumably the Greeks and other Europeans will eventu-
ally develop their antibodies too. But, to return to the
general point from which we started: the disintegration of
values, of which we have been speaking, is not a local
American phenomenon, but is endemic to the whole in-
dustrialized (and industrializing) West.

Let me say this, however: whatever the future holds,
whatever deterioration occurs, or whatever recovery of
values should be achieved, the role of religion in a culture is
tremendously important. Historically, religion has been
the great binding force. That, of course, is not its only
quality or function. It could, for example, flower in a great
poem like Dante's *Divine Comedy*, a great mythic enactment
of the heights and depths possible to mankind; but, unlike
any poem which needs demand only a willing suspension
of disbelief, religion actually gripped the whole society at a
deep level of conviction. I would argue that the breakdown
of traditional religion is the best index of what is happening
not only here in America but in varying degrees all over the
Western world.

THE SOUTHERN IDENTITY

WARREN: Various people have said in regard to the American Civil War that the South had no continuing sense of identity because it had no binding religion. But the Irish, for instance, had a cohesive force in their religion and were not subjugated. They kept on making trouble for the British for hundreds of years. For the Confederates, once Appomattox had happened, it was all over except conversation.

BROOKS: Well, I demur a bit there. I think that there has been a resistance that is still alive, though with the general point I agree.

WARREN: The South's resistance is not a political resistance. It's another kind. It has various manifestations and sometimes, I must say, some that I don't approve of.

BROOKS: So with me.

WARREN: We accept as a fact that the South had nothing to fall back on once Lee had surrendered. They had no cohesive force except sentiment after that. Not religion.

BROOKS: Well, I think that's basically true, but again, I have some reservations. I think that as recently as twenty-five years ago the South could have been said to be the one part of the United States that still believed in the supernatural.

WARREN: In a broad way, perhaps. But it wasn't a binding force as is generated by a universally shared religious center. There was no church, no articulated faith to fall back on as the Irish had. The South had no—it had a regional "set" of a kind, the kind you found in the "backward" part of the country, but it didn't have a hard central point of reference, you see. Southern nationalism—and the South almost did become a nation, was one for four bloody years—anyway, southern nationalism was a peculiar thing. It was real, God knows; people died for it. But it was, and is, competing with another "nationalism," for southerners felt that the Revolution was theirs, just a little bit more than anybody else's. Southern nationalism competed with the older nationalism, even in the same bosom.

BROOKS: To go back to the question of religion. The Irish have distorted their religion by making it a kind of bulwark of nationalism.

WARREN: Yes.

BROOKS: The South, in formal terms at least, had the same religion as the rest of the country—nothing that could set it off against the "ungodly" North, for example. And of course the South was fractionated with all kinds of sects and cults. In general, I agree with the proposition that, if the South had had a coherent religion, highly articulated, which set it off from the religion or lack of religion or different religion of the rest of the country, that fact certainly would have made a great deal of difference.

WARREN: Well, there are other facts than that. I don't want to raise, to discuss, the point, but to me the doctrine of states' rights was in itself a suicidal doctrine in the Confederacy.

BROOKS: I suppose it was, though again one could play with the term. But remember what we were saying just a few minutes ago. Continued centralization through industrialization, urbanization, and the growth of the executive branch of the federal government might also prove suicidal—suicidal, that is, to any concept of democracy.

WARREN: It may well be.

BROOKS: If, for example, it's going to sweep out the artist, if it is going to disintegrate the culture.

WARREN: Well, I'm simply thinking about Governor Brown of Georgia—his behavior—the fact that the states were so jealous of their states' rights in the Confederacy that they

had a hard time in achieving an effective central govern-
ment to wage the war.

BROOKS: Yes. They dismembered themselves in the face of the
enemy. Brown's policy was insane. There's no question of
that. Perhaps this is the best reason for regarding the
southern cause as being, from the very beginning, a "lost
cause."

WARREN: One more question, Cleanth, about religion. For a long
time, for more than a century, there's been a tendency to
assume that the arts—most frequently it is poetry that is
singled out for this—can take the place of religion, can
perform the same function that religion has performed in
the past. Matthew Arnold, of course, is the famous exam-
ple of this, as we mentioned earlier in this conversation. Do
you want to talk to that a little more?

BROOKS: Yes, though I concede that here I'm taking a minority
position. There are not only many who would affirm Ar-
nold's position; they number amongst themselves some of
the best literary minds that we have. I would therefore be
foolish to adopt a dogmatic tone in what I shall say. In the
first place, I concede that art and religion have much in
common, but I see them as having rather different roles. A
little while earlier I talked about literature as presenting a
kind of total, dramatic picture of the world, a picture that
could be accepted with no more than a willing suspension
of disbelief. Thus, you can put down your Dante and you
can pick up your Homer and, again, you have a view of the
world which is dramatistic, which makes a certain sense,
which has a certain dignity and beauty. You don't have to
choose between them—at least as a *literary* man you don't
have to choose. I think that a society profits from having a
group of people who are aware of some of the human
options and who are able to see the world under different

great governing metaphors. By providing such perspectives, literature becomes a civilizing force.

WARREN: Malraux's notion of the museum without walls applied to literature.

BROOKS: That's right. I think that for me, at least, this is the basic role of the arts. They have been always a civilizing force. I prefer to regard them in this way rather than as prophetic, that is, demanding dedication and commitment. (If one means by "prophetic" simply that the work is a profound human utterance, that's a different matter.) I think the real issue is whether the civilizing function is enough to undergird a culture or a community. After all, there have been, and are, barbaric religions. I hasten to say that I prefer a civilized religion. But, if the religion, however attractive, becomes merely a charming and beautiful cult, so tolerant that it can accept almost anything, a ceremonial sword with no cutting edge, then its value has been reduced to that of an aesthetic experience. It is no longer a religion.

WARREN: In making the comparison to a ceremonial sword that has no cutting edge, are you implying that literature has no connection with action?

BROOKS: No, but I do mean to say that it has no *immediate* relation to action. Even a novel that changes men's minds is different from a political pamphlet. It is by contrast reflective, detached, and contemplative. It possesses a certain aesthetic distance which allows its subjective matter to be seen massively, "in the round." The rhetoric urging direct action is stripped down for action, stripped of all that might distract one from action.

WARREN: Let me ask you a question. You're saying that we look at the arts for the civilizing of society. We look at the arts and see Homer, Dante, Milton, Dreiser, Baudelaire; we read them with something like the same spirit. We can put ourselves inside their skins and learn about their society. Scholarship allows us to enter deeply or less deeply into that society so that we can read them with some sympathy. But there's another question. Do works of art originate in this kind of sympathy? Quite a different question. Can the individual artist be thus catholic or not? Must his work not grow out of some deep personal commitment? Won't it almost inevitably show a personal focus? This is not to say, of course, that a writer may not have a large grain of skepticism in him. Skepticism may in fact be a dominant attitude toward reality but, if so, that's part of his personal world view and something rather different from the uncommitted catholicity about which we've been talking. On the contrary, it's another example of the writer's personal focus. We know less about Shakespeare's views than we know about the views of Balzac or Baudelaire or Melville. But we do feel an overarching basic vision in Shakespeare. We don't find just scholarly catholicity; we find a powerful personality and a certain world view, however we may choose to define that world view.

BROOKS: That's a very important point. I find it hard to believe that anything except a very special and limited kind of art could come out of a totally uncommitted spirit. Surely most authentic literature reveals some deep personal vision. The reader need not adopt the writer's conviction; but the writer himself will probably need to have convictions.

WARREN: I feel that too; that's why I think that the modern world has another split in it. On the one hand, as civilized viewers of art, listeners of music, and readers of literature, we aim constantly toward a catholicity for deeper understanding of the various possible views. We strive to live in the museum without walls. But, on the other hand, can the artist do that? Isn't he bound to stay with what is the hot thing for *him*?

BROOKS: Right. Isn't every artist at some level an existentialist? I want to be cautious about using this now overworked term, but it does seem to have a special relevance to the artist, for every artist must find his own particular way of seeing the world. He never, of course, comes to his own vision from an absolutely fresh start. He always is in some relation to the culture that produced him, though his response may be partial acceptance or redefinition or even complete rejection. But he's got to make his view of the world *truly* —experientially—his own. Even if he has inherited from his culture a great controlling metaphor, he will probably have to make his own modifications of it. The artist, in short, is not out for an adventure among masterpieces or even among basic metaphors through which to interpret the world.

WARREN: The artist can, of course, have sympathy for the various kinds of people who figure in his work, and the dramatist must. He may even take a skeptical view of their values—values are very hard to come by in the world and often they tend to cancel out. But that's a world view too.

BROOKS: Well, to go back a bit. I set a very high value on the arts and particularly the one I know best, literature. But I doubt very much that you can found anything but a very limited community on the arts alone. Granted their civilizing value, can they undergird a culture? Thus, I am skeptical about the success of what Stephen Dedalus promised to do. You will remember that at the close of Joyce's *Portrait of the Artist*, Stephen resolves to be "a priest of the eternal imagination" who will forge the uncreated conscience of his race. In terms of Joyce's novel, it is just and proper that Stephen Dedalus should see this as his role. But Stephen would have been more modest and accurate if he had determined only to try to remake the "consciousness of his race." This latter resolve in fact makes lots of sense. The artist is constantly showing us what we are as well as exploring what we might be. But conscience, unless you're using the term in the old eighteenth-century sense in which conscience can mean merely consciousness, does not represent what the artist characteristically creates.

Though literature obviously deals with morality—"with concrete moral problems," as Allen Tate puts it—nevertheless the realm of the aesthetic has to be distinguished from the realm of the ethical, and, as a corollary, literature properly dramatizes a situation rather than offering an ethical principle. This is not to say that the artist does not have his own personal ethics, which may, in particular instances, put to shame those of most other people. We cited earlier the example of an intellectual like York Powell who, according to Yeats and Eliot, was a man of intellectual dignity, probity, and absolute sincerity.

WARREN: Like a Lucretius or a Marcus Aurelius.

BROOKS: Yes.

WARREN: Was the problem the same in the pre-Christian world as it is in the Christian world here?

BROOKS: I would think so. One of the things I want to do soon is to read again the history of the Roman Empire in a good deal more detail and, I hope, with a more discerning mind than I read it long ago. One might learn from it something pertinent to our own situation. There are certain parallels between our immense, terrifically successful civilization with its superhighways and luxurious bathrooms, like those of the Romans, and its order and decency and general efficiency, like the Roman, yet a civilization which, again like the Roman, shows a deep dissatisfaction with its own success. Many Roman citizens apparently felt a hunger for something to believe in, something to hold onto, something to give direction to their lives. At the end, the Roman

Empire was indeed a decadent empire. It was the rose that was beginning to wilt.

WARREN: It wilted for a long time.

BROOKS: Yes. Rome wasn't built in a day and it didn't go to pieces in a day. It did wilt for a long time. If our own society is indeed wilting, that will probably take a long time too. Our barbarians will be of our own nurture. As we remarked before, they will come up through the cracks in the floors of our civilization.

WARREN: Or down from the Senate house—or White House.

BROOKS: Yes. In any case they will be *insiders*. I'm not nearly so much worried about the threat from outside. I am not particularly worried by Chinese or Russian Communists, for example. Our downfall, if it comes, I suspect will have to be put under the heading of autotoxemia. But I don't prophesy. I think that one of the most profound things that Eric Voegelin ever said was that we delude ourselves if we think we can predict the course of history.

WARREN: No, there's no reason for believing that. At best, the past can show only possibly fruitful parallels.

BROOKS: You can't outguess the course of history and that's a good thing. I would like to think, for example, that my own somewhat gloomy view of the future will prove to be quite wrong.

WARREN: Well, whatever the prognosis about the outcome of history, the individual must act. "Arise! thrust in the sickle," Henry Vaughan writes, out of his Bible. You have your own role to play, whatever the prophets of doom may say.

BROOKS: At the very least you would want to go down making an effort, not just lying supine. The unforeseen and even unlikely event is always possible. Besides, if you hold that the values in which you believe are eternal, you have to act upon them even if the civilization does go under.

WARREN: Robert E. Lee confessed at the end that he had "never believed in victory." But, to get back on the track, there are a number of people like me who stand outside any formal religion or even outside the Christian religion in any strict sense of the word. We are beneficiaries of the Christian religion, the Christian tradition, but we still want to find our way and can't find it in terms of orthodox Christianity.

BROOKS: Well, on this point I'd rather talk of the general situation than in terms of individuals. For this preference I have two good reasons. First, I think that the former raises the bigger issue. Second, one doesn't want to risk saying things that might sound like self-righteous priggishness. To claim that one is a believer, at least in our present secular civilization, smacks of pharisaical self-congratulation. To maintain the doctrine doesn't mean that one claims that he has succeeded in living up to it or even wholly understanding it. My friends who profess no religious faith at all number some of the "best" people that I have ever known. I wish I possessed their personal virtues. But to come back to what I think are the basic issues: I'm not worried so much about the individual in our civilization as I am about what is happening to the civilization itself.

WARREN: Well, I am too. And I think we are probably fairly close in our worries. Also, I agree with you about the matter of the arts being no substitute for religion. But a world without art would be a world, I would guess, incapable of religious sense.

BROOKS: I think it probably would be. Or it would yield only a very thin, barren, and barbarous religion.

WARREN: I've overstated it. It would be a thin and rather brutalized religion.

BROOKS: Yes. And the history of Christianity itself reveals just that when we look back at some particular periods—for example, the deficiencies of sympathy for other human beings as revealed in an auto-de-fé or in the wars of religion in the sixteenth and seventeenth centuries. And later, in the seventeenth and eighteenth centuries, the period in which this country was being settled, "Christian" nations such as Britain, Holland, Portugal not only tolerated slavery but themselves engaged in the slave trade. Slavery was not invented by the American South. New Englanders in the colonial period owned slaves, and even that generally humane and peaceable sect, the Quakers, had members who sailed slave ships. Christianity has often been affirmed when its precepts were not fully understood or, if understood, not lived up to. Less scandalously, there have been, and still are, societies that claimed to be democracies but tolerated all sorts of undemocratic anomalies. It's a sad human failing. My present point, however, is this: can one hope to have an integrated civilization without some kind of religion as the integrating force?

WARREN: All right. I would agree with that completely. Yet, Christianity, in its orthodox form, is unavailable, I think, for many people. Unavailable to me. I can take it as a big governing metaphor which speaks the deepest about human experience. It has to be that. But by using the term "metaphor" I'm not reducing religion to a work of art. It's not a work of art; it's a work of something else—a spiritual work—which undercuts and underlies works of art. I'm not saying that I take it as just another metaphor in a merely figurative sense. I take it as a metaphor for existence—that it penetrates existence. That isn't making any sense.

BROOKS: Yes, that is making sense.

WARREN: Cleanth, there's a very striking sentence in your last book. I wonder if you could gloss it, explain it. It might touch upon a lot of things you have said before. It just might. Here is your sentence: "If modern man wears the daytime face of Prometheus, his nighttime face is that of Narcissus, and the modern writer usually shares both experiences and may indeed feel torn apart by them." Well, Narcissus is clearly in some way the antithesis of Prometheus. But could you spell out a bit their relationship?

BROOKS: *Prometheus* is, of course, Greek for "forethought." Prometheus is a demigod, the semidivine man who brings technology and scientific knowledge to mortal men. For them he steals fire from heaven. In the Greek story, Zeus, the king of the Olympian gods, punishes Prometheus because he's gotten above himself. He is making man too powerful. He will eventually enable men to challenge the reigning deity. Certainly Shelley, in his *Prometheus Unbound*, welcomed the Promethean age, looked forward to it as an epoch in which man would become indeed divinized, would get control not only of nature but of history as well—would be able to direct the course of history. Prometheus would enable man to make the world what the world ought to be.

Ours is certainly a Promethean age. We are worried unless our gross national product is getting larger every year. We are confident that our knowledge of the universe will be rapidly enlarged. We mean to emancipate ourselves from every kind of restraint. We've actually landed men on the moon, a truly spectacular feat. There is something quite grand and splendid about it. Those successful applications of theoretical science are truly marvelous achievements, whether they are the triumphs of modern surgery or the moon shot. On the other hand, the strain exerted on modern man by his very achievements is tremendous. For these achievements to become possible he has had to live in a certain way and at a certain tension. Therefore, a part of modern man turns away—turns inward. Modern man is not only like Prometheus. He is also like Narcissus, gazing into the pool, trying to discover himself. I think that there is some kind of relationship, perhaps causal, between our great technological advances that have made man in the "developed" countries so powerful and in these same countries the number of desperately unhappy, frustrated people who don't know what to believe in and who have difficulty in knowing what kind of persons they really are. But modern man as Narcissus is not the poetic Greek boy, in love with himself, gazing into the pool to contemplate his own features. The love of, or at least confidence in, the self belongs to the modern Prometheus. The modern Narcissus gazes into the deep pool of self with desperate anxiety. Too often he finds in it no reflection of a familiar face.

WARREN: This is a little like Pascal's note on the two infinities. Man stands on the knife-edge between the infinitely small and the infinitely great. Such would be the outward and inward aspect of infinity for us and, on the knife-edge between them, man unable to understand himself—the infinity of the self and the infinity of the objective, space-time world.

BROOKS: Or, one could go to another great Frenchman of Pascal's age, Descartes, who split the world in two: the inner world of the psyche, which, in our day, becomes more and more mysterious and difficult to deal with, and the immense world outside, which includes the moon shot and all the other great technological achievements, a world amenable to almost any kind of scientific investigation.

WARREN: With reference to both of those infinities I often feel lost. My relation to the world of great scientific achievement is so tenuous. I can admire it, but I understand so little that I feel left behind. You can grope toward an understanding of it and feel a pride in man's power of mind and in the character too of those great achievements. But, in much the same way, you also look toward the abyss of the self and attempt to explore it, and you can feel equally frustrated, equally torn between the two things. I understand all too well the sense of isolation for the man who cannot really penetrate either. It must be a very common experience.

BROOKS: It must be. But I must hurry on to make one reservation. I don't mean to imply that the men who landed on the moon tossed on midnight couches, distraught and frightened by the abyss of self. *They* at least may not be like either the ancient or the modern Narcissus.

WARREN: Better not be.

BROOKS: My impression is that few if any of them were split and divided men. In fact, they seemed to have been not only healthy in body but untroubled in mind. Most of them seem to have left behind them wives uttering prayers for them and on Sundays sitting in their pew in some evangelical and often fundamentalist church. Understand, none of what I say here is meant to be disparaging or to express surprise. You would hardly expect our lunar Argonauts to be "Hamlet[s] thin from eating flies," to use a phrase from W. B. Yeats. It's probably a good thing that they were not introspective Hamlets.

WARREN: Why should they have been? We don't want to put poets and philosophers on the moon. We want to put technicians on the moon.

BROOKS: Yes, technicians with stout hearts and few neuroses. But then, by any account, our moon men were extraordinary. Most of us, however, are ordinary, closer to the average; and even average citizens, including the less sensitive, have been affected by modernity. In short, one doesn't have to be a professing intellectual to have felt the stresses and strains of our epoch, to have been pulled—pulled apart, sometimes—by contemplating either one of the infinities.

WARREN: In fact, the jails and mental hospitals are full of casualties who are functionally illiterate.

BROOKS: But we can view our plight in more positive terms. It has made for some very great writing. It has furnished our writers with perhaps their most persistent theme: the loss of cultural unity, the crisis in civilization, and the great challenge to mankind generally. In sum, the widening rift in the culture and in man has put in a new perspective nearly all of the stock situations with which our Western literature has dealt for some 2,700 years.

WARREN: Let's turn again to the South for a little. Some distinguished historians, for example Vann Woodward in *The Burden of Southern History*, as well as some literary men, have probed at the question of the "unity" of the South and, to put it in another way, what makes the South the "South." Let's probe a little more. To begin with, how would you treat the idea that the presence of the black, and all which that entailed, created the South?

BROOKS: The black man influenced the South tremendously, and still does, of course. But, "created" seems a little strong to me. I am inclined to say that the southern experience created the South, just as the English experience created England and the French experience created France. The presence of the black man was a very important part of that experience. But to say that his presence created the South oversimplifies a very complicated situation.

WARREN: Let's look at another statement: the fact that the Confederate states lost the Civil War made possible the "cultural unity of the South"—in other words, made possible the myth that defines the "South."

BROOKS: I have to resist that notion, too, though it contains a good deal of truth. Men remember the wars that they lost, not those that they won. The causes that refuse to die are nearly always the lost causes. Undoubtedly the South's attempt to get its independence in 1861 gave the southern states and the southern people a sense of unity that was all-important for the southern consciousness. The fact that we lost the war was in a sense even more important. In the first place, the war had important consequences. It helped lock the South into a colonial economy, and this was the basic factor in making the South from 1865 until the 1930s what Roosevelt called America's "economic problem number one." I'm even willing to accept your phrasing "made possible the myth that defines the South," though I would add that the entity that we call the South is indeed *supported* by a myth. But I'd like to look into this matter of myth a little further. I'd have to claim the same thing for the unity of America: in great part it's a complex of intangibles that holds America together. If it weren't so, I don't think that our continental empire, with all of its diversity and competing sectional interests, would necessarily remain one nation. If there is a myth of the South, there is also a myth of America.

There's another connection with myth that I'd like to develop a little further if I may. Any myth that has shown the endurance and vitality of the myth of the South always involves some sort of important truth, even if one can't always state that truth in scientific or sociological or historical terms. I mentioned the American myth with all that it connotes of man's fresh start, the great experiment in democracy, the liberation of the common man from all sorts of oppressive overlordships. To take up something closer in character to the southern myth, let's look at the New England myth, which we both know is very much alive today. The New England myth, in fact, supplied the most powerful genes for the present American myth, but the New England myth has its own particularities. The Pilgrim Fathers brought that myth with them, or maybe it would be fairer to say that the myth in its power and vitality brought them to these shores. They were a chosen people, leaving their Egyptian captivity to set up in the wilderness God's own polity, the kind of society in which Jehovah had indicated in the Scriptures he wished men to live. The quest for the perfect society was, as we know, secularized, but it has continued to be a quest, a march to the New Jerusalem, though the New Jerusalem is no longer conceived as the heavenly city but as the radiant democratic metropolis.

It's interesting to compare the southern myth with the New England myth. If New England was from the beginning millennialist, one can say that the southern myth was not so much millennialist or utopian as arcadian. It looked not to the future but to the past. If, however, we insist that any new beginning cannot help being future-minded, the future toward which the South looked was a *re-creation*, on a new and more bountiful soil, of the Roman republic.

Do you remember Horace's sixteenth epode, and especially the lines that go something like this: "To discover the good life, good men must leave the city and sail off to the west." It was, from the beginning, an agrarian dream—life lived close to nature in which an American Cincinnatus could, when needed, leave the plow and take up the sword and where, in the senate hall, wisdom would be dispensed through learned eloquence. Southern political oratory has played upon this theme for decades, and the theme is sounded even today. John Peale Bishop, if I remember right, wrote a very fine poem in which his southern ancestors were likened to Aeneas, sailing to the west to preserve a heritage, and Allen Tate has written at least two or three very fine poems on this same subject.

Mind you, I am not forgetting the material side of things, as if dreams and ideals determined everything. The Jamestown colony was founded in Virginia to make money, and Boston was very quickly producing its merchant princes. Yet material causes and selfish motives rarely squeeze out cultural myths. You could even argue that they need them and nurture them. But, before leaving this myth business, let me say that the myth of the Old South has gotten its bad name by being used too often to provide situations on which to base very bad literature, much of it written by southerners, but some of it written by their yankee cousins. Such fiction usually does portray an unreal world, and the southern plantation as depicted in such fiction is about as sleazy and unreal as you can imagine. But that doesn't mean that we can't get glimpses into a real plantation world when, say, we read Mrs. Chesnut's *A Diary from Dixie* or Robert M. Myers' *Children of Pride*. I'm not forgetting that the plantation South was only a special part of the Old South. Yet some such world, magnolias, white columned plantation houses, masters and slaves, and all the rest, did indeed exist, and the masters and mistresses were solid enough human flesh. Some of them, like Mrs. Chesnut, could apparently even be charming and, as the world goes, decent and likable people. A good many, like Mrs. Chesnut, were deeply concerned about the problem of slavery.

WARREN: To what degree can it be said that many of the special qualities of the South, or what may be thought of as such, are really qualities that simply belong to old America, qualities that can still be observed in backcountry New England and elsewhere? Qualities both bad and good?

BROOKS: A great many of the qualities of the South are simply holdovers from the older America, qualities good and bad that have persisted in the southern states after they had pretty well died out in other parts of the country. Even in the matter of speech, the South is a museum of old speech forms, pronunciations, vocabulary, as well as of customs and manners. There's no reason why the older South shouldn't resemble in many respects the older parts of the Northeast. The first settlers to both regions came from the same relatively small island at about the same time in its history and from essentially the same strata of society. (No one believes anymore the fiction that the first settlers to Virginia were younger sons of English noblemen.)

I think that during 1974 a good many people in this country, during the televised hearings of the Senate committee on Watergate, felt that they were witnessing a survival—in this instance, for most of them, a welcome survival—of the older America, as they watched and listened to the three southern senators talk. (I'm leaving out Senator Gurney of Florida because his voice, manner, and even mode of dress proclaimed him a modern easterner. As we both know, southern Florida is basically now an eastern state.) In this trio, Senator Ervin was the most conspicuous example of what I'm talking about, though he had obvious cultural affinities with his two younger colleagues, Talmadge and Baker. What do I have in mind in particular about Ervin? Not merely his accent, but his phrasing, his unfashionable fervor, even evangelical at times, his quotations from the Bible and the English classics, a certain innocence (real or feigned), a certain courtliness, and so on.

But I am not forgetting the qualification in your question,

"qualities both bad and good." The South on the whole has had a bad press for a long time. Everybody knows what its obviously bad qualities are. To mention one: frontier unruliness and violence have hung on in the southern states, particularly those in the great central valley, long after they died out in the rest of the United States. Any southerner hopes that the worst traits of the older America can be eliminated, and I think there is good reason to think that in the southern states they are being eliminated. But I, and I expect you too, hope that the good traits that have survived in the South won't disappear along with them. Even if they have been retained by accident—even by what some people would call the cultural stagnation—good traits they are. I'd hate to see them lost.

WARREN: Some ten years ago, when I was having a great number of interviews as background for a book I was doing called *Who Speaks for the Negro?*—what a different world that was, only ten years ago!—a young black, a girl just out of college, a native of Alabama who had firsthand acquaintance with some of the violence of that period, remarked to me that she had more hope for racial peace in the South than in the North. But I should add that a little later she changed her mind—a growing pessimism about the whole race question in our country. I have often wanted to see her and find out what she now thinks. But back to the question.

BROOKS: I too would like to know what she now thinks. But, earlier, she may well have had in mind the relative concreteness of the South. Life there is still less abstract than I find it in the Northeast. Even the sharper polarization in the South may have its helpful aspects. I heard just the other night on a television program a Negro man who had moved back from Chicago, I believe it was, to Montgomery, Alabama. He was talking about being a little more comfortable in the South. He was glad he had returned and, though he didn't gloss over the fact that bigotry and prejudice continued to exist, he could better put up with them there because their expression was blunt and forth-right. You knew where you stood, whereas in the North he had found that prejudice was often there, all right, but it was so guarded and buffered that you really couldn't be sure of your relation to the person in question.

WARREN: Saint Augustine says that the virtue of children is more the result of the feebleness of their members than of purity of heart. I am inclined to think that the same thing may be said of some of the qualities sometimes attributed to the South as special virtues. The product of backwardness, isolation, and poverty. But now the South is changing at an astronomical rate. Let me interpolate that I am in favor of change. But the question is: do you see any chance for the South, in its accelerating "modernization," to escape some of the things that have fouled our country and made our cities into cesspools of violence, degradation, and poverty?

BROOKS: Your citation of Saint Augustine doesn't exactly warm the cockles of my heart, but it doesn't chill the marrow of my bones either. I think that there is truth in what the tough-minded old saint says, and I am perfectly willing to apply it to the South, provided we are willing to apply it everywhere else. Original Sin right across the board— that's a ticket I can support. But, if we do apply it right across the board, let's remember that it will play hob with a good many American virtues. It will suggest that our vaunt-ed efficiency comes from a trained imbecility, that our tolerance of the people and customs and actions we don't like is not so much tolerance as our indifference and lack of commitment, and that such dissent and revolutionary en-thusiasm as we show may be no more than an exhibitionism, the chance to get our pictures in the paper and become heroes of our peer group.

To turn our attention specifically to the South, however. What you are really asking is how many of the special virtues that we attribute to the South are the accidental products of backwardness and isolation, and how many are indeed active virtues, conciously chosen and adhered to. It's sometimes hard to draw the line between them. Let me give an example. For the first five months of 1974 I lived in Baton Rouge. The house we rented from a professor on sabbatical leave came equipped with a pleasant Labrador dog that insisted on being taken for a walk once or twice a day. I quickly gave in—I needed the exercise too—and took her faithfully every afternoon through some part or other of the neighborhood. I think that every person within a radius of a quarter of a mile of my house, from five years old to seventy-five, spoke to me and usually inquired about my dog, not perfunctorily, but pleasantly and with what seemed a genuine human interest. Now I happen to like this kind of mannerliness. If it's just a built-in habit from an older and more leisurely civilization, I still like it. But, though it may well have been with some of my temporary neighbors only a formality, I got the impression that I was regarded not just as a thing but as a human being, a person. If so, the greeting, however unimportant, partook of active virtue and represented a civilizing force.

WARREN: I was in Utah recently for a couple of weeks. It's like Baton Rouge in that way.

BROOKS: Let me now move up to something that I think is truly important. I am thinking of the South's resistance—I think the South is still resistant—to American utopianism, to the notion that man is an unlimited creature who can do anything that he thinks desirable simply by putting good old

American know-how to work under a full charge of good old American willpower. I won't say that the South has been utterly untouched by millennialism, but I repeat what I said earlier: the southern ideal has been essentially arcadian, harking back to a simpler golden age, rather than millennialist, pressing forward to the secular New Jerusalem. Besides, millennialism feeds on urbanization, technology, and industrialization. Up to the present, the South has had comparatively little of these.

More important still, the South had the stuffings knocked out of it in the Civil War when it attempted to gain its own independence in an effort to control its own destiny. The loss of war and the long period of relative poverty that followed gave the South a salutary dose of realism. I think that Vann Woodward is quite right when he says in *The Burden of Southern History*: "The utopian schemes and the gospel of progress that flourished above the Mason and Dixon Line never found very wide acceptance below the Potomac during the nineteenth century. . . . The experience of evil and the experience of tragedy are parts of the southern heritage that are as difficult to reconcile with the American notion of innocence and social felicity as the experience of poverty and defeat are to reconcile with the legends of abundance and success."

How much of this admirable caution with regard to millennialist schemes still lingers in the southern states? I don't know, but I have an impression that the antimillennialist instinct is still strong. Insofar as the Americanization of the South means more elaborate stands for the Hamburger King, more commercialism of the spirit, more sociologizing of the language, and an increasing apathy toward the centralization of political power, then I hope the South will resist such "Americanization."

I am not naïvely optimistic. I am personally aware of how many of the vices of the Old South linger, and occasionally in the last several years on visits to the South I ran into instances of what I would regard as a new hard-nosed, business-before-anything-else philosophy. But I am heartened by certain things which I expect would cast a pall of gloom over other people. I am heartened, for example, by the stubbornness of the southern accent. Fifty years of radio and twenty-five of television have made, as far as I can see, almost no dent in it. It is an old-fashioned English, basically from the southern half of the island of Great Britain, with lots of archaic seventeenth- and eighteenth-century pronunciations, and, furthermore, liberally sprinkled with dialect pronunciations from counties like Devon, Somerset, Wiltshire, and Sussex. I see no good reason for changing it, and I think that the variety of American life will be impaired just to the extent that it is changed. I am also heartened by the persistence of all sorts of little personal habits, gestures, and attitudes such as make social life more interesting, more pleasant, and I should say more civilized.

I have mentioned small and what may appear unimportant things to indicate the stubbornness to change, but in this context they may be the most significant of all, for it is in matters of this sort that a life-style most visibly shows itself and its ability to maintain itself. But, that the South is changing in the sense that people have gone out of farming and moved into town, I readily agree. That the cities are growing and that Atlanta and Houston in particular have become great cities, American style, is obvious. Will the South simply become absorbed into America? And, for that matter, let me ask whether England, France, Italy, and Germany will also become "Americanized"? Will their life-styles also become variations on the American life-style?

Before answers are ventured, one may ask how much have Wales, Scotland, and Ireland been able to retain their cultural identities in spite of the tremendously larger and more powerful kingdom of England with which they are so tightly associated. For, though Ireland is a republic, politically independent, it is powerfully affected economically by its proximity to England. None of the parallels I have suggested fits perfectly the cultural situation of the South. Ireland and Scotland have their own dialects, and Wales has its own language, though it is beginning to disappear. The truth is that we don't know, but I have a great deal more confidence in cultural stubbornness and resistance to change than most of my friends, including most of my southern friends. I know that all over the world airports are alike, that supermarkets are alike, and that skyscrapers are alike. But I think that the importance of such likeness can easily be exaggerated. I can remember prophecies made nearly fifty years ago about cultural change, and note that many of them are still unfulfilled.

A final word on this subject on which I cannot be nonpartisan. I am an interested party and my bias against the change is clearly evident. But I would like to say this: it would be a shame for the South to change so fast that it would lapse into uncritical millennialism or else into the world-weary cynicism of the alienated intellectual before it had fully rid itself of its barbaric vices.

WARREN: And virtues.

BROOKS: Yes. Yet the possibility is real, for the vices of our great world cities and the vices of barbarism seem to get along very well together. Moreover, whether or not the South would lose by becoming Americanized, America itself, I am satisfied, would lose. One could be bitter and ask what would the rest of the nation use as a convenient whipping boy if the South simply became undubitably American? Or more genially, one could ask whether we don't have enough monotony already; it's to everybody's interest to preserve as much healthy variety as possible.

WARREN: What about writing in the South?

BROOKS: I think we would agree that the great period began after the First World War. We would also agree, in general at least, with the thesis of Allen Tate's essay "A Southern Mode of the Imagination," in which he argues that it was at this time that the southern writer achieved enough detachment from his own subculture to see it, perhaps for the first time, in the round and to understand it and to understand himself. Allen, of course, stresses the dialectical aspect of the matter: a southern writer was at last free to criticize his culture rather than compelled to defend it against attack and against even critical inspection. Allen's argument, which he comes at, of course, in his own way, is very like that of William Butler Yeats—to wit, that though we can create rhetoric out of our quarrel with others, it is only through a quarrel with ourselves that we can create poetry.

Yeats's position, as a matter of fact, was very much like that of the southern writers of the twentieth century. Though Yeats was born in 1865, his drastic alteration of style—and, with it, his quarrel with his romantic self and with his native land—occurred only ten or fifteen years before the much younger southern writers won their emancipation and entered the dialectical mode. To put the matter in a slightly different way, both Yeats and the southern writers rejoined the mainstream of Western literature and began to concern themselves with the plight of modern man. Where Yeats principally differed from his great contemporaries such as Eliot and Pound was in having a base in a backward-looking, traditional society which had hardly yet, as a culture, entered the modern world. Yeats turned that heritage, one that many people would have regarded as a liability, into an immense advantage. The southern writers of the 1920s were very much in Yeats's position: their culture, like Yeats's, had managed to preserve something of the wholeness, spontaneity, and concreteness of an earlier day and thus furnished the necessary other term for the dialectic—that is, passion as against intellection, poetry as against science, tradition as against modernity, an agrarian life as opposed to an industrial life. The backward South, FDR's "economic problem number one," filled with memories of a lost cause, but rich in personal relations, violent passions, and undying memories, was for the new southern writers not a liability but an asset: it was a necessary condition for a dialectical literature.

One could illustrate the matter from any of a dozen writers of our century. Faulkner is an obvious example, but the work of Allen Tate or Andrew Lytle or Flannery O'Connor or yourself, for that matter, would make the point just as emphatically. The question whether one loves his native section or despises it does not matter, though the question of whether he loves it uncritically or loathes it absolutely would matter very much. The authentic writer is too much the product of his own society and its culture is too much a part of himself for the either/or option to be valid. That is why Yeats's apothegm is really so much to the point. If the South sufficiently possesses the southern writer's imagination—if it is truly a part of himself—then his quarrel with it is truly a quarrel with himself, and the result can be poetry, often poetry of the most serious kind, including tragic poetry.

WARREN: In a world in which the contempt for the past becomes more and more marked and in which the mastery of mere techniques is more and more demanding, can you see any place for the study of history? I have in mind here something more than southern history; I refer to any kind of history. What can we get from the study of history? Is it more than the lies that we must tell ourselves in each period in order to be able to live with ourselves?

BROOKS: There is no doubt about the contempt for the past, a contempt that, I suspect, is a necessary part of the Promethean age. Prometheus was "forethought," whereas his brother, Epimetheus, was mere "afterthought." Most of us, consciously or unconsciously, associate the study of history with Epimetheus. If he had only thought about matters beforehand, he wouldn't have been put in the position of having to say along with the judge in Whittier's "Maud Muller": "For of all sad words of tongue or pen,/The saddest are these: 'It might have been!' "

We want matters operational, and the social sciences carry implications of operational value that history, alas, does not. What I'm going a long way around to say can be put more succinctly: if we believe that man essentially does not change, then history becomes the study of man, universal man, unchanging man, and thus a valuable study of ourselves. But, if we are so confident that modern man is really a new article, who has been reshaped by modern technology and has the means to reshape himself further and more radically, then why shouldn't we dismiss the study of history as antiquarianism, valuable finally for its entertainment matter, costume drama at best and, at worst, a drab record of the kind of mistakes that benighted men made but that we enlightened beings won't have to make in the future.

WARREN: But can't there be a history of how man changes?

BROOKS: Yes, but I am connecting the dismissal of history, insofar as it is a real phenomenon of our time, with what we earlier talked about as millennialism, man's confidence that he can, through his increasing knowledge, project himself on reality and create a kind of paradise on earth.

One of the most interesting things I've seen in the last several years on the subject is a set of remarks made by Eric Voegelin in an article in which he is arguing for philosophy and the study of human values as opposed to mere opinion-mongering or the adjustment of ourselves from time to time to some new climate of opinion. He rather slyly suggests that the student unrest in the last decade came about quite as much from the students' dissatisfaction with their professors as from their dissatisfaction with the war in Vietnam. He goes on to say that "even the spiritually and intellectually underprivileged, who live by the breath of opinion alone, have become aware that something is wrong with our institutions of higher learning, though they do not quite know what." The students, in short, want somebody to tell them the truth about reality. They want teachers who believe that it may be possible to ascertain the truth about reality—part of it at any rate—not merely to shuffle through the pack of various opinions. In short, Voegelin asks for the inquiry of Socrates rather than the opinion-mongering of the Sophists. (I ought to make it plain that Voegelin doesn't claim that the students, specifically those of the sixties, put it this way. Indeed, he points out that, if the reasons they advanced for condemning their professors were bad, it was because those professors had cut them off from the life of reason so effectively "that they could not even articulate the causes of their genuine unrest.")

Voegelin, however, goes on to point out that the genuine study of man is hard to suppress. It has, he says, begun to creep back deviously into our universities once more "under the respectable cover of comparative religion, comparative literature, the history of art, the science of the myth, the history of philosophy, intellectual history, the exploration of primitive symbolisms in ethnography and anthropology, the study of ancient civilizations, archeology and prehistory," and so on. He gives great credit for this revival to "the splendid advance of the historical sciences" which have "become the underground of the great *resistance* to the present climate of opinion. In every one of the fields enumerated, we find the men who devote their life to it, because here they find the spiritual integrity and wholeness of existence which on· the dominant level of the universities has been destroyed. No critical attack on the insanity of the 'Age' can be more devastating than the plain fact that men who respect their own humanity, and want to cultivate it as they should, must become refugees to the Megalithicum, or Siberian shamanism, or Coptic Papyri, to the petroglyphs in the caves of the Isle-de-France, or to the symbolisms of African tribes, in order to find a spiritual home and the life of reason." These statements may seem extreme, but they come from the pen of a man who knows a great deal of history and philosophy and who has taught for many years in Austria and Germany as well as in the United States. In any case, it's interesting that he sees the study of history as part and parcel of a genuine concern to understand the nature of Man, not simply to adjust or condition groups of men to fit into a particular climate of opinion or to keep them quiet as they live under the strain of a highly technological civilization.

In this general connection, however, I want to return, if I may, to the South once more. The issue of millennialism and history comes up in a very remarkable essay by Lewis P. Simpson first published in the *Sewanee Review* and then in his recent book called *The Dispossessed Garden*. Simpson describes the resurgence of southern literature in the third, fourth, and fifth decades of this century pretty much in terms that you or I or Allen Tate have used to describe it. But he puts a great deal of emphasis on what he calls the southern writer's "covenant with memory and history." The southern writers of the twenties and thirties and forties had not only a concern for history, but they had a lived history close at hand. They could actually talk to Civil War veterans and people who had lived through the Reconstruction. History, in all of its vicissitudes, touched them closely and was much alive. This sense of history and the drama of their own region could be brought to bear on the alienated and fragmented world that writers outside the South, writers like Joyce, Lawrence, and Eliot, were concerned with. Simpson sums up the matter by saying that throughout this period the focus of the southern literary imagination was on "the contention between the truth of history and the compulsion to gnosis." By "gnosis" Simpson—drawing on Voegelin as I do in my own remarks here—means the confidence in man's know-how and his orientation to the future, roughly what I have been calling millennialism. This is Simpson's way of describing the dialectic that characterized southern literature of the period.

The essay is very tightly argued and I am not quite sure that I understand the detail of the argument, but clearly Simpson is concerned with the fact that the southern writer today is further removed from history—that is, lived history—than the generation before him and that he is unable to rely on what a writer like Faulkner relied on. I believe Simpson's phrase is that the modern southern writer has been "dispossessed of the reality of memory and history—and so of the reality of human community—by gnostic modernity." The southern writer is thus driven back upon himself in order to find meaning or, as Simpson puts it, "the covenant with memory and history has been abrogated in favor of a covenant within the existential self." Simpson illustrates by saying that Faulkner's work was an attempted ratification of the first covenant, but William Styron's novels, for example, are an attempted ratification of the second.

I hope that Simpson will develop his argument in more detail. I find it, for obvious reasons, very persuasive. But it's gloomier about the prospects of southern literature than I would like it to be. On the other hand, it would provide a very interesting answer to your question about what we can get from the study of history. Someone might call the study of history a study of the human community, a study of man himself, which cannot be replaced by anthropology, sociology, or psychology, important as they are. That would be my line. I do think that the study of history is essential, but I think that the study of literature is essential too. For, with all of their differences, the subject matter is basically the same.

WARREN: The human being regarded in his humanity. Is that right?

BROOKS: Yes.

Allen Tate

What I Owe to Cleanth Brooks

E VEN THEN, in December, 1929, he was wearing his thick spectacles, and one had the fleeting thought that like Eliot's Donne he was looking into one's skull beneath the skin. The amusing, if somewhat disconcerting, thing about this was that it seemed to be a one-way scrutiny: his lenses were so thick that I couldn't see through to his eyes to surmise what he was thinking. And I can't to this day, forty-six years later. We know what Cleanth is thinking only after he has thought it and put it down on paper; what he doesn't put on paper we never know. Cleanth Brooks is one of the most mysterious men I have ever known. I couldn't have known then that back of the mystery was an acute intelligence so formidable that I have not to this day been able to fathom it. This small, mild-mannered man, so perfect a gentleman that one cannot understand that he has faced Eliot's "horror and boredom," is in my opinion, formed over more than four decades, the foremost American critic.

1929: Cleanth and I were brought together in Paris, at the Café des Deux Magots, on a chilly December afternoon by a

125

man named Charles Pipkin, who was somewhat older than I and, I believe, a former Rhodes Scholar who was already dean of the graduate school at Louisiana State University. I could not have known then that "Pip," as we later called him, was planning to bring Cleanth, after his Oxford degree, to Louisiana. Red Warren and Cleanth knew each other at Vanderbilt and in 1929 at Oxford; and, although Red was in Paris about this time, I didn't see them there together. Red got his B.Litt. degree at the end of the summer term; Cleanth received his B.A. a year later, in 1931, and in 1932 his B.Litt., and went directly to LSU. (Red did not go there until 1934, after teaching at Vanderbilt and Southwestern at Memphis.) I could not have known in 1929, and neither did Cleanth and Pip, that the triumvirate, Pip, Red, and Cleanth, would found in 1935 the *Southern Review*, the great literary quarterly of the 1930s. After Cleanth was established at LSU he began to write parts of his famous critical work *Modern Poetry and the Tradition*—slow and painstaking work which was not published until 1939. This distinguished book was dedicated to me; I take great pleasure, forty years later, in calling public attention to the dedication, in spite of the mysterious fact that I still do not know the reason for the dedication, for I have during all these years learned more from Cleanth than he could possibly have learned from me.

Just when in the thirties he began to send me first drafts of parts of the book for my "criticism" I don't remember, perhaps it was in 1937. The point I want to emphasize, a point that his modesty will not let him acknowledge, is that my ideas of the metaphysical tradition in English poetry derived order and coherence from those tentative chapters of the book. When *Modern Poetry and the Tradition* was finished we had for the first time a synthesis of the critical works of I. A. Richards, T. S. Eliot, John Crowe Ransom, and, to a small extent, myself. I had not known that such a synthesis was possible; and this, among other valuable insights, is what I learned back in those days from the interchange of ideas with Cleanth Brooks.

In the years that followed, up to the present, Cleanth has published a number of volumes which place him as the most versatile and the most resourceful American critic. The animadversions of erudite mediocrities like Douglas Bush to the contrary, Cleanth cannot be pinned down as a "New Critic" who limits his range to the routine of *explication de texte*, for, in addition to his subtle readings of poetic texts, he is also a learned historical scholar. He differs from most historical scholars in knowing how to use literary history: he knows that the poem is not merely its historical background.

There is the great book on William Faulkner: this is total criticism. (It will be followed by another volume on Faulkner.) There is *The Well-Wrought Urn*, a landmark in modern criticism; and then there is *The Hidden God*, a book that a mere explicator of texts could not have written. And now, in 1971, we have *A Shaping Joy*, a collection of eighteen essays, the range of which is so wide and the insight so deep that I look around in vain for another critic who could cover so authoritatively so much ground.

I conclude this inadequate eulogy of an old friend with the certainty that he is young enough, in spite of his recent retirement from Yale, to give us many more books for our instruction and delight.

Robert B. Heilman   # Cleanth Brooks: Some Snapshots, Mostly from an Old Album

IT IS A truism that Cleanth Brooks has greatly influenced the criticism and teaching of literature since 1935. He helped provide a vocabulary, and behind it a set of attitudes, that seemed to change the nature of literature. The beholder gained a new eye, and with it he saw in poetry what, though of course it had always been there, had not been readily or steadily beheld. "Beholder," however, is slightly misleading, for inevitably there were beholders and beholders: many stubborn adherents of the old vision, many enthusiastic readers by the new light, and another breed who I think best reflected the Brooks and Warren cast of mind, the bifocalists who were aware of literature both in its dependencies (the stamping ground of the old history) and in its independencies (where the New Criticism was breaking new ground). Whatever the varieties of literary experience, the overall change was so great that the "revolution in literary studies" is a historical cliché. In its most important aspects, that revolution is likely to be permanent; unless we are very unlucky we will not lose our knowledge that literature exists in its own right, not as a subheading of social history, and that its structures define its essence. At the same time the revolution had the "popular success" that begets its own penalties. Some enthusiastic converts seized new terminologies and brandished them so relentlessly that useful instruments seemed hackneyed. For years it was as if some seductive ad had proclaimed, "Symbols can be fun" or "Make every day your symbol day." (As late as 1971 a British play, Simon Gray's *Butley*, could base a farcical scene on an undergraduate paper solemnly dishing up image-and-symbol, paradox-and-levels, birth-and-death, night-of-the-soul criticism.) Then after some years a new generation, never having known the New Criticism as a struggling newcomer, saw it only as an established orthodoxy needing remedial rebellion. One persistent form of remedy has been political abuse; at times Brooks and associates have been called fascists, and recently I have heard them called racists (this by a black critic). But ordinarily reapportionism elects a more staid politics of headshaking over wrongheadedness, lengthy listing of shortcomings, announcing the decline of the oppressive doctrines, or alluding to their demise at some past time: "We have done with all that." To charge Brooks with error has become one way of symbolizing one's professional reliability, independence, and deserts.

I sketch this well-known history only for context. Since it is a history of some magnitude, it reveals how much more Brooks has been than even a well-known academic figure. To associate with him was inevitably to feel the energy of his mind, its habitual probing in many directions, its trying out of hypotheses, earnestly of course but many times playfully too, the rigor of thought infused with an imaginativeness that would often add gamesomeness to an enterprise serious enough at heart. I found in him a largeness of spirit that appeared not only in the deployment of knowledge and ideas, as hardly needs saying, but also—and this kind of thing does need saying—in generosity to the ways, the styles of others and in habitual authentic courtesy (I would say "courtliness" if that would not connote, in days of diminished self-discipline, an archaic heaviness) in relations with others. I have not slipped unawares into an anticlimax here: manners do image the man, the man is my subject, and graciousness is the everyday version of magnanimity. Magnanimity, or its cousin urbanity, does not always mark the intellectual, who alas may be given to the unawareness of others, the self-righteousness, and even the arrogance that betray malnutrition of spirit.

Though I say that the man is my subject, it is principally the man that I knew at Louisiana State University in the 1930s and 1940s. "Portrait of the critic as a young man" would imply both too much and too little: a portrait is more than the sum of a few snapshots (which I think is the right image for these informal notes), and "young man" wrongly suggests that all belongs to the past. Neither virtues nor crotchets disappear with time, and in Cleanth Brooks a greater than usual stability of being may be assumed.

Since I have elsewhere expressed my professional indebtedness to Brooks (and of course to Robert Penn Warren), I will stick to another kind of history here. When a flock of us new Ph.D.'s from the North came to an expanding LSU in the thirties, the liveliest members of the department were the Vanderbilt-*cum*-Oxford young men who were beginning to have some impact on literary and social criticism. Since newcomers such as myself knew nothing about the South or southerners and were not prepared for the innovating thought of some southerners and since the southern critics were not convinced that an influx of nonsoutherners with the old-style graduate training was the *deus ex machina* for higher education in the South, the situation was more than usually favorable for antagonisms and feuding, which are a central way of life in more than one English department. But as I remember it there was little more than initial cautiousness or tentative suspicion, the preliminary feeling out of others to see what human realities lay beneath styles that to either side may have seemed alien or even a little threatening. What developed was at least a thorough working amicability among men of different ways or beliefs, whether personal relations were more or less intimate. I introduce this agreeable history to make clear that it was not an accident and to give Cleanth Brooks credit for an important part in it. I have already said that he was a generous and courteous man; he could win confidence even when he did not win converts, and liking if not allegiance; he did not carry commitment into contentiousness or private judgment into the expectable next step of semivisible antipathy. What he had was not so much "tolerance" or *laissez vivre* as friendliness or social sense or disposition to keep doors open: a spontaneous getting on with people without modifying his dislike of that liberal spirit which in fear of being dogmatic tends to make no judgments at all. When we got better acquainted I knew that he made many judgments, always probing for the moral center and therefore often severe and doubtless sometimes as biased as other people's. But the constant need to be clearheaded was quite compatible with an easiness of intercourse that could survive almost anything short of indecency or failure of obligation. I am glad to be unable to say that Cleanth did not suffer fools gladly, for this banal pseudocompliment nearly always means that a man is rude to those who do not share his prepossessions. Cleanth gave fools the benefit of the doubt: they might be re-prepossessed. But he did have an extraordinarily vivid expression of dismay and pain—a plaintive, mildly accusatory falling and dimming of face—when nonfools did not get the point.

There was a lot of getting along with diversity among a number of faculty members who in 1939 joined in a move that had unexpected repercussions. "Liberals" and "conservatives," anti-Francoists as well as sympathizers with the New Germany and with Trotskyism and perhaps the New Russia generally, we had in common mainly a feeling that LSU was capable of improvement, and we got out a statement on this subject, naming a few things that could be done. To our astonishment, its appearance filled the air with the noise of denial and denunciation. Nineteen of us had signed the statement, and "the 19" became the day's strongest term of opprobrium; some 160 faculty members signed a counterstatement (several, they said, because they had been given no opportunity of signing the first one, as well as several of "the 19"), asserting that LSU was a treasury of academic excellences; and there was some vague talk of "haircutting," *i.e.*, nonreappointment, nonpromotion, etc., for the 19. (Of the 19, a number have died. Some went on to distinction, there and elsewhere—Brooks and Warren; Robert Harris, until recently dean at the University of Virginia; Charles Hyneman, Distinguished Professor at Indiana and sometime president of the Political Science Association, the only really good floor man in the 19; and one later became a vice-president of LSU.)

The affair of the 19 is relevant here for two reasons. One is that Cleanth Brooks was very active in it; we often held meetings at his house. He had a high degree of institutional concern and, if I may use an almost defunct word, loyalty; unlike many members of the profession, he did not use the pressure of other concerns (teaching, editing, an extensive program of criticism and scholarship) to justify indifference to the university. The second reason lies in the fact that one of the ways of discrediting the 19 was the old southern one, historically understandable but not quite expectable in a university, of calling them "damn yankees." One night Cleanth said, to a group of us who were at his house, "Let's check this out." We simply had not thought about origins before, and we began counting on fingers; the truth was that the 19 were almost evenly divided between northerners and southerners. What is more, we checked as many of the 160 as we could remember and found them to be likewise a mingling of northerners and southerners. There were two lessons in this affair. One, this use of "damn yankee" was an amusing example of a low-grade literary method that Cleanth had been inveighing against for some time—the easy use of stock terms to get a quick-trick stock response. Two, all of us were finding bonds, not in regions, but in qualities that have nothing to do with regions. Perhaps I seem a bit wide-eyed in naming this as a lesson and in valuing it, but I hope I am doing more than revealing my own naïveté. Even today we still manage to feel strong regional barriers, but that feeling surely had more grounds in the 1930s. More than that, Cleanth and like-minded men were sometimes stigmatized as "professional southerners," and their ways of defining and defending southern interests were not always acceptable to other southerners, not to mention northerners, who doubtless did not always find it easy to reconsider long-held assumptions. Hence the professed regionalists might easily have antagonized many and become withdrawn, indrawn, holier-than-thou, combative, and therefore unable to find common ground with anybody else. The point is that that is precisely what they never did in any way become, and to say that is to provide some evidence for what I have been saying about Cleanth. He contributed not to divisiveness, but to *esprit de corps* and even before that to assembling the corps itself.

His institutional concern led Cleanth to invest a great deal of time in seeking desirable appointments when the department chairmanship and the university presidency became vacant—

time for caucusing, trying to persuade colleagues, trying to reach the powers that were, and so on. Since most people want to put allies into chairmanships, it is worth reporting that Cleanth's candidate shared with him, I am sure, not one literary or social or political idea; Cleanth was simply supporting an honorable man. The presidency became vacant when the incumbent, a genius of a sort, a big thinker before thinking big had been thought of, an imaginative man who like other men of imagination felt the letter of the law to be irksome, found history and the market refusing to cooperate as a financial dream had told him they would and decamped. We were immensely busy about the succession, saved from hopelessness by ignorance of our own impotence. One Sunday Cleanth and several others in our thirties (volunteers? commissioned representatives? and if so, of whom?) drove several hundred miles to call upon the president of the Board of Supervisors at his home, hoping to urge our candidate upon him and to register dismay over the rumored front-runner, an army officer (who was soon to get the job). On such occasions Cleanth adopted what seemed to me a very ingratiating approach: a sort of naïvely earnest throwing of us appellants on the mercy of a court admittedly dedicated to all worthy ends. Cleanth did not have to be a serpent to be a little less the dove that he was content to appear, trusting to the goodness in men who have crumbs to toss to hungry mouths.

The sixtyish-or-so president (lumber? oil? sugar? I don't recall) was courteous and friendly, professed gratitude for our concern, and said he had the best interests of the university at heart. Then with Cleanth and me he took a tack that was devastating in effect, though I am unsure whether he just fell into it, made honest use of a good thing, or took a deadpan demonic revenge for our bothering him. Having found that we professed literature, he took on the air of a kindly benefactor: "Gentlemen, I know that you will be interested, etc." Then he revealed to us a manuscript or privately printed pamphlet, the poetry of his wife, and introduced us to the maker herself. He was like a plantation owner letting an oil prospector in on a hidden gusher in the back forty. I am not sure whether we were to assay the crude on the spot or send in a laboratory report by mail. On the scene I limped in clichés while Cleanth managed benign words, in which the chilly critical spirit was somewhat muffled in the folds of courtesy and in which he gave only the mildest of gentlemanly turns to the screw that might have capped that well of English a little defiled by gentle reading and unfettered memory.

I have especially wanted to picture Cleanth as at once the very responsible man and the very genial man. I will only allude in passing to a strong filial piety of several kinds and to a quasi-paternal devotedness that exacted much in time and energy; Cleanth took on large responsibility for a younger relative and probably surpassed most fathers in giving literal day-to-day assistance with studies and other problems. Various family calls upon him were, I suspect, unusually demanding, but they never elicited any sign of his being burdened or harassed. Patience is the link between this side of his personality and the social and academic sides, in which openness, concessiveness, and forbearance prevented casual touchiness and unintentional sharpness and mitigated the criticalness which no first-rate mind is without. It was a matter of common report that, if a student's recitation were even faintly capable of being interpreted to the student's credit, Cleanth unfailingly came up with that interpretation. He tried to pull the student in rather than put him down. (I borrow the latter phrase from students whom, when I was department chairman, I often heard use it to complain of instructors rather less gifted than Brooks.) He would make as much of a concession as he could even to self-confident prejudice and perverse attitudes, somehow gain a foothold in the student's terrain, and try to lead him from there to better ground. He was quick to find the tactics suitable to the occasion. He could be very persuasive and certainly was winning even when not wholly persuasive. I can imagine him in class, in an effort to guide the student, using the mild invitation that we often heard in personal talk, "Now looka here." Behind the urbane manner was the basic social act of giving the student (or for that matter the colleague) confidence that Cleanth had confidence in him. He did have that confidence or its surrogate, a practical acceptingness, to a marked degree; this could even make him a little vulnerable to an occasional academic calculator or self-deceiver who managed to seem more of a true believer, or a true thinker with worthy beliefs, than he was. Having accepted, Cleanth would be slow to revalue—a steadfastness once or twice enjoyed by people who might have felt an earlier chill in associates quicker to judge. To those of us who tended to start with a protective suspicion and to yield trust only when it seemed earned, it was rather a lesson to see a style in which trust came first and suspicion was reluctantly granted even when it seemed earned. Cleanth would guard against possible harshness in the public or formal evaluation even though in the confidential assessment among friends he did not button up his acute sense of reality. There used to circulate a charming story that Cleanth once said of a student, "He is no good. He doesn't know anything. He can't write a sentence. In fact, he is illiterate. I just had to give him a B."

It is only a small leap from one kind of family piety to another, from kindness to colleagues and students to kindness to animals. For some years the Brookses had a little dog, a Boston bull I think, to which they were much devoted. The story was (as these pages may suggest, stories tended to accumulate about Brooks—the makings of a saga) that Cleanth had participated in a caesarean section by which the dog was brought into the world, and I think the beast was named Caesar. The true kindness of his foster home seemed to have little impact on this dog, in whose case benevolence was evidently, in our more recent cliché, counterproductive. Perhaps a birth trauma had rendered him constitutionally uncooperative. In "training" he managed only to distinguish between floor and paper (an achievement that would have counted for more in a nonwriting and nonreading household), and he was paranoidally aggressive, able, with his ears back, teeth out, and voice piercing, to cause trepidation among timider guests. Once when some caucusing group was meeting at Cleanth's house, Charles Hyneman, who was not at all timid but probably got weary of sitting protectively on legs and feet, barked at the host, "Cleanth, if you don't do something about that dog, I will never come here again." Charles had the gift of combining candor with geniality, he and Cleanth remained good friends, and he continued to visit. David Nichol Smith, Cleanth's tutor at Oxford, once visited Baton Rouge and in similar circumstances expressed himself differently. Caesar did not so much chew on Nichol Smith as run all over him, yapping and snarling. Once when the Brookses were both busy in the kitchen (Cleanth did not establish himself as an intellectual by conspicuous incompetence on the food-and-drink front; he was always a most helpful husband), Caesar ran up Nichol Smith's long legs, which were stretched out and forming a sort of ramp from floor to chair, and began a noisy demonstration on the distinguished guest's middle. With a very quick but just perceptible turning of his head toward the kitchen as if to be wholly sure that he was not seen and heard, Nichol Smith made a vehement, sweeping brush-off, hissing fiercely at Caesar, "Get down, you cur!"

Cleanth was a frequent host not only to colleagues, as I have been saying, but to visitors from elsewhere. At his house we met not only Nichol Smith but John Ransom, Cleanth's old

Vanderbilt teacher; Katherine Anne Porter, for many years an intimate friend of the Brookses; Andrew Lytle, novelist and for a long time editor of the *Sewanee Review;* I. A. Richards; Marshall McLuhan. Cleanth was always indefatigable in chat and jesting, in good-tempered argument, in elaborating delightful fantasies for the discomfiture of the erring, in drawing Red Warren and Lytle into the storytelling of which they were both great masters, and occasionally in organizing charades. It is not easy to forget one episode in which the team that I was on failed miserably to interpret a charade, even after demanding alternative enactments and sweating it out for an hour or more. Our opponents' monstrous images, obscure and immorally ambiguous, were devised, as I recall it, by Mrs. Brooks, Lytle, and Warren. With glee they finally revealed the words presented, "The World's Body"—the title, of course, of Ransom's book of not long before. It was a little comforting that the defeated team was headed by Cleanth and John Crowe Ransom himself.

From Cleanth as host we can move in two directions: to an analogous activity that tells us more about the Brooks mind and to reminiscences that lightly highlight the personality. The hospitality that Cleanth practiced at home appeared in another way in his work as editor of the *Southern Review*, work which may not be remembered now. (Obviously one cannot separate the role of one editor from that of another, but one may assume that each editor helped create the policy evident in editorial practice.) Here *hospitality* is applicable in two ways—as an openness to contributions by writers who held beliefs not shared by the editors but who developed their positions with acuteness and depth and as a welcoming of many new writers who had to be judged on their typescripts alone. The latter offers the opportunity of getting new writers off to a start, as with Eudora Welty, and also involves the risk of giving space to one-story or one-essay people. The *Review* had some of these too; the only point is that the editors were willing to take the risk instead of playing it safe with writers already arrived or on the way. On the other hand they could subject the latter, who might be acquaintances or even allies, to the same independent critical scrutiny that they gave to known and established writers studied in class.

On the side of reminiscence I have to record what happened some time after I. A. Richards had been a houseguest of the Brookses. Richards wrote to ask about a pair of shoes he thought he had left behind, and the Brookses looked everywhere, but fruitlessly. Then suddenly Mrs. Brooks said, "Cleanth, what do you have on your feet?" Cleanth, I believe, resisted the imputation, but his wife insisted that the shoes he had on were too long and narrow to be his. Cleanth's reply, according to legend, was, "But you know my shoes don't fit me." In a similar episode—missing articles, surprising reappearance, and reasoning by the wearer—the property that changed hands was some gloves I had left in the office occupied by Cleanth and me. This was during the war when most of us were teaching an ASTP English course that included some logic lessons prescribed by the government syllabus. The clothes episodes led someone fresh from struggles with logic (I think it was the late Esmond Marilla) to say, "Cleanth, you watch your enthymemes. Your implied major is, 'All clothes which do not fit me are mine.'" Well, the foggy man has had his run in anecdote and fable, and every campus has its specialist in absentmindedness. But the Brooks story, aside from its lesser role as an amusing footnote to biography, serves mainly to illustrate the paradox advanced by someone a year or two ago: that absentmindedness is the other face of presentmindedness, a firm focusing of attention on essential matters, whatever others become blurred in the process. This applies exactly to Cleanth, who may have had more hazy moments than most people about extrinsic matters, but who never failed in lucid attention to the intrinsic ones.

The lucid attention is of course richly established in his manifold writings, which are not my subject. But I want to make one observation: that lucidity is not the by-product of unwavering adherence to a party line, for which consistency of thought is sometimes mistaken. Loyalty to causes, for instance, has not made Cleanth any less clear eyed about either the devotees or the raw materials of causes. In *The Hidden God*, speaking to a Christian audience, he chides Christians who have taken up T. S. Eliot because they have heard of him as a "good churchman." He could chide southerners who found the "southern cause," however defined, a good thing. His objectivity should be taken for granted, of course, but I make the statement precisely because many people who do not know or digest the record have thought of Cleanth as an unwavering apologist for all things southern or once southern. I am sure that he more than once felt pushed into the apologist's position by stereotyped attacks upon the South—ones that continue even after northerners have unveiled some aptness in vices once thought to be southern specialties. In public combat one does not always have much choice. But lest the figure of public combat seem all of the man, it is worth noting that, in contexts where the object was understanding and personal confidence rendered misunderstanding unlikely, no nonsoutherner could be more incisive than Brooks in detached evaluations not only of the present South but of the past South too. His persistent sense of ambivalence even in areas of devotion appears in some words he uses to define the "special heritage of the South" (the subject of Chapter 14 in his *William Faulkner: The Yoknapatawpha Country*): "the past experienced not only as a precious heritage but as a crippling burden." In looking at traditions that he valued, he was no less hesitant in cutting through any accumulated flimflam than he was in seeing through contemporary intellectual fashions. One of these fashions, now doubtless forgotten, had a great run in its own day: the fashion, set off I think by some words in *Partisan Review*, of screaming "failure of nerve" to demolish anyone not irrationally devoted to the current metropolitan rationalisms. Cleanth's shrewd comment was, "They've given themselves away. That's all they're going on—nerve."

The lucidity of mind is reflected in a lucidity of style that has always stood out in a day when professorial critics often achieve a gruesome murkiness of vocabulary and syntax, whether by lack of discipline, by a sentimentally self-indulgent trust that whatever tumbles or writes out is invaluable in its initial form, or by a cynical sense that impenetrability tends to pick up some market value because many people don't like to say that they can't understand the impenetrable and hence quote it more than they would otherwise. How much conscious disciplining of style Cleanth found desirable I do not know; my impression is that his easy naturalness and unpretentiousness were almost congenital. On special occasions he could strive for, or perhaps fall into, a very muted irony, sometimes a little too *sotto voce* for complete effectiveness if one did not have a special key. His written style is really a spoken style with a barely perceptible heightening through ordinance and embellishment. His conversational style was perhaps a shade less colloquial than informal faculty discourse tends to be, but easy, plain, essentially decorous, and expectably much freer with punch lines than his platform style; it was quite varied, ranging from literary wit to pungent or racy earthiness, the former neither self-conscious nor buttonholing, the latter keeping its force through a restraint and appropriateness prodigally discarded in our present adolescent phase of the free-speech epoch. This style reflected a thorough familiarity with nature in all her aspects, and Cleanth delighted to observe her workings in individuals who seemed to inhabit a higher plane (as in the high-toned sculptress whose male nudes were hyperbolically male). There was much contagiousness in the merriment with which he laid bare somebody's pettifoggery or self-deception or logical or Freudian slips (he rather enjoyed playing games with this last mode of thought, of which he has made only sparing formal use). There was always an impish glint in his eye in jest and banter; he was the gleeful rather than the deadpan phrasemaker or epigrammatist.

His deftness in words and tenacity in issues naturally made him a leader in academic matters in which he took part. He led best in smaller group meetings, in sessions to identify ends and plan means; he had a mildness, courteousness, and inclination to subtlety that were not the best equipment for open combat. When planning became, as it could, a sort of exercise for freeing emotions, Cleanth could gaily extemporize fanciful schemes for capturing the citadel, booby-trapping the ungodly, etc.; he delighted in ingenious war games which by deception and unexpectedness would have to confound even the wary. I suspected that in some little corner of consciousness he harbored the notion that, if some of us were only a little less unimaginative and stolid, we could execute some blueprint of his to storm the heights and make the bad guys cry uncle. One trifling example, though only by analogy. Junior faculty members of our department would occasionally get into a game of touch football with our opposite numbers in other departments. It was about all we could do to get the ball from the center to a back, and then get it handed off to a runner for a sweep or passed to some receiver (I have a clear picture of myself throwing horrible passes on one such occasion). But Cleanth would devise, and urge upon us, complex reverses and hidden-ball plays, and his characteristi-

cally good-natured face would stretch into sad lines of disap-
pointment in us when in our self-doubt we clung to less taxing
offensive designs. Not for nothing had he come from the Van-
derbilt that invented what was then called razzle-dazzle foot-
ball. Besides, he was an instinctive quarterback, and in univer-
sity affairs he loved the metaphor of the quarterback sending
the fullback crashing through the enemy line (single-wing
power plays had their lure too). The only trouble was that in the
academic game our side tended to be weak at fullback.

Not a large man physically, Cleanth had not a trace of the
Napoleonic. In him, behind the mildness of manner, one felt the
solid strength. Along with the confidence springing from talent
there was much modesty about given performances. Of a com-
pleted lecture script he could say, "It ought to be better, but it's
too late now." Or of lecture assignments undertaken: "Well,
back to the scissors and paste." Along with the firm mainte-
nance of position there was a sweet reasonableness about op-
position, a disarming effort to find the common ground rather
than a well-armed rush to the battleground. Along with great
patience with young learners about or in literature (students
and writers), there was considerable impatience with old boys
to whom literature hardly existed as literature. Along with a
basic charitableness that I have mentioned more than once,
there was a vigorous challenging of what I might call the clichés
in the atmosphere, the positions apparently accepted by every-
body but examined by nobody, the faculty club fashions and
unconscious assumptions. Was the *New Yorker* really a wise and
sophisticated journal? Was the New York *Times* really an exem-
plar of omniscience and dispassionate right reasoning? Why did
faculty rationalism miss so much of reality? Was standard
liberalism an instrument of truth or a device for shirking hard
decisions? A freedom from dogmatism or a ragbag of counter-
dogmas? Such inquiries, offered gently but repeatedly, made it

difficult to beg questions or to suppose that there were no questions to be asked.

Other images, recollections, tales. The story that Cleanth delayed the start of his honeymoon to fill his suitcase with books; the story that he was racing through dozens of detective stories to find the central key or pattern that would enable him to turn out a master sleuth tale to ease the bite of the thirties depression. He did have the makings of a figure of myth. His having enough energy left, after everything else, to learn bookbinding as a hobby and to become rather proficient at it. His becoming interested in the construction of an outdoor fireplace, following through with the project, and, on the day of topping out, asking his wife whether she happened to have at hand any "raw dough" with which to test the new construction. His blueprinting, at least in words, inventions of various kinds: there was a series based on the football ethic, as he rightly read it, that anything goes which is not specifically prohibited. The most memorable of these, for me, was a defensive uniform covered with external suction cups that would make it impossible for any ball carrier to break a tackle unless he tore out the arms of the tackler. His and my making a long automobile trip to do lectures at another university in a dry state, taking along a carload of spirits needed by thinking men there, and, after what seemed to be the perils of rum-running over the border, being taken slightly aback when the consignees felt some of the goods to be too costly (one price that raised eyebrows, as I recall it, was $2.10 for a fifth of bourbon). Cleanth's regularly riding a bike during the war, perilous as it was for a nearsighted man, and several times, once to avoid hitting a dog, pitching into the street and coming up bloody—but ungrounded. The total absence of anything like self-pity even when there were heavy strains of institutional uncertainty, special family responsibilities, and the depression generally. Cleanth going to the

University of Chicago for a year and giving us a taste of depart-
ment life without the intellectual vitality and the general zest
which he contributed. Then, finally, the offer from Yale. On a
very beautiful moonlit spring night in 1947 the Brookses and we
were driving back to Baton Rouge from what had been an
especially pleasant party at a country home in Mississippi. Try-
ing as one does at such times to strengthen the irrational barriers
against departure—the apparently rational ones are always the
most fragile—and knowing that anything rhetorical would not
do, I came up with something no more eloquent than, "You
would miss all this very much." These flat words may have
contained some truth, but any nostalgia that he did feel was
clearly no brake upon an impressive career at Yale.

After we both left LSU for opposite coasts it was a decade and
a half until I again saw Cleanth with some regularity. This was
in 1964–1965, when my sabbatical spent in London coincided
with his first year as cultural attaché at the American embassy
there. His basic virtues were unchanged. He maintained
equanimity under difficulties (bad prior information about ren-
tals, persistent housing difficulties, several robberies, the
strenuous demands of a new kind of life). For me, as for many,
Cleanth's work pace would have been exhausting: his keeping
in touch with academic and literary figures both English and
American, setting up lectures at the embassy, keeping up with
embassy life generally, being a host in a variety of situations,
taking part in literary symposia and other such gatherings in
Britain and on the Continent, lecturing often at universi-
ties and schools—all in two years. Of many occasions at
which he was an official American representative I saw him at
two—the memorial service for T. S. Eliot at Westminster Abbey
and the ceremony at which the Society of Authors made an a-
ward to the laureate John Masefield (at eighty-seven an impres-
sively sturdy figure)—enough to glimpse his unobtrusiveness

but alertness and readiness to play his part. I do not think any man could have performed a great variety of tasks more willingly or with more consistent dignity and graciousness. We were fortunate to have a rare kind of public servant abroad— one who could meet the intellectual and artistic communities with the infrequent combination of high intelligence and an unstraining and unfeigned amiability. Behind the scenes Cleanth had less inclination for the merry or impish *jeux d'esprit*, the playful fantasies that imaged the pretensions and inconsistencies and vulnerabilities of the world around. Doubtless there is less incentive for jesting invention when one perceives more sharply the precariousness of such order as we have. But he still exercised the large talent for asking hard questions about prevailing attitudes and fashionable assumptions, both British and American, about truth, belief, policy. The physically nearsighted man had, if anything, sharpened his eye for the dubious clichés of thought that flourish because many remain blind.

But these reminiscences of the London year are only a brief postscript to recollections of earlier years. Though the years are long gone, these pages are not an elegy, which would be a bit early. Nor are they a eulogy, which would be too easy. I have considered them rather a collection of snapshots which might, in sum, give an impression of a more varied personality than could be known through the critical writings. Even if that personality had seriously altered with time or disappeared, it would still have the interest that naturally attaches to an individual active at a crossroads both in a very colorful institution and in a larger academic and literary scene. In general, the scholar-critic is no less likely than the poet or novelist to be interesting as a person. Of course, the writer may have the easy appeal of a talent for creating spectacles or of a hyperactive id or libido, and the professor that of eccentricity or the faculty for histrionic self-display on many topical stages. Even an essayist may make his pages a projection of an emotive and turbulent self, a quivering body of sympathy, antipathy, and prophecy. Cleanth, on the contrary, has always been an unusually well-disciplined and self-contained man, no heart on sleeve either on printed page or in social intercourse. The easy friendliness and the generous ways that I have several times mentioned accompany a fundamental reserve that I suspect is not often penetrated even by regular associates. Hence the possessor of old snapshots cannot suppose that he is presenting more than a few surfaces. He can only hope that there are enough of these to give a general impression of the man that will seem valid to those who know him and at least a little revealing to those who have known the writer less than the writings. In showing snapshots one knowingly risks the trivial, and, as a hedge against the solemnity which one's sense of quality may betray one into, one admits some touches of the innocently amusing and some glimpses of occasional foibles that do not diminish essential largeness. If one is lucky, he contributes to the pleasure which we ordinarily take in the personality of the gifted man as it appears on the less public side and in remoter doings and which survives even the absence of the discreditable.

I started with a brief sketch of the historical context in which we see this gifted man, and I will finish with another short note on it. Not so long ago a talented younger man said to me, "Your generation revolted against the old history, found out about literary structure, and discovered the major tools for understanding structure. What is left for my generation to do?" I thought of Cleanth Brooks at this time, and now I remember the rhetorical question because the need for self-creation which it implies is one of the reasons for thrusts against critical methods which Brooks helped establish long ago. It is a much less distressing reason than a self-conscious and all-but-pathological mobility in our day: the delusion that all change makes for improvement and hence the worship of chronic innovation in the very academy that ought to know better. I am not complaining about the gradual perennial revisionism that is the substance of literary history or the restatements that come with changes in perspective or with terminological wear and tear. Neither of these, I suspect, would seriously endanger the indispensable insight on which Brooksian criticism relies—that the work is independent, a thing-in-itself, obviously not without significant external relations, but in the end to be understood and judged by internal relations (the kinds of elements related and the ways in which they are related). That is what in my initial statement I predicted would not be lost. But it would be wrong not to see that it is indeed threatened by one recent academic fashion—the fashion of interdisciplinary studies. Whatever advantages these may have in social and scientific fields, they tend when including literature to lose sight of the literary and to treat literature as only one of a mass of undifferentiated printed objects that go along with other sorts of objects to prop up whatever kinds of synthesis the researcher is concerned with. This development is especially clear in "American studies." The trouble with the every-man-his-own-Toynbee program is that truly significant syntheses can be made only by very exceptional minds and by them only after long, hard thinking and heroic assimilation of facts. It is depressing to see graduate students who at best have a skimmed-milk knowledge of literature thin it out still further in order to secure a still more watery knowledge of other fields under the illusion that this pale mix of assorted superficialities will be intellectually enriching. This process can have only trivial results, but what is worse is that it will trivialize any one literature by cutting it off from its proper relationships with other literatures, by destroying the boundaries between literature and nonliterature, and by failing wholly to secure the in-depth, inside knowledge by which the stature and the value of literature are known.

This brief note of disappointment in "trendy" literary studies is not, I hope, an excrescence in what is mainly a personal memoir. The memoir comes into being because the subject of it has done notable things; the personality interests by belonging to a person whose works naturally excite interest. Retrospective as it is by definition, the memoir is still prospective in tone; it implies the durability, the future of the man's work. I only make that overt when I point to new fashions through which, contagious as we find the flux, we could drift away from solid ground slowly won. I would like to see and hear Cleanth Brooks, in a congenial group, pinking such fashions—the shrewd, heart-of-the-matter analysis coming through either in sober, trenchant argument or in mild-mannered but cutting jests, the serious point outlined directly with firm and sober mien or translated into a merry game with its own light fantastic steps, the nimble imagination wittily pricking modish masks and brightening the fencer's face with delight in the rational and figurative cut and thrust.

Walter J. Ong, S.J.   From Rhetorical
Culture to New
Criticism: The Poem
as a Closed Field

A poem should not mean
But be.
—Archibald MacLeish, *Ars Poetica*

THE NEW CRITICISM and the poetry
which arose with it deserve to be examined in fuller perspectives than those in which they have commonly been viewed. Both are still too often described largely as ad hoc reactions to what went immediately before. The Hulme-Eliot-Pound-Leavis-Richards-Ransom kind of criticism is set against the impressionistic and often autobiographical performances of William Hazlitt, Walter Pater ("the presence that thus rose so strangely beside the waters"), or Oscar Wilde. The doctrine of clear, precise images which entered into the fiber of the New Criticism as well as into the more or less contemporaneous imagist poetry is set against the vagaries of Edwardian and

Georgian verse. And eventually the story winds down with the anticulture movement which compromised the New Criticism at mid-century.

We are, however, becoming increasingly aware that the New Criticism calls for more than such short-range description. It was somehow a major cultural development. Some new insight into why and how it was can be gained if the New Criticism is examined in relation to the antecedent rhetorical tradition, which had dominated the theory and practice of expression from antiquity to the romantic age, when the remote beginnings of the New Criticism can be detected in Samuel Taylor Coleridge.

So far as I know, the New Criticism has never been examined in this way. Even at first blush the rhetorical tradition would appear relevant to the New Criticism not only because the older rhetoric had registered and controlled the dominant attitudes toward poetry for two millennia, but also because the New Criticism from its beginnings has had a lot to say about rhetoric. One of I. A. Richards' earliest books was *The Philosophy of Rhetoric* (1933); and in the United States, where verbal rhetoric is more studied and less practiced than in Great Britain and its dismantled empire, Cleanth Brooks and Robert Penn Warren have influenced millions of teachers and students, directly or indirectly, not only through their *Understanding Poetry*, but also through their companion volume *Modern Rhetoric* and through other textbooks treating poetry and rhetoric under the same covers.

Basically, the relationship between the old rhetoric and the New Criticism is one of opposition. The New Criticism was concerned with rhetoric because by overthrowing the old rhetorical tradition it made imperative an overhauling of the entire noetic economy. The old rhetorical tradition was no small thing. From antiquity the study of rhetoric had encapsulated the most ancient, central, and pervasive tradition of verbalization and of thought known to mankind.

Elsewhere I have tried to explain how, until the beginning of the modern technological and romantic age in the later eighteenth century, Western culture in its intellectual and academic manifestations—and, *mutatis mutandis*, very likely all human culture everywhere—can be meaningfully designated rhetorical culture.[1] Basically, rhetorical culture means culture in which, even after the development of writing, the pristine oral-aural modes of knowledge storage and retrieval still dominate noetic activity, including both thought itself and verbal formulation and communication. When writing first appeared, it did not immediately wipe out or supplant oral-aural modes of thought and verbalization. Rather, it accentuated and codified them. Writing made scientific analytic thought possible. Directed to the consideration of communication, such analytic thought produced "rhetoric" as a formal, reflective *technē* or art.

It is paradoxical and thought provoking that rhetoric was one of the first fields of knowledge worked up as a formal art with the aid of writing, for rhetoric means primarily oratory or public speaking, for which the Greek word is *rhētorikē*. The written art of rhetoric at first focused primarily not on written but on oral communication, which outproduced and outranked writing not only at the time when writing first timidly began, but also for several millennia afterwards. New inventions normally at first reinforce what they will eventually transform or supplant. The automobile at first encouraged prolification of the kinds of roads devised for horses. Superhighways came late. Writing undermines the oral noetic economy, but only after it first strengthens it by giving it status in the new "scientific" world which writing made possible.

From the time the first scripts had been invented around

1 Walter J. Ong, *Rhetoric, Romance, and Technology* (Ithaca and London: Cornell University Press, 1971), 1–22, 255–83.

3500 B.C., the old oral culture had been threatened; but before the age of letterpress print, beginning around A.D. 1450, writing had not greatly altered some of the major features of the oral noetic economy: the organization and exploitation of knowledge through *loci communes* or commonplaces, the use of academic procedures centered upon oral reaction and upon the agonistic intellectuality which preliterate orality fosters, and an overall attitude toward expression which, at first overtly and later less openly but still actually, regarded oratory as the paradigm of all verbalization. Through the Renaissance and even into the romantic age, textbooks on "rhetoric" regularly and dutifully included a section on delivery (*pronuntiatio* or *actio*), which is to say oral performance, even though most of their users were being trained in fact chiefly for "literacy," which is to say for writing. We no longer include a section on delivery in a book on writing, but we have retained the term "rhetoric" for such a book, thereby attesting unconsciously the still residual force of pristine oral culture.

The rhetoric of the New Criticism represents, however, a rather final break with the older rhetoric in the way it fixes the eye unflinchingly on chirographic and typographic expression. On the one hand, the New Criticism descends from the old academic rhetoric matured in the orality of classical antiquity and rooted in the pristine oral world of mankind, an oral world dominated by male ceremonial contest—fliting, disputation, and formalized debate—and marked by heroic male bonding structures of which the war party was the paradigm. But, on the other hand, the New Critical rhetoric descends also from the vernacular, bourgeois, account-keeping schools designed for training in "reading, writing, and 'rithmetic," with very little of the heroic-oral-combative in them. The vernaculars moved into academia first in the lower grades, from which they worked their way up in the curricula. The New Criticism arose as the universities shifted their central linguistic focus from Latin to

English.[2] Before this shift there had never been any developed university criticism of English literature as a whole.

The hallmark of the old rhetoric in the West was the use of Latin, since the sixth century not a mother tongue any more but exclusively a sex-linked, public, male language encoding the agonistic structures of the agora and the academy. Into the twentieth century, the requirement of Latin, in however attenuated a form, marked the schools which trained boys and young men not for business but for academic or public life, for taking positions on issues and fighting them through, for diplomacy and other verbal jousting. The vernacular schools, by contrast, trained boys and, somewhat later, girls for managing the economy, commercial or household, and for other practical, noncombative uses of literacy. The two types of schools influenced one another and often intimately coexisted; in the United States, as late as the 1920s, the same secondary school often housed two clearly marked courses: the "classical" course (training, roughly, debaters) and the "commercial" course (for, roughly, account keepers). By and large, women entered the older, "classical" academic world where it was most amenable to influence from the vernacular schools. They seemed to want classical education, but the psychological structures were against it. As women came into academia, Latin went out.

The older rhetorical Latin tradition stood for a committed, agonistic approach to learning and to life. In this tradition, even the study of literature was programed to prepare for taking a position and defending it or for attacking that which another was defending. "For by the reading of his [Homer's] work called *Iliados*, where the assembly of the most noble Greeks against Troy is recited with their affairs, he gathereth courage and strength against his enemies, wisdom and eloquence for

2 Walter J. Ong, *The Barbarian Within* (New York: Macmillan,1962), 177–205; see also Ong, *Rhetoric, Romance, and Technology*, 113–41.

consultations, and persuasions to his people and army," Sir Thomas Elyot explains in 1531 in *The Book Named the Governor*. It was still much the same more than three centuries later in *Tom Brown's School Days* (1857). This educational world prepared for contest, for struggle, taking for granted the existence of violence. Significantly, the last bastions of Latin in the British Isles, the public schools, are also the last bastions of the programed use of physical punishment. George Orwell once ventured that without physical punishment it was impossible to teach Latin; on the whole, though not in every particular case, he has been proven right.

In this setting, as was to be expected, poetry as a purely aesthetic activity had little, if any, place. From antiquity through most of the nineteenth century, poetry by and large was conceived of academically as a part or a subsidiary of rhetoric, which was ordered not to creativity but, paradigmatically, to public decision making. Generally speaking, whatever contrary theories may have been more or less in circulation privately, poetry was in fact taught academically not for itself but as an ancillary subject, or semisubject, to develop the linguistic skills and the sensibility required for an orator or man of public affairs. And academic practice reflected the dominant nonacademic views. Poetry was supposed to teach, to move, and to delight, with a heavy emphasis on the first two, from Dionysius of Halicarnasses, probably the most aesthetically oriented ancient rhetorician, through Sir Philip Sidney and John Milton—who wrote *Paradise Lost* for agonistic purposes, to "justifie the wayes of God to men"—and on into the beginning of the romantic movement. In the last analysis, academia felt that speech was essentially for the committed man, an accomplishment to be used in making and implementing practical decisions. Deviations from this activist position there were from antiquity, but most of them were in favor of "philosophy"—that is, the speculative life, as this was cultivated in the study of logic, "physics" or natural philosophy, or metaphysics—not in favor of poetry or any other performance conceived as purely aesthetic. When humanists such as Lorenzo Valla spoke out in favor of eloquence, the practical art of winning assent and getting things done, they identified the enemy not as poetry but as the pursuit of knowledge for the sake of knowledge, the speculative tradition of the universities.[3]

In these longer historical perspectives, many of the features of the New Criticism and its concomitant poetry take on much wider meanings. We can examine one feature here in particular, the characteristic doctrine concerning the integrity of the literary work itself. Criticism must begin, the doctrine teaches, by examining a poem or other work of literature on the work's own grounds, asking of the work itself what it is undertaking to do and adjudicating its success in terms of its discernible aims. The literary work exists in its own closed field. This doctrine finds somewhat different expression and different emphasis in different critics, but in one or another guise it is present in virtually all New Criticism and nowhere more significantly than in Cleanth Brooks's cardinal book, *The Well-Wrought Urn: Studies in the Structure of Poetry*, which, we are advised on the dedicatory page, was worked out in greater part in a seminar at the University of Michigan in the summer of 1942, during the heyday of the New Criticism. Here, in a variety of ways and through the patient study of diverse texts, the reader is shown over and over again the unity in diversity, the paradoxes, the ironies, the tensions—how the poem's parts are indeed very much parts in that they can tend to fly away from one another, but are nevertheless convincingly held together in the unity of the

3 See Jerrold E. Seigel, *Rhetoric and Philosophy in Renaissance Humanism* (Princeton, N.J.: Princeton University Press, 1968), 141–44, 160–69.

poem. This holding together, the closed field, *is* the poem, the work of art.

The poem, in other words, is what it is because of its interior economy, not because of the way it ties in at specific points with "life" or with anything else. In this sense a poem does not "mean" or "signify." To say that something has meaning or signification is to refer it outside itself in one way or another. The word *tree* means or signifies a physical object, which is not the word itself. A person's life or actions have meaning when they are referred to something or someone beyond themselves. Meaning or significance thus breaks open any closed field. If, as in typical New Criticism doctrine, the poem is a closed field, to give it "meaning" threatens its whole validity as a poem. "A poem should not mean/But be," Archibald MacLeish proclaims in his *Ars Poetica* (1926). If the poem is related to life, as it of course is, the relationship must be not from without but somehow from within, interior to interior: life relates to the poem and the poem to life in terms of the poem's own inner consistency. This relationship yields meaning, but of a special sort, meaning growing out of the dialectical relationship between art and nature, play and work—terms which define each other.

Even laws of decorum do not refer characters or situations beyond the poem itself. In Appendix 1 of *The Well-Wrought Urn*, "Criticism, History, and Critical Relativism," Professor Brooks speaks strongly for the interrelationship between poetry and life, but he protests that decorum itself is not a matter of relating poetic language point for point to real-life situations—making sure that poetic swains speak and behave like real-life swains—but of relating poetic language to the poem. Within the poem itself, in a sense anything goes. But only in a sense, for the organization of any poem worth the name imposes its own demands, which must be honored. If they are, decorum is achieved and morality guaranteed, for poetry is such that, if it is not of a piece with life, nevertheless it is always consistent with life when it is consistent with itself, with its own unity. "To thine own self be true," and all will be well poetically. There is no way to have a good poem which will be indecorous or morally debilitating. The interior consistency of the poem, if honored, rules out or expels any incipient disaccord. The total poem, if it is good, accords with extrapoetic reality, though its parts individually may not match extrapoetic correlates. How the inner consistency of the poem relates to that of life is a further question we need not broach here. Propounded by its best advocates the doctrine is rigorous and consistent.

To a certain extent, it appears that this contention—that each poem must be approached on its own grounds and judged for what it is—is not new. Had not Alexander Pope taken a position like this when he wrote in *An Essay on Criticism*, "A perfect judge will read each work of wit/With the same spirit that its author writ"? Pope does here urge a certain deference to a poem's integrity, but the integrity appears less isolated than what the New Criticism has in mind. Pope seems willing to view the poem as being in contact with external reality through its author. The poem is something someone has said, not a detached existence whose business is simply to "be." Pope does not demand the author's absence once the poetic work is composed with quite the insistence of the New Criticism. He is concerned with fairness to the author at least as much as with fairness to the poem. Hence he does not devote any particular thought to the depersonifying effects of aesthetic distance.

The New Critics do, and their thought is part of us now. In "Tradition and the Individual Talent," T. S. Eliot writes, "Poetry is not the expression of personality but an escape from personality."[4] This echoes John Keats's statement about "negative capability." It is of course quite true and, to us, even

---

4 T. S. Eliot, *Selected Essays* (New York: Harcourt Brace, 1950), 10.

obvious. Shakespeare's own personal problems cannot be construed from *Macbeth* or *Hamlet* or *A Midsummer Night's Dream* (although if you know Shakespeare's personal history from other sources you can conceivably relate these plays to it). Some of Eugene O'Neill's personal hang-ups can be construed from *Mourning Becomes Electra* or *Long Day's Journey into Night* and, insofar as they can be, the dramatic effectiveness of these works suffers. They hold together not entirely because of what they are, but partly because of what O'Neill was and the way they touched his life—which means they do not hold together all that well. They sound contrived. Ernest Hemingway's stories tell you much more about Hemingway's lack of maturity than William Faulkner's tell you about Faulkner's problems with alcohol, and Hemingway's inability fully to transcend his own problems in his writing excludes him forever from the rank where Faulkner and Shakespeare and Sophocles stand.

This objectivity or relative dissociation of the work of art from its author has in one way or another been a quality of true art from the start. It was a feature of oral performance before literature began. Individual epic singers had their own styles, but these were not expressions of "personality" in any usual sense. You cannot find Homer's personality in the *Iliad*, although you might find the personality of an entire culture there. But with the New Criticism these matters—disinvolvement with personality, "objectivity" in art, insulation of the poem from direct existential interactions—became burning issues. As never before, it became imperative to treat the poem as a conspicuously closed field, an object disengaged from real persons and indeed from all else. Such an imperative lies back of the "classicism" advocated from T. E. Hulme on, back of T. S. Eliot's "objective correlative," a "set of objects, a situation, a chain of events" which will evoke a "particular emotion," to some extent back of Wallace Stevens' "supreme fiction," and of course back of imagism in all its avatars.

A strong feeling for the poem as a closed field signals the end of the old rhetorical world by recasting the readers or "audience" in a spectator's rather than an interlocutor's role. So long as a poem was assimilated to rhetoric, it operated within the agonistic framework of real life, of decision and action. The rhetorician addressing his audience is struggling with the audience, interacting with it, though the audience for the moment is mute. And so is the original poet, the oral poet, who remained, unconsciously if not consciously, the paradigmatic poet so long as the old rhetorical tradition survived.

A few years ago, I asked two graduate students of mine at St. Louis University, one an Ibo from Nigeria and one a native of western Ireland, how long it took one of their skilled oral storytellers—"poets" in Sir Philip Sidney's sense, a common sense—to tell a story. The response of both was the same: "How long? It depends on the audience reaction. The same story may take ten minutes or an hour." The Irishman added, "You always knew what he was going to say, but you never knew how long it would take him to say it." Fiction or poetry in this tradition is truly "creative," but it is of a piece with dialogue and with real life in a way the written product is not. (Written narrative or poetry has other ways of being in contact with real life, no less honorable, of course, but different—as, for example, the calculated use of colloquial speech, rare or unknown in artistic oral performance of cultures without writing.) Writing seals off its product from direct dialogue: the writer creates his text in isolation. It is this isolation of his which makes credible and, more than credible, meaningful the doctrine of the poem as a closed field.

The doctrine of the poem as a closed field reveals not only the chirographic roots but also the deep romantic roots of the New Criticism. With romanticism, the old agonistic poetic had been replaced by a new doctrine of creativity. The poet is irenic, or at

, least neutral, uncommitted, free of dialogic struggle with an audience, since for the "creative" romantic imagination the poem is no longer a riposte but a simple product, an "object" rather than an exchange. This insulation of discourse from dialogue on aesthetic grounds has evident similarities with the isolation or insulation fostered by writing, as just noted, and suggests a subtle alliance between literacy and romanticism complementary to the alliance between rhetoric (oratory) and classicism, as I have attempted elsewhere to show.[5]

The insulation of poetry from dialogue allows poetic in the romantic age (in which we still live) to deflect attention which had been earlier directed to the audience, back to the poet's own self. John Stuart Mill registered the changed emphasis, with no evident awareness of its deeper implications, when, in his "Thoughts on Poetry and Its Varieties," he stated that "eloquence is *heard*; poetry is *overheard*."[6] Earlier, when "eloquence" would have included poetry as akin to rhetoric, poets wanted desperately to be heard; even when they were not actually competing with one another, they sang to audiences for applause. But not romantic poets, at least in implied principle. They wanted to be alone—which means in effect, of course, that they felt themselves more as writers than as oral speakers.

The romantic feeling for isolation of the poem is strikingly illustrated in the felicitous halftone print on the dust jacket of M. H. Abrams' deeply perceptive recent book on romanticism, *Natural Supernaturalism.*[7] The print reproduces in black and white a painting, *The Bard,* by the romantic John Martin (1789–1854). This painting is certainly one of the most unwittingly informative anachronisms in literary and art history. High on a

---

5 Ong, *Rhetoric, Romance, and Technology,* 255–83.

6 John Stuart Mill, *Dissertations and Discussions: Political, Philosophical, and Historical* (New York: Henry Holt, 1874–82), I, 97.

7 M. H. Abrams, *Natural Supernaturalism* (New York: Norton, 1971).

precipice in a mountain fastness, an ancient bard stands. Harp in hand and wildly gesticulating, he sings at the top of his voice—utterly alone, to no one at all, for the awesome landscape is completely unpeopled. In the castle on a rocky outcropping opposite, across a deep valley cut by a torrent, no one at all appears. Martin has gone Mill one better: this poetry is not even overheard.

The actuality of all bardic performance, so far as investigation can ascertain, is entirely the opposite of this earnest but grotesque representation. Bards were and are extraordinarily gregarious folk. The real bard encountered by folklorists, anthropologists, or students of oral verbalization will do anything for an audience. He depends on audience reaction, as has been noted, to shape his performance, so that he badly needs an audience, generally speaking, even to get under way. Albert B. Lord shows how bards themselves learned their bardic skills by long hours of listening in such audiences,[8] not by sounding off on mountain crags.

The old poetic tradition associated with rhetoric had socialized the poet in another way, too. It had kept the poet engaged, struggling, not only with an audience but with other poets as well. Rhetorically colored poetic was a poetic of virtuosity, setting poet against poet. The earlier poetic was not always explicitly conscious of its agonistic underpinnings, but the underpinnings were there nevertheless, to be seen if you looked. Contest, ceremonial polemic, was a constitutive element in the noetic organization of the old preromantic rhetorical world and of the poetic this world enfolded. Pope speaks for the dominant poetic of two thousand preromantic years when, in *An Essay on Criticism*, he allies wit with Nature and assigns to the poet the task of producing "what oft was thought, but ne'er so well expressed." This is the pristine rhetorical world speaking,

---

8 Albert B. Lord, *The Singer of Tales*, Harvard Studies in Comparative Literature, XXIV (Cambridge, Mass.: Harvard University Press, 1960), 20–29.

thinking of composition, including poetry, as proceeding by "invention" (*inventio*), retrieval of matter from the accumulated stores of mankind, stores organized by means of the places or commonplaces or topics (*loci* or *topoi*.) This topical poetic clearly calls for an agonistic stance for, if the poet deals with the common store of awareness accessible to all, his warrant for saying or singing again what everybody is already familiar with can only be that he can say it better than others. The invocation of the Muse can be paraphrased, "Let me win, outdo all the other singers." In preromantic, rhetorical culture, the poet is essentially a contestant. He must do his work, make his poem, as conspicuous competitor within the dialectic of existence, the struggle—basically not lethal, as Thomas Hobbes and Herbert Spencer thought, but ceremonial—between man and man.

In the oral or residually oral cultures in which rhetorical culture is rooted, the originality which romanticism was to erect into a poetic and artistic principle is normally wasteful and counterproductive, for, in the absence of writing and hence of records, available energies must be channeled into repeating what is already known, lest it slip away forever. The novelty esteemed in such cultures is the novelty of supreme skill with the known, virtuosity in handling the familiar, the ability to excel in a situation where all the factors are in hand, are the same for all, and hence challenge all equally, as in an athletic contest. This is the "exquisiteness" looked for when the Welsh mercilessly graded bards by degrees of proficiency at periodic bardic contests. Hence, in oral or residually oral cultures, contests between poets or other verbal performers are quite normal, from the fliting in the *Iliad* and in *Beowulf* through the poets' contests in the medieval courts of love (real or fictional) to the present-day eisteddfod survivals in Wales and the "dozens" still practiced by our young American blacks.

Poets today still have rivalries (and indeed, on the average poets' egos are very likely more assertive than those of nonpoets), but modern romantic poetic no longer enforces ceremonial virtuosity as the older rhetorical poetic did. Expertise in exploiting a common store of matter is no longer the announced aim of the craft. "Creativity" is, and creativity implies that each poet starts not from a storehouse but *ex nihilo*, making poems which in principle are unique lock, stock, and barrel. "Creativity" is not all of romantic poetic, and it is tempered in fact by doctrines such as Eliot's doctrine of tradition. But the concept has certain basic implications and it is a central feature of romantic poetic— including, incidentally, Eliot's concept of tradition itself.

In a poetic focused on creativity, the sense of struggle weakens at two points. First, involvement with a living audience weakens; in place of rhetorico-poetic concern with teaching, moving, and delighting (*docere, movere, delectare*), poets programed to be "creative" develop concern with image and symbol, which tends to be concern with production in terms of sight, however mediated by words—the "audience" here turns into spectators. Between the spectators and the performers there is no struggle, although there may be communication.

Second, as just suggested, combative involvement of poet with poet weakens. There is no contest, for the common grounds needed for contest have been eliminated or minimized. Instead of bardic contests, the romantic world has poetry "readings," which may be covertly agonistic but are seldom openly programed as combative. Where a sense of poetic contest survives, as it does certainly at points today, the agonistic action is often also muted by being focused on poems in writing (which provide something "objective" to look at, to "examine"), not on recitations or readings.

Such are some of the implications of romantic poetics and of mountaintop bards. Romantic actuality, including modern poetry, of course did not always conform to such implications. But it frequently or usually did. It is difficult to imagine Wordsworth at an eisteddfod singing *The Prelude* or anything else he wrote. The creative romantic poet does *his* thing, not the communal thing. Wordsworth was his own hero, and had to be.

Seen in these perspectives of the old rhetorical world antecedent to it, the age of the New Criticism clearly is tied in with evolving psychological and social structures more extensively than might otherwise appear. From as far back as we can go into the beginnings of academic history, *agonia* or contest had constituted the mode of instruction in all academic subjects. From rhetoric itself to logic and physics and on through medicine, law, and theology, learning was acquired and tested by oratorical contest, dialectical debate or disputation, defense of theses or attacks upon those which others were defending. These procedures derived from the orality of early culture and from the very nature of oral performance. Oral performance favors not impartial investigation but contest. The typical orator's stance is not, "Let me objectively work through this matter with you, for I do not know the answer as yet," but rather, "Here I take my stand." An orator does in fact typically stand, a combative and precarious posture, inviting overthrow. A writer sits, or squats. He also revises, as an orator can seldom afford to do. The procedures of early oral or rhetorical cultures were typically of a piece with the world of male ceremonial combat, which was held at high value in a literary and academic world powered at its center by the ceremonial male language of Latin, a language resonant with the orality of antiquity and acquired with the help of physical punishment through rituals carried on in the tradition of puberty rites.

The age of the New Criticism provides us with a different setting. Contest as a conspicuous institution for instruction and learning no longer figures in the classroom setting. Deweyan educational reform ruled contest out, although it was on its last legs long before John Dewey intervened. Physical punishment, Latin as an instructional medium and linguistic paradigm, testing by oral defense of theses, academic focus on preparation for the public agora and political arena rather than for commercial or social service, though they remained vestigially here and there, were by World War I moribund. All disappeared from the academic scene about the same time. Their disappearance coincides with the use of the vernacular and the entrance of women into higher education. So far as I know, there was never a formal, scholastic disputation in the old, rigorously formal, ceremonially combative style conducted in English or conducted by women. Women tend to fight when they truly have to, for realities, not for laurels, and to speak the mother tongue, which is truly their own.

If this very sketchy description of one aspect of the state of affairs is valid, it suggests the question, Where have the polemic or agonistic drives gone? It is hard to believe that they have simply disappeared from poetics and from academia generally. The most inclusive answer is that nobody quite knows, although it is certain that the presence of women in the literary and academic world has basically shifted the psychological and noetic structures there toward declared irenicism. What matters here is that by the advent of the New Criticism the verbal world had strikingly downgraded ceremonial combat. The New Criticism generated its own economy of hostilities, but, however fierce, they were largely incidental, not operational.

It adds further to our perspectives to note in conclusion how verbal hostilities have been reconstituted as the age of the New Criticism has shaped itself into a new age. Student demonstrations have revivified verbal polemic, not in the formerly controlled, ceremonially agonistic educational setting, where even scurrilities were ritualized, but in an essentially callow setting of raw confrontation. The rhetoric of liberation movements has fed other hostilities into newly opened verbal channels. Poetry of liberation movements is rhetorical and polemic, in this resembling that of the oral or residually oral culture of the preromantic past. Such resemblance is understandable in many cases because liberation movements are powered largely out of oral cultures—in the case of black liberation, a very highly developed oral culture, complexly related to the literacy around it and to the secondary, literate orality of technological popular art culture.

Moreover, in our day the verbal *agonia* of politics has become real in portions of academia often most shielded from it a few years ago, notably the field of poetry. Poetry, we are told, is and must be an activist political event. Although political stances were being imputed to poetry at the onset of the New Criticism in the 1930s—by Christopher Caudwell, for example—such imputations were pretty well disabled by the aesthetics prevalent in the New Criticism. The reopening of activist approaches to literature recalls the earlier poetic, which was part of or subordinate to the practical concerns of rhetoric, and alerts us to the curious ways in which electronic, secondary orality, though derivative from and permanently dependent on writing and print, reproduces some noetic structures characteristic of early or primary (preliterate) orality.

The new activism will soon be no newer than the New Criticism is, but its emergence has made it clear that the psychological and cultural and intellectual forces which produced the age of the New Criticism no longer act in concert as they once did. *Mais, plus ça change, plus çest la même chose.* If the forces of the New Criticism once acted in concert, we can remind ourselves that "concert" means struggle, contest, *agonia.* The forces in the New Criticism, even in their ascendancy, were never quite at ease with themselves, but were in fact always struggling. Their struggle produced the tremendous outburst of energy and achievement marking the work of Cleanth Brooks and those who have learned from him.

Thomas Daniel Young A Little Divergence:
The Critical Theories
of John Crowe Ransom
and Cleanth Brooks

WHEN CLEANTH BROOKS came
from his home in West Tennessee to enter the freshman class of
Vanderbilt University, John Crowe Ransom was awaiting reac-
tion to _Chills and Fever_, his second volume of verse. Since his
return from service in France in World War I, Ransom had
offered regularly his courses in advanced composition and
modern literature, courses that had enrolled, among others,
Merrill Moore, Andrew Lytle, Allen Tate, and Robert Penn
Warren. Then in its third year and to live one more before its
demise in December, 1925, the _Fugitive_, to which Ransom had
contributed most of his mature poetry, was already proclaimed
"one of the best journals of its kind available." Although the
administration of Vanderbilt University had not formally rec-
ognized the existence of the group of faculty members and
students who were participating in one of the most significant
literary ventures of this century, students of Brooks's cast were

168

well aware of what was transpiring in those Saturday evening meetings in the home of James M. Frank. One of Brooks's sensibility surely found the atmosphere on the campus exhilarating. In the corridors of College Hall he passed every day men who not only were writing poetry but were publishing their verse, his first association with poets outside the pages of a textbook. But, as he wrote many years later, "My Vanderbilt years were—as far as having John's tutelage was concerned— largely wasted. A melancholy reflection. I have only myself, in my ignorance and innocence, and my confused romanticism, to blame."

Because he was "too much in awe" of the man who had already received national notice as poet and man of letters and because he felt he "was not ready for the work the class was doing," Brooks dropped Ransom's course in modern literature, in which he had enrolled at the beginning of his sophomore year. Although he never acted on his resolution to take the course before he graduated, he did complete during his junior year the advanced composition. But Ransom's earliest influence on Brooks, unlike that on Donald Davidson, Tate, and Warren, was not in the classroom but through his poetry. "I couldn't make much of his poetry," Brooks wrote in February, 1973, "until my senior year. Then, one evening, idly looking at one of his volumes lying on a table before me, I started reading the poems and something happened. I found them fascinating and wondered how I had missed their quality before. This is not to say that I suddenly understood every word and phrase. But their general import was clear and their stylistic brilliance hit me hard." What Ransom had done for the brilliant and sensitive young student was to take "literature off the library shelf, blow the dust off," and convince him that it "is alive and wonderfully important." This conviction undoubtedly assisted Brooks in determining his formal vocation.

In September, 1928, after his graduation from Vanderbilt the previous June, Brooks enrolled in Tulane University, from which he earned the master of arts degree the following June. While he was in New Orleans, he "began to see Ransom's poetry for what it was"; he began to "read him hard and continued to do so in the years that followed." From Oxford, where he studied as a Rhodes Scholar from 1929 to 1932, he wrote Donald Davidson that he had just read *God Without Thunder* and that Ransom's statement of the place and function of religion in twentieth-century society was the most plausible and convincing treatment of that subject he had seen. "I was frankly surprised at Ransom's position," he wrote, "and delighted—partially perhaps because his book represents a more mature and sensitive statement of the position I had been working toward; e.g. I found the same significance in C. C. Ayres' *Science: A False Messiah*. I had the same interpretation of Kant and Hume. I had found the same hostility and withering skepticism in the anthropologists. . . . I am at this time writing Ransom a long letter telling him what I think of his book."

This letter was followed by others and during the winter and spring of 1931–1932 Brooks visited Ransom in Devonshire, where he and his family were living while he was studying on a Guggenheim grant. After receiving a B.Litt. degree from Oxford in the spring of 1932, Brooks accepted a position at Louisiana State University, where two years later he was joined by Robert Penn Warren. In 1935 the first issue of the *Southern Review* appeared, with Brooks and Warren as managing editors, and during the next few years that distinguished journal carried more of Ransom's essays than any other publication. Although any contribution from Ransom was cordially received in Baton Rouge, its acceptance for publication was not always assured, as indicated by the reception of Ransom's controversial "Shakespeare at Sonnets."

On October 18, 1937, Ransom wrote Brooks: "I enclose the 'Shakespeare at Sonnets' about which I spoke to you at Allen's last summer. It is the last piece I have felt it necessary to do for completion of my MS [*The World's Body*], which I have delayed sending in till this one was off. . . . I note that I am being a little rough on Shakespeare in a magazine edited by two great Shakespeareans." The response by the "two great Shakespeareans" to the essay is apparently lost, but its general tone is suggested in a letter Ransom wrote Allen Tate on November 11:

> The boys deal pretty pedantically with my poor paper, you will see. . . . I wrote them a pretty warm letter but after thinking it over withheld it and wrote another. I also revised the thing, adding a bit, taking account of points of theirs which seemed to be worth anything, generally improving it. . . . I really stepped on their toes a little come to think about it. For Red is a Shakespearean and would not like my irresponsible knocks for the comfort of the Philistines; and Cleanth is an expert on metaphysical poetry, and thinks everybody ought to discuss the thing in his minute terms. They are a bit magisterial, or is it just my own over-sensitive imagination?

Whatever the objections, they must have been satisfied by Ransom's revisions, for he wrote Tate on November 17: "A nice note from the boys at Baton Rouge says they're printing my piece. I suppose they felt aggrieved at my high tone, but they don't extend the argument further." The essay was published in the winter issue, 1938.

A few months later Brooks sent Ransom the proof sheets of *Modern Poetry and the Tradition*, most of the essays in which Ransom had not read, and asked for the "honest reaction I always get from you." From Austin, where he was serving as visiting professor for the summer, Ransom responded immediately. "The book stands up," he wrote; "the most unified of all the fine critical books of our day, with [the] possible exception of Empson, coming to a fine climax with the chapter on reform of literary history." That Ransom could not accept some of its major conclusions, however, is indicated in the paragraph following the previously quoted sentence:

Your position is argued with patient and persuasive logic and illustration. It is an extreme position, as I think, and held with extreme almost dogmatic tenacity. You never discuss any *limit* to complication, and you tend to think that any complication in a modern is logical or functional complication, whereas poor Burns' *my love's like a red, red rose* is not functional or logical. To most readers it will seem that *Waste Land* is excessive complication and no unit poem at all, after reading your exposition. You do a similar disservice to Yeats. You put into the 17th century tradition poems that no 17th century poet would have approved. You use *wit* too broadly or else you do wrong to the poetry in requiring it; and *irony. Lycidas* and Vergil and Greek poetry fall by your estimate. . . .

Yet I believe this is about the ablest book that's appeared. Its error if any is on the side of the angels.

As soon as the book was published, a copy came to the office of the *Kenyon Review,* and Ransom wrote Brooks apologizing for not being able to review it immediately. Since he already had a twelve-page essay in the current number, he was extremely reluctant "to appear on more pages than that of my own journal." But in the next issue he planned to "editorialize and give it the very best send-off, with a haggling reservation or two towards the end to make the review decently 'objective.'" This "haggling reservation or two" is anticipated in the comments with which he closed the paragraph referring to the book: "As I have pondered on your general position I am most doubtful about your references to science. I have the idea that any definite and positive structural pattern discoverable in the poem, or anywhere on earth for that matter, is an act of science, not a peculiar act of poetry; unless you want poetry to rate merely as superior science. Science is not as simple as you imply . . . you . . . seem to be primarily interested in displaying functional structure. For me, at the present, that's not quite the main cue."

The association between the two men became closer during the late thirties and early forties. In addition to the frequent exchange of letters and manuscripts, which always included requests for reaction and comment, there was considerable discussion of joint editorial ventures of the two journals. Some of their most ambitious plans were interrupted, however, by the coming of World War II and its effect on the national economy. Ransom wrote Tate on January 5, 1942, that Warren had warned him of the demise of the *Southern Review* and, on January 28, that there was a strong possibility that the *Kenyon Review* would have to be discontinued. The faculty committee appointed by the president of the college to study the budget might decide, he feared, that the *Review* was a luxury rather than "an educational necessity." Whatever that committee's decision, he was faced with the immediate prospect of having to decrease by one-half the honoraria to contributors, of having to employ a student-secretary, and of being able to publish only three times a year. "But here's a possibility," he concluded; "upon the announced demise of the *Southern Review*, I wrote the boys to please come in and merge with the KR." If such an arrangement could be worked out, he intended to use the cover of the *Southern Review* and print on it the names of both journals. He would publish all of their accepted contributions, honor their unexpired subscriptions, and list on the title page all three names as editors. "We'd make this joint editorship real in every workable sense," he wrote, "and we could easily by arranging some sort of exchange have one of them up here a part of each year, on the faculty and on the grounds."

While the necessarily involved negotiations were continuing at Baton Rouge and between Brooks and Warren there and Ransom in Gambier, the financial condition of the *Kenyon Review* considerably worsened. Ransom was convinced that he could not continue publication beyond 1942 unless he could discover a generous outside donor; nevertheless he prepared a budget anticipating the merger of the two journals, and he wrote Tate in early February outlining in minute detail his plans for the combined publication. As late as April 22 no decision had been reached concerning the proposed merger, although Brooks and Warren had announced the previous fall that their journal faced "suspension of publication with the spring issue of 1942." At this time there appeared the statement, "The Editors regret that with the present number the *Southern Review* ceases publication" but that "unexpired subscriptions will be filled by the *Kenyon Review*." Although a complete merger of the two journals was never effected, the *Kenyon Review* was paid $750 to fill the unexpired subscriptions of the *Southern*, and the masthead of the *Kenyon*, beginning with the autumn issue carried as advisory editors the names of both Brooks and Warren.

That Brooks took his appointment seriously is indicated by the steady flow of reviews and articles he submitted and by his detailed and generous comments on the prospective contributions on which Ransom asked his opinion. While serving as advisory editor, he contributed more than a dozen articles and reviews to the *Kenyon Review*. During the fall and winter of 1943–1944 he spent a considerable amount of time arranging for a symposium on the poetry of Gerard Manley Hopkins, which included contributions by Austin Warren, Josephine Miles, Marshall McLuhan, and Harold Whitehall and was published in the autumn issue, 1944. From the inauguration of the Kenyon School of English in 1948 and for the three years of its existence, Brooks served as one of its Fellows, and for its first session he joined a distinguished faculty, including Eric Bentley, Richard Chase, F. O. Matthiessen, William Empson, Austin Warren, Allen Tate, and Ransom. Each member of the faculty taught one course and made at least one appearance before the entire student body. Brooks offered a course in Milton and gave as his public lecture a discussion of Milton's metaphors. As soon as possible after his return to Yale, he wrote Ransom his impressions of that innovative educational experience. "I should have written earlier," he began, "to tell you what I have told others, that the first session of the K[enyon] S[chool] seemed to me a brilliant success. The students to whom I talked, particularly the more mature students and auditors, were unanimous in saying this. Actually none of us who were personally involved can be the most impartial judges; even so, having made this discount, I think all of us have a right to think the school was brilliantly launched."

Over a period of forty years or more Ransom and Brooks were close friends. Although they were never able to spend a great deal of time together, they often lamented this fact, and their letters contain repeated references to needing and desiring the opportunity for long discussions of literary and personal matters. Whenever busy schedules would permit, visits were arranged, even at the expense of further complicating travel arrangements already uncomfortably involved. At the same time, each followed closely the development of the other's professional career. Ransom wrote extensive and masterful reviews of Brooks's books as they appeared; Brooks, in turn, produced some of the most helpful commentary yet available on Ransom. In addition to the sections devoted to him in both *Modern Poetry and the Tradition* and *The Well-Wrought Urn*, Brooks analyzes and evaluates Ransom's theories and practices, both as poet and critic, in some of the most informative and convincing of his essays.

In spite of the mutual affection and respect these two men shared for more than four decades, they did not always agree on literary theory. In both we have the insistence that literature embodies the highest values of the culture from which it comes and that these values cannot be transmitted to its consumers—

to the readers of poetry, for example—unless the art object is given the closest scrutiny possible. The manner in which this examination should occur was always of first importance to Ransom and remains a major concern for Brooks. When Ransom once wrote that he and Brooks were about "as like as two peas from the same pod," he was referring to personal similarities. Both grew up in small Tennessee towns, the sons of Methodist ministers; both were educated at Vanderbilt and Oxford. In spite of these similarities "we have diverged a little," Ransom wrote; and although he was concerned about some of Brooks's "departures," it was always with the feeling that he was contending with his alter ego. For, he concluded, if "Brooks and I were being landed on the desert island, I have no doubt that the books we would severally take along would be the same books, and chosen in the same order, and we would read them in unison." Here, it would seem, Ransom was suggesting the nature of their critical disagreement. Both agreed on the function of poetry. It assumes a necessary place in the life of the civilized man because it contains a unique kind of knowledge; he can learn from it that which he can get nowhere else. But this consensus of opinion regarding the uses of poetry did not carry over into their discussions of its basic nature. Ransom believed that Brooks had overstated his case in insisting that wit, paradox, and irony are essential elements of poetry; Brooks was not persuaded that Ransom's argument for logical structure in a poem does not destroy its essential unity by suggesting a split between form and content. A review of the published commentary on each other's work not only reveals these similarities and differences but also reminds us of the extent to which both Ransom and Brooks have influenced literary theory and practice during the past three or four decades.

In the autumn of 1937 Ransom published in the *Virginia Quarterly Review* his well-known essay "Criticism, Inc.," in which he proposes to inform his readers of the "proper business of criticism." For too long, he writes, our critics have been amateurs, men without the specific qualifications to perform the highly specialized function they have undertaken. Readers of criticism in the past have looked to three sources for the kind of competence the critic needs, but the results have been disappointing. First, there is the artist, who "should know good art when he sees it," but his "understanding is intuitive rather than dialectical." Although he may serve admirably as critic as long as he sticks to the "technical effects" of the artwork with which he is familiar, his weakness is usually apparent when he attempts to expound a theory of art. The second source from which we might expect sound criticism of art is the philosopher, but his weakness as critic complements that of the artist. Although the philosopher can render a real assistance in expounding a theory of art, he is usually not well enough acquainted with individual works to comment helpfully on their specific technical effects. If the readers of poetry cannot expect the kind of critical assistance they need from either the poet or the philosopher, they must look elsewhere for help.

The logical source of the kind of help readers of poetry need and deserve, the essay continues, is the university professor of English. But those who look to the universities for this kind of assistance will surely be disappointed. Although the professors of literature are learned, they are not critical, and they spend a lifetime compiling the "data of literature" and seldom if ever render a literary judgment. They are often good textual, philological, and historical scholars but, as important as these activities are, they are not adequate substitutes for the precise and systematic literary criticism the world of art must have. The essay ends with a call for a "Criticism, Inc., or Criticism, Ltd.," so that this important activity "may be taken in hand by professionals" rather than continued as a part-time, avocational interest of amateurs.

Even at the time Ransom wrote this essay, he was undoubtedly aware that he was not alone in his request for a new approach to literary study, for criticism concerned with formal analysis and literary judgments, for specific examples of the kinds of insights one can obtain only from the study of the literary documents themselves. Since the inception of the *Southern Review*, Robert Penn Warren and Cleanth Brooks had been seeking for publication critical essays and reviews based upon the intensive and sensitive experiences with the works of art for which Ransom was calling; as a matter of fact, during the three years of the journal's existence more than a dozen of Ransom's own essays and reviews had appeared in its pages. In 1938, the year Ransom's *The World's Body*, which included "Criticism, Inc.," was published, Brooks and Warren issued *Understanding Poetry*, a textbook which carried into the classroom the critical approach that Ransom desired.

The "Letter to the Teacher," with which this popular textbook opens, leaves no doubt where its emphasis is placed. The editors agree with Ransom that one can get from poetry, properly read, insights into the nature of human existence that he can get almost nowhere else, but if poetry is to provide this kind of illumination it must be read as poetry and not as history, biography, or moral philosophy. The temptation to which too many readers and teachers of poetry have succumbed in the past is that of substituting something else for the poem. The most common substitutes are "paraphrase of logical and narrative content," "study of biographical and historical materials," and "inspirational and didactic interpretation." Although all of these may be important to one degree or another in the study of a poem, they should always be regarded as means and not as ends. The accumulation of this kind of information should not be confused with the essential literary activity, that of reading the poem itself. To teach poetry adequately and properly, the editors insist, one's teaching methods must include the following principles: "(1) Emphasis should be kept on the poem as a poem; (2) the treatment should be concrete and inductive; and (3) a poem should always be treated as an organic system of relationships, and the poetic quality should never be understood as inhering in one or more factors taken in isolation." In an anthology of several hundred poems—arranged in order of increasing difficulty and complemented by analyses of individual poems and discussions of such poetic techniques and topics as "metrics," "tone and attitude," "imagery," and "statement and idea"—the editors demonstrate how this approach to poetry should function. It is hardly an overstatement to say that this book and its two companion volumes, *Understanding Fiction* (1943) and *Understanding Drama* (1945), the latter done by Brooks and Robert B. Heilman, have revolutionized the way literature is taught in the classroom.

In 1939 Brooks published *Modern Poetry and the Tradition*, which he says is dedicated to helping the reader, whose "conception of poetry is . . . primarily defined . . . by the achievement of the Romantic poets," understand and appreciate the poetry of his own age. Convinced that his generation of readers was "witnessing . . . a critical revolution of the order of the Romantic Revolt," he proposes to show the relationship of modern to traditional poetry and to demonstrate that the poetry of W. B. Yeats, T. S. Eliot, and their contemporaries, though sometimes difficult and obscure, is not incomprehensible. Many modern readers, Brooks argues, have difficulty with contemporary verse because they are accustomed to reading poetry in which images are mere ornaments used for clarity, vividness, and beauty and are not prepared for poetry in which much of the imagery seems to "demean rather than adorn . . . darken rather than illuminate." Two other concepts, which go at least as far back as Joseph Addison, have prevented contemporary verse from receiving a fair hearing: certain words and objects are intrinsically poetic and the intellectual faculty is opposed to the emotional or poetic faculty.

To get the proper perspective on the intentions of the modern poet, the argument continues, one must look beyond the romantic and Victorian poets to the metaphysicals, the last group to make full use of the prosaic, the difficult, the daring, the fanciful, and even the unpoetic. This study of the metaphysicals is necessary because the significant relationship between this group and the moderns is their "common conception of the use of metaphor" as opposed to the neoclassical and romantic poets. Following Thomas Hobbes, the neoclassic poets looked upon the role of the poet as that of copyist; the modern poets, like the metaphysicals, think the proper role of the poet is that of maker. The play of intellect in a poem is not necessarily hostile to the presentation of a sincere emotional experience. Often the complex attitudes which a poem expresses combine both emotion and intellect. The proper basis for judging the quality of any figure is to determine how it functions either positively or negatively; it "may serve irony as well as ennoblement." The only appropriate question, then, is, how well does it function in its own context?

In the metaphysical poem, metaphor is essential because it *is* the poem. "Metaphor is not to be considered," Brooks argues, "as the alternative of the poet, which he may elect to use or not, since he may state the matter directly and straightforwardly if he chooses." Metaphor is often the only means of expressing the complex attitude with which the poet is concerned. This line of thought leads Brooks to two of his best-known critical statements. One, metaphorical language is not decoration or ornament; it *is* the poem and to remove it is to destroy the poem. Two, for this reason no poem can be reduced to paraphrase.

Two of poetry's worst enemies, Brooks believes, were Thomas Hobbes and Matthew Arnold. Hobbes insisted that poetry is essentially statement and that the poet should endeavor to express "high poetic truth"; therefore he will use clear illustrations, "illustrations which dignify and heighten." He will neither indulge in fanciful playfulness nor give the reader any reason to misunderstand his meaning. Arnold would remove everything from a poem which would seem to contradict what the poet wishes to communicate. Such views result in two common fallacies. The first is the didactic heresy which insists that the end of poetry is to "instruct and convert." Those who hold this view are simply misinformed about the kind of truth poetry gives. A poem is "not a more or less true statement in metrical garb, but an organization of experience." The second fallacy insists that the poet should present his view of the experience simply and directly—a false conception which forces the poet into sentimentality, the result of the poet's sacrificing the totality of his vision and adopting a particular interpretation.

Like Ransom, Brooks favors metaphysical poetry, a poetry which does not oversimplify the poet's view by omitting opposing and discordant elements but includes such elements and attempts to resolve them into a larger unity. Irony may result from the bringing together of the opposing impulses, and wit, as Eliot had previously defined the term, is the "poet's ability to synthesize diverse materials." The limiting term "metaphysical" may be applied to that kind of poetry in which the "opposition of the impulses which are united is extreme." Therefore, the poet is a maker with almost absolute confidence in the power of the imagination to remake his world "by relating into an organic whole the amorphous and heterogeneous and contradictory." A year earlier in his "Poetry: A Note in Ontology," Ransom had expressed his inclination for metaphysical poetry, in which the poet asserts his "unscientific and miraculous predications," over either physical poetry, a poetry almost devoid of idea, or Platonic poetry, which "discourses in things, but on the understanding that they are translatable at every point into ideas."

Brooks summarizes the neoclassical age in this manner:

The weakening of metaphor, the development of a specifically "poetic" subject matter and diction. The emphasis on simplicity and clarity, the simplification of the poet's attitude, the segregation of the witty and the ironical from the serious, the stricter separation of the various genres—all these items testify to the monopoly of the scientific spirit. This process of clarification involved the *exclusion* of certain elements from poetry—the prosaic, the unrefined, and the obscure. The imagination was weakened from a "magic and synthetic" power to Hobbes's conception of it as the file-clerk of the memory.

The romantic movement was a reaction against many of these assumptions and, specifically, it attempted to liberate the imagination. But the revolution was not severe enough and was not able to free itself from the conception that the function of poetry is didacticism. The importance of the new revolution, led by I. A. Richards, Eliot, Ransom, and Tate, is that it is attempting a complete liberation of the imagination. The most obvious result of the present critical revolution is in the successful use of "prosaic or unpleasant materials," in the "union of the intellectual with the emotional," and in the ability of the modern poet to "rid himself of clichés, worn-out literary materials, and the other stereotypes of Victorianism." The serious and intelligent reader of poetry will not refuse to give modern verse the kind of attention it deserves just because the poet refuses to oversimplify the experience he is presenting. If the scope and breadth of the experience he is assimilating is complex, this kind of reader will know that the poetic representation of that experience will necessarily be complex and may be even esoteric and obscure. The remainder of this book comprises detailed analyses of poems by Eliot, Yeats, Robert Frost, W. H. Auden, Tate, Warren, Ransom, and others. These exegeses are the kind of criticism Ransom called for in "Criticism, Inc." They concentrate on the poem as poem, they are concrete and inductive, and they insist that the poem is an indivisible unit, an organic system of relationships. Of most importance is their demonstration that, properly read, poetry presents, in Ransom's terms, the "kind of knowledge by which we must know what we have arranged that we shall not know otherwise."

In his review of *Modern Poetry and the Tradition*, which appeared in the spring, 1940, *Kenyon Review*, Ransom complimented the *Southern Review*, "the organ of the most powerful critical discussion in the language." Its editors have been particularly "sympathetic with modern experimental poetry," and the book under consideration defends this editorial interest to the "point of brilliancy." He pointed immediately to Brooks's greatest strength; he is, "very likely, the most expert living 'reader' or interpreter of difficult verse." One of the greatest contributions of the book is in the exposition of difficult or obscure passages of modern verse, the significance of which would likely go by a less sensitive and imaginative reader.

In spite of Ransom's genuine admiration for the book, however, some of its theoretical assumptions and the conclusions based on these assumptions troubled him. In the first place "its dialectic skims rather lightly over some of the deep places." He could not agree with Brooks's argument that "our difficult modern poetry, with all its 'wit' and 'richness,' has returned to the 17th century." Modern poetry differs from that of the metaphysicals in at least two important respects: the moderns have not had the "patience to achieve firm metrical structure" and their poetry is "equally lacking in firmness of logical argument." The seventeenth-century poets were infinitely superior in logic to those of either the eighteenth or the nineteenth century, and logic, he believed, is "more organic to the imaginative effect than Mr. Brooks will admit." Although Brooks argues convincingly for the superiority of twentieth-century poetry—with its irony, wit, and inclusiveness—over that of the eighteenth or nineteenth century, Ransom could not accept Brooks's thesis that symbolist poetry is very much like that of the English metaphysicals. The symbols of the English religious poetry of the seventeenth century were public and convention-al, whereas those of the symbolist poets, and Eliot's *The Waste Land* belongs in this category, are esoteric, eclectic, and unsys-tematic. "Mr. Brooks," he concluded, "probably is the most accomplished reader of symbolist poetry who has spread his interpretations upon the record; but his critical faculty has not yet attacked its problem, nor perhaps yet even acknowledged it."

In *Modern Poetry and the Tradition*, Brooks comments upon poetic unity and the manner in which logic functions in a poem:

The only unity which matters in poetry is an imaginative unity. Logi-cal unity when it occurs in a poem is valued, not in itself, but only as an element which may be brought into the larger imaginative unity—that is, it is not valued in itself unless we value the poem as science or as exhortation to a practical purpose. Logic may be used as a powerful instrument by the poet, as for example by Donne, but the logical unity does not organize the poem . . . the logic, though bril-liant, is bad logic if we are to judge the poem on its value as a logical exercise. The show of logic, it is true, is justified; but it is justified in imaginative terms—not in logical terms. The logic is used to dictate a particular tone. It is really employed as a kind of metaphor. Nonlogi-cal relationships are treated here as if they were logical.

Ransom's reaction to this passage is predictable. "I cannot think this is a satisfactory disposition of the function of the logic," he wrote, "and I would particularly covet a fuller treatment by Mr. Brooks of the relation of imagination to logic. The logic is proba-bly more organic to the imaginative effect than Mr. Brooks will admit." The degree of Ransom's dissatisfaction with Brooks's treatment of the function of logic in the poem is most obvious in

"Wanted: An Ontological Critic," the essay in which is given the best summary of the critical principles he held at this time. Particularly important to this discussion are his comments on the "odd structure" of the poem:

> What is the value of a structure which (a) is not so tight and precise on its logical side as a scientific or technical prose structure generally is; and (b) imports and carries along a great deal of irrelevant or foreign matter which is clearly not structural but even obstructive. . . . we sum it up by saying that the poem is a loose logical structure with an irrelevant local texture. . . .
>
> The structure proper is the prose of the poem, being a logical discourse of almost any kind, and dealing with almost any content suited to a logical discourse.

Ransom develops his argument by pointing out that the structure of a poem includes not only rhyme and meter but its logical content; the "logical texture" is composed of diction, imagery, sound, and other "irrelevant" elements of art.

Brooks's reaction to Ransom's "texture-structure formulation" is most clearly expressed in "The Heresy of Paraphrase," a chapter in *The Well-Wrought Urn* (1947). The structure of poetry, he states emphatically, is dramatic: a poem, like a play, arrives at its conclusion through conflict, and its resolution, which is also dramatic, is reached through analogical rather than logical means. The essential structure of a poem is a "pattern of resolved stresses . . . a pattern of resolutions and balances and harmonizations, developed through a temporal scheme." Although a prose statement about a poem may follow a logical pattern, the poem itself seldom does, for a poem is itself an action and not a statement about action. Ransom's description of the dual nature of poetry suggests too obviously to Brooks the age-old dichotomy of form and content and may lead to the erroneous conclusion that a poem consists of a "prose sense decorated by a sensuous imagery." An idea may be extracted from a poem by paraphrase, but its importance as far as the poem is concerned lies in its "dramatic propriety," in its relation to the total context of the poem. The conclusion of a poem is the "working out of the various tensions—set up by whatever means—by propositions, metaphors, symbols." The unity of a poem, therefore, is achieved by a dramatic, not a logical process. His definition of structure differs from Ransom's:

> The structure meant is a structure of meanings, evaluations, and interpretations; and the principle of unity which informs it seems to be one of balancing and harmonizing connotations, attitudes, and meanings. But even here one needs to make important qualifications: the principle is not one which involves the arrangement of the various elements into homogeneous groupings, pairing like with like. It unites the like with the unlike. It does not unite them, however, by the simple process of allowing one connotation to cancel out another nor does it reduce the contradictory attitudes to harmony by a process of subtraction. The unity is not a unity of the sort to be achieved by the reduction and simplification appropriate to an algebraic formula. It is a positive unity, not a negative; it represents not a residue but an achieved harmony.

To think of a poem as a statement—and here he may be thinking of Ransom's assertion that the structure of a poem includes its paraphrasable content—sets up a false dilemma. The critic must avoid any kind of critical principle which suggests that the "prose sense" of a poem is a "rack on which the stuff of the poem is hung." Instead he should think of the prose paraphrase as a scaffold thrown around a building and not a part of the building itself. "To repeat," Brooks concludes, "most of our difficulties in criticism are rooted in the heresy of the paraphrase. If we allow ourselves to be misled by it, we distort the relation of the poem to its 'truth,' we raise the problem of belief in a vicious and crippling form, we split the poem between its 'form' and its 'content.'"

Ransom's response to this argument is included in "Poetry:

The Formal Analysis," which appeared in the summer,1947, *Kenyon Review*. The New Critics, he writes, have brought about a "linguistic revolution in [their] reading of poetry." Although he agrees in general with their intensive and analytical emphasis upon the "total connotation of words," he is also aware of some weaknesses in their approach. "The critic goes straight from one detail to another," he insists, "in the manner of the bee who gathers honey from the several blossoms as he comes to them, without noticing the bush which supports all the blossoms." In their intensive study of the *texture* of the poem, the critics have neglected its *structure*. They have shown us the "exciting turns of poetic language," but they have not been able to give us an acceptable definition of a poem. No one has done more than Brooks, he concludes, to establish this kind of criticism; no one has demonstrated more ingenuity than he in "reading the obscure meanings of many well known poems." The essays in *The Well-Wrought Urn* indicate, furthermore, that Brooks is attempting to conceive of the unified poem. He does not succeed in this new role, however, because, although he has "various formulations" for the poem, the terms he uses to define the poem are themselves undefined. Brooks insists that the "unity of poetic language has the form and status of a verbal paradox," but paradox, Ransom argues, is a "provisional way of speaking." We are not content to leave a paradox as a final meaning. Either we resolve the paradox or we sense its solution, which we feel is too obvious to require formal statement.

In this essay Ransom restates his agreement with Brooks that the meaning of a poem and that of its paraphrase are not the same because the paraphrase always reduces the text and leaves out some of its meaning. But a poem has two kinds of meaning: one is its "ostensible argument," which can be rendered by paraphrase, and the other is its "tissue of meaning," which cannot. Like a Freudian dream, a poem has both a "manifest and permissible" and a "latent and suspected" content. Not only is the paraphrase possible, but it is also useful because it "straightens out the text and prunes the meaning down." He explains when and how the reader may find the paraphrase useful. If the literary text is long and involved, the paraphrase will assist him in getting "perspective and proportion." But, Ransom cautions, the critic must never think his work is done when he has made the paraphrase, even of the most difficult poem. Some texts do not demand a paraphrase because the reader receives their meaning intuitively and immediately. The serious reader of poetry, he concludes, will realize that a "poem is not included in its paraphrase," but a "poem must include its own paraphrase, or else a logical argument capable of being expressed in a paraphrase." After all, a poem is public property. It must "make contact with its auditors"; therefore it "must be decent enough to make formal sense."

Brooks addresses himself to this objection to his argument against paraphrase almost as if he had anticipated the very language in which Ransom would express his demurral. The reader must ask, he says, whether it is possible to frame a statement that will "say" briefly what the poem "says" as poem. If he had chosen, could not the poet have provided such a statement? Cannot the sensitive and intelligent reader frame such a statement?

The answer must be that the poet himself obviously did not—else he would not have had to write his poem. We as readers can attempt to frame such a proposition in our effort to understand the poem; it may well help toward an understanding. Certainly, the efforts to arrive at such propositions can do no harm *if we do not mistake them for the inner core of the poem*—if we do not mistake them for "what the poem *really* says." For, if we take one of them to represent the essential poem, we have to disregard the qualifications exerted by the total context as of no account, or else we have assumed that we can reproduce the effect of the total context in a condensed prose statement.

In "The Concrete Universal: Observations on the Understanding of Poetry" (1954), Ransom returns to this discussion of the value of paraphrase. First of all, he would like to withdraw his statement made fifteen years or so earlier that a poem has both a logical structure and a texture "whose character was partly irrelevant to the logical form and purpose." Now he would say that the poem is an organism with three organs: the head, the heart, and the feet. Each organ speaks a different language: "the head in an intellectual language, the heart in an affective language, the feet in a rhythmical language." The language of the head presents an intellectual action; therefore the poem will have a beginning, a middle, and an end. In a complex modern poem the reader may not be sure of these respective parts, so he performs first an *explication de texte* and "then a translation of the composite language into the exclusive language of the intellect, which we call the logical paraphrase." Then Ransom asks, what is the use of this paraphrase?

I think perhaps I used to make it a point of honor to intimate that the intellectuals with their paraphrases were abusing and spoiling our poems. But now I think that may be arrogant and wrong, and surely it is unreasonable and vain. There is nowhere in the world for the logical paraphrase to have come from except the poem, where it is implicit; and it is the intellectuals (in their capacity of formal logicians) who are masters of explicating what is implicit. Nor do they harm the poem by taking their use of it. When we look again, the poem is still there, timeless and inviolable, for the other uses.

In "Why Critics Don't Go Mad" Ransom says the particular fascination with Brooks's view of poetry is its nearness to the "ancient doctrine of divine inspiration." For Brooks the poem exists in its metaphors; all else is insignificant. His approach to a poem is to go directly to the "dominating figure," to a "paradox or an irony which is vivid" and which is likely to have "philosophical or religious implications." Then he wrestles as "much of the poem as possible" under this central figure and therein is the essential sense of the poem. He does not "want the poem to have a formal shape, but simply to unfold its own metaphorical energy." Although Ransom agreed with Brooks that the "poetic object must be defended in its full and private being," he also insisted that the critic must define that "character in the poem which makes it discourse." The poem has "generality and definition," it is a "species of Aristotelian discourse," and it has a beginning, middle, and end if the argument is large enough to include these characteristics; if not, it has a "point," an "act of predication," and "that minute kind of order which we call syntax." The metaphors in the poem have to accommodate themselves to this much "logical formalism." Finally, Ransom suggested to Brooks that both of them might have been wrong all these years about the essential nature of a poem:

A little while ago I was urging Brooks to acknowledge the logical form of the poem as something fixed and . . . invincible; which the showy metaphors, episodic or "dominant" as they might be, had better make their peace with . . . and I had the idea of a poem as a great "paradox," a construct looking two ways, with logic trying to dominate the metaphors, and metaphors trying to dominate the logic. . . . But now I suggest that we must reckon with the meters too, and the poem assumes the form of a trinitarian existence. For the meters in turn enforce themselves against the logic and the metaphors, but against resistance.

When one looks back through the critical writing of Brooks and Ransom, he is impressed with the number of similarities in their theories. Both men insist that literary criticism is an aesthetic criticism; no other approach is valid—not psychological, humanist, or Marxist. Both deplore the affective fallacy and argue that the intention of the poet is of little consequence. The critic must examine the poem itself, and this examination should concentrate on its form or structure. Ransom would surely have applauded this statement by Brooks: "If the artistic form, the dramatic structure of the poem, defines, fortifies, and validates what the poet has to say—if the poet speaks to us more meaningfully when he speaks as artist through the medium of his poetic form, then we will do well to take into account the niceties of that form if we want to know precisely what he has to tell us."

Both Ransom and Brooks agree on the cognitive function of poetry. Poetry provides a means through which man can know a great deal that science cannot teach him. "Poetry," Ransom argued, "intends to recover the denser and more refractory original world which we know loosely through our perceptions and memories." In an unpublished book-length essay, the chief concerns of which can be reconstructed from his correspondence with Allen Tate, Ransom described this cognitive function. There are, he wrote Tate on September 5, 1926, three moments "in the historical order of experience." The first is the experience itself, which is "pure of all intellectual content, unreflective, concrete, and singular." The second is a period of thought, analysis, and application. During this period a record is made and concepts are formed; abstract ideas are conceived by subtracting "from the whole experience." The third moment is one of reflection; it begins with memory and a "sense of loss. We become aware of the deficiency of the record. Most of the experience is quite missing from it." When one realizes that the abstract ideas do not reproduce the initial experience, the sense of loss may become so acute that he will attempt to recapture that elusive first moment through an act of creation. Thus he may construct dreams, fancies, morals, art, or religion. All of these employ images, but these images exist alongside the previously conceived concepts. This "mixed world" is presented in all its complexity through this combination of ideas and images, of "the conceptual and formal and the individual and concrete." From this pronouncement of a theory of poetic knowledge, Ransom moved easily to his statement of preference for the poetry that presents the opposition and then the reconciliation of the concept and the concrete image. Physical poetry is about things and Platonic poetry is about ideas; only metaphysical poetry introduces a "miracle," a figure that combines conceptual speculation and the concrete particularity of the world's body. This miraculism "arises when the poet discovers by analogy an identity between objects which is partial, though it should be considerable, and proceeds to an identification which is complete."

With much of this mode of thought Brooks would certainly agree, as indicated in his discussion of the poem as an imitation of reality, a presentation of a unified experience:

> It is not enough for the poet to analyze his experience as the scientist does, breaking it up into parts, distinguishing part from part, classifying the various parts. His task is finally to unify experience. He must return to us the unity of the experience itself as man knows it in his own experience. The poem, if it be a true poem, is a simulacrum of reality—in this sense, at least, it is an "imitation"—by *being* an experience rather than any mere statement about experience or any mere abstraction from experience.

But it is surely wrong to conceive of Brooks's criticism as a mere copy of that of his older contemporary. The reader who makes an intensive examination of their critical writings will be more impressed by their differences than by their similarities. Brooks is basically a practical critic. Although he does engage in theoretical speculations on the nature and function of poetry, he theorizes only to the extent necessary to provide a base for his commentary on individual poems. He has expressed his dislike of being known as "an indefatigable exegete," but the truth of the matter is that he is probably best known for his stimulating and illuminating analyses of significant literary works. If he, in Ransom's words, is "the most forceful and influential critic" of his generation, this reputation rests in large part on the fact, to quote Ransom again, that "he is the best reader of difficult verse around." Ransom obviously believed the Brooks's analytical criticism furnishes many examples of how poetry should be read, but he himself wrote few detailed commentaries of individual poems. In spite of a few glaring exceptions to this statement (one thinks immediately of "Yeats and His Symbols" and "Shakespeare at Sonnets"), most of Ransom's critical energy was expended in philosophical speculation on the nature and function of poetry. It is ironic that he was a critic who abhorred the kind of abstraction essential to philosophic exploration, one who in poetry demanded the specific and concrete; nevertheless he was convinced that criticism must become more philosophical if it is to encompass the vast range of human experience which only art can render. Ransom set out to broaden and deepen the base of literary criticism, to provide it with an ontology that would enable it to deal meaningfully and systematically with the aspects of human behavior revealed in the art object. It is for this reason that he was critical of the formal critic who did his verbal analysis and stopped. Although he believed that a close reading of the text must precede any other critical operation, he insisted that a critic's job goes beyond exegesis.

In spite of his assertion that Brooks's defense of poetry rests on some "fairly impenetrable esoteric quality" when it should be defended because "of its human substance and on the naturalistic level," Ransom approved of the younger critic's insistence that poetry is a means of perception and cognition. It is not primarily a vehicle through which a poet may express emotion, feelings, or moralistic attitudes. But, if the two critics agreed on the function of poetry, they disagreed on its nature.

Brooks argues that the coherence of a poem depends not upon logic but upon an attitude given life in a poem by its dominant metaphor. Ransom insisted that a metaphor cannot be a whole poem; neither can its unity depend upon the attitude embodied in the metaphor. The unity of the poem, Ransom argued, comes through an ideational core set against the metaphor, whereas Brooks believes that the unity of a poem "lies in the unification of attitudes into a hierachy subordinated to a local and governing attitude." Thus, he insists that the unity of a poem is achieved through a dramatic process and not a logical one. Ransom held the contrary view.

This difference of opinion regarding the means by which a unified poem is formed probably accounts for the different demands Ransom and Brooks make upon the metaphor. Ransom insisted that there be a single and consistent development of the metaphorical comparison because the way in which the figure is developed often reveals the emotions of the poet. Brooks's demands are less rigid, allowing some "emotive meanderings," to use James E. Magner's phrase, as long as these seeming digressions contribute to the dominant tone of the poem. Ransom expected consistent development of the metaphor in order to give the poem logical completeness; only through this kind of development, he insisted, can a poet give his creation a stable and unified structure. Brooks does not believe a metaphor has to be made to conform to any "prose line of . . . argument"; there may and should be associative meanderings as long as they contribute to the central attitude of the poem. Brooks would say that the strength of a poem comes from the force of its tone and attitude; Ransom, from its consistent and logical development.

But these differences, though significant, are not irreconcilable. Both critics try to reach the same goal but from slightly different directions. They both would argue that the "rich and contingent materiality" of an experience cannot be explained in scientific terms and that the purpose of poetry is to do what science cannot: to render the experience, not to comment on it. For both, poetry is a profoundly serious activity that should attract, in its creation and consumption, the best minds of this, or any other, generation. As long as poetry is regarded as a trifling fiction, of no real use when compared to the demonstrated "truths" of the physical and social sciences, it will continue to be ignored and its creators regarded as eccentric misfits in the social order. Several years ago Donald Davidson warned us that no civilization has ever lived without poetry and that ours can hardly be an exception. Few men in this century have contributed more energy or more genius than Ransom and Brooks in an attempt, if not to avoid, at least to postpone that tragedy. If Ransom attempted to convince us that poetry is valuable because it contains truths that are otherwise unavailable, Brooks has demonstrated how these truths may be recognized.

René Wellek

Cleanth Brooks, Critic of Critics

C LEANTH BROOKS is usually iden-
tified with one method, "close reading," and with a search for
such devices as paradox and irony in English poetry from
Shakespeare to Yeats. He has been accused of "critical monism"
by R. S. Crane in an article included in the Chicago symposium,
Critics and Criticism.[1] If one looks for a theoretical defense of his
point of view, one frequently will be disappointed by his delib-
erate, sometimes sudden dropping of the issues by quoting and
analyzing a poem. Thus Brooks's article "Literary Criticism"
soon becomes a discussion of Andrew Marvell's "Horatian
Ode."[2] The piece "The New Criticism and Scholarship" turns
into an interpretation of Bishop Corbet's "The Fairies
Farewell."[3] The address "The Quick and the Dead: A Comment

1 R. S. Crane, "The Critical Monism of Cleanth Brooks," in R. S. Crane *et al.*
(eds.), *Critics and Criticism: Ancient and Modern* (Chicago: University of
Chicago Press, 1952), 83–107.
2 Cleanth Brooks, "Literary Criticism," in *English Institute Essays, 1946* (New
York: Columbia University Press,. 1947), 127–58.
3 Cleanth Brooks, "The New Criticism and Scholarship," in W. S. Knicker-
bocker (ed.), *Twentieth-Century English* (New York: Philosophical Library,
1946), 371–83.

on Humanistic Studies" revolves around a poem "The Fall" by
Sir Richard Fanshawe.[4] The paper "Literary Criticism: Poet,
Poem, and Reader" treats us to an analysis of "The Grasshop-
per" of Sir Richard Lovelace.[5]

Still, focusing on Cleanth Brooks's brilliant and sensitive close
readings, most easily accessible in his two best-known books,
Modern Poetry and the Tradition (1939) and *The Well-Wrought Urn*
(1947), does grave injustice to the totality of his work. I can only
allude to his early study *The Relation of the Alabama-Georgia
Dialect to the Provincial Dialects of Great Britain* (1935) and to his
editing of the multivolume *Correspondence of Thomas Percy*,[6]
which shows his competence as an antiquarian eighteenth-
century scholar. I shall barely refer to *William Faulkner: The
Yoknapatawpha Country* (1963), which studies the fictional world
of William Faulkner very closely. I want rather to make a plea for
Cleanth Brooks as a historian of criticism, as a critic of critics. His
comments on criticism constitute an extensive part of his work
that has not received the attention it deserves. It includes not
only the 166 pages in the collaborative *Literary Criticism: A Short
History* (1957) with William K. Wimsatt, in which Brooks took
upon himself to discuss the major English and American critics
of the twentieth century from A. C. Bradley to Northrop Frye,
but also many scattered essays and reviews, as well as passages
in his books commenting on almost all prominent figures in the
history of English and American criticism.

Much of Brooks's comment on other critics is, no doubt,
self-defense, *apologia pro domo sua*. He knows that criticism is, as

4 Cleanth Brooks, "The Quick and the Dead: A Comment on Humanistic
   Studies," in Julian Harris (ed.),*The Humanities: An Appraisal* (Madison: Uni-
   versity of Wisconsin Press, 1950), 1–21.
5 Cleanth Brooks, "Literary Criticism: Poet, Poem, and Reader," in Stanley
   Burnshaw (ed.), *Varieties of Literary Experience* (New York: New York Univer-
   sity Press, 1962), 95–114.
6 Six volumes of the Thomas Percy correspondence have been issued to date
   (1942–1961), and another is being readied for publication.

Benedetto Croce knew and so said repeatedly, "criticism of criticism."[7] In criticizing others, Cleanth Brooks defines his own position, sometimes clarifying or modifying it in the context of the history of criticism or with rival currents of literary theory in this century. But his criticism of criticism is not only an attempt at self-definition. It has, predominantly, an objective aim and value, taking "objective" to mean Brooks's success as an expositor of ideas often alien to his own way of thinking. Brooks is an eminently fair-minded, text-oriented, conscientious examiner of ideas who is rarely openly polemical. After all, motivation in self-defense and self-definition does not dispose of the validity of arguments. Although we are all "situated" in history, in a specific time and place, we can reach out into the realm of ideas which—without any Platonic implications—we should recognize as timeless or at least constant in the sense of their being with us throughout recorded history, debated and debatable perennially.

Something like a general history of criticism emerges from Cleanth Brooks's writings, though the emphasis is comprehensibly on the situation of his own time. I shall try to survey and comment on his views, pulling together scattered passages, trying to construct a picture which might make details stand out to those not conversant with all of his writings.

Aristotle, undeniably the fountainhead of literary theory for centuries, is not in the center of Cleanth Brooks's interest. But Brooks appeals to his example on one crucial point: he sees Aristotle as the prototype of a critic concerned with the technical analysis of works of literary art who at the same time is, in his other writings, overwhelmingly concerned with moral, political, and metaphysical issues.[8] Brooks approves of this division

---

7 Benedetto Croce, *Poesia e non poesia* (Bari: G. Laterza, 1948), viii.
8 Brooks, "Literary Criticism: Poet, Poem, and Reader," 96–97. Cf. Cleanth Brooks, review of Alba Warren's *English Poetic Theory, 1825–1865,* in *American Oxonian* (January,1952), 52–53.

because he is convinced that the amalgamation and confusion of literary theory with morals, politics, and religion has been at the root of many difficulties of critical theory. He insists on a clear distinction between poetry and religion. Aristotle is thus upheld as a model of a great and exemplary man who implicitly denies Matthew Arnold's prophecy that "most of what now passes with us for religion and philosophy will be replaced by poetry."[9] Brooks confesses, "I am not one of those people who believe that man can live by poetry alone." The Arnoldian promise of a fusion of poetry and religion leads to a "real distortion of poetry and to nothing better than an *ersatz* religion."[10] He insists that "precisely those critics who, by and large, manifest a deep concern for religion are also concerned to maintain the independence of literature and its distinction from religion." He rejects the view that science has disposed of religion and that the values of religion have to find refuge in poetry. Literature would then become "the rhetorical garb for truthful propositions which are to be derived from science or philosophy."[11] The artist would be "a kind of super-advertising man—a specialist in arousing sympathetic emotions for the propositions he elected to present. In this scheme of things, poetics disappears into rhetoric." He suggests, "The shadow of Matthew Arnold still rests heavily upon our era."[12]

The American new humanists are, in Cleanth Brooks's eyes, a brand of Arnoldians. Brooks has not commented *in extenso* on either Irving Babbitt or Paul Elmer More. He praises Prosser

9 Matthew Arnold, *Essays in Criticism: Second Series* (London: Macmillan, 1888), 2.
10 Cleanth Brooks, "Implications of an Organic Theory of Poetry," in M. H. Abrams (ed.), *Literature and Belief: English Institute Essays, 1957* (New York: Columbia University Press,1958), 77–78.
11 Cleanth Brooks, "Metaphor and the Function of Criticism," in S. R. Hopper (ed.), *Spiritual Problems in Contemporary Literature* (New York: Harper, 1952), 130–31.
12 Cleanth Brooks, "A Note on the Limits of 'History' and the Limits of 'Criticism,'" *Sewanee Review*, LXI (January, 1953), 135.

Frye's *Romance and Tragedy* (1922) as "one of the ablest documents produced by the New Humanists" but remarks that Frye "out-Hegels Hegel in the sternness of his ethical demands." "As in so much of the work of this group there is a certain note of desperation. . . . He gloomily notes that almost from the very birth of tragedy there has been a falling off, with no real recoveries . . . Frye is carrying on a stubborn rear-guard action." [13] This is also what Brooks thinks of Douglas Bush and his Christian humanism when he casts doubts on Bush's hope that literature can be "put to work to save the situation." [14]

Though Brooks can appeal to Aristotle's separation of poetics and ethics, he cannot relish the peculiar reinterpretation of Aristotle's poetic theories in the Chicago group. This is due not only to a reaction against the sharp criticism of R. S. Crane, whom he has singled out as a "good example" of "elaborate system building, admirable as a display of sheer dialectic, almost for its own sake." [15] Rather there is a fundamental disagreement about the role of language in poetry. The Chicago group, Cleanth Brooks asserts, has a false view of language as "a mere phonetic protoplasm without inherent character," as the inert "material" of poetry. [16] These critics overemphasize plot and construe a theory of genres that leads to their indefensible proliferation. [17] Somewhat slyly, he draws a parallel to the conflict between John Dryden and Thomas Rymer with Rymer cast as "the worthy champion of plot." [18] We may remember that T. B. Macaulay called Rymer "the worst critic that ever lived."

13 William K. Wimsatt, Jr., and Cleanth Brooks, *Literary Criticism: A Short History* (New York: A. A. Knopf, 1957), 560.
14 Brooks, "A Note on the Limits of 'History' and the Limits of 'Criticism,'" 134.
15 Cleanth Brooks, review of Allen Tate's *On the Limits of Poetry*, in *Hudson Review*, II (Spring, 1949), 129.
16 Brooks, "Implications of an Organic Theory of Poetry," 66.
17 Wimsatt and Brooks, *Literary Criticism*, 694n.
18 *Ibid.*, 687n.

Aristotle as a theorist plays no prominent role in Cleanth Brooks's ancestry; one must assume that he sympathizes with John Crowe Ransom's dictum that "Aristotle does handsomely by the plot, and has nothing very impressive to say for the poetry." [19] Brooks, in any case, is not particularly interested in drama as stagecraft and plotting.

Samuel Taylor Coleridge's saying (derived from Goethe) that men are either Aristotelians or Platonists has been quoted *ad nauseam*. It does not apply in the case of Cleanth Brooks. I am not aware of any comment on Plato beyond a few casual allusions, but Brooks is undoubtedly indebted to Coleridge, who can be described (and has described himself) as belonging to the Platonic tradition. Brooks, however, completely cuts off Coleridge's thought from its metaphysical roots. He does not bother about the dialectics of subject and object, about the reconciliation of man and nature, the distinction between poetry and poem. He rather singles out the definition of imagination as the reconciliation of opposites and quotes it in several contexts, as T. S. Eliot has also done. The passage is used as if it were merely an endorsement of Dr. Johnson's characterization of metaphysical poetry as using "heterogeneous ideas yoked by violence together" deprived of any pejorative implication or else a definition of the "poetry of inclusion" or synthesis Brooks knows from George Santayana and I. A. Richards.

Coleridge is an authority for the view that a work of art is a totality, a unity in multiplicity, an organism. Brooks stresses that this multiplicity can be and should be contradictory, should be a multiplicity of tensions. He expressly disapproves of what he considers the romantic perversion of the organic concept of poetry to a mystical unity. [20] He has no use for Coleridge's

19 John Crowe Ransom, *Poems and Essays* (New York: Vintage Books, 1955), 97.
20 Cleanth Brooks, "The Poem as Organism: Modern Critical Procedure," in *English Institute Annual, 1940* (New York: Columbia University Press, 1941), 27.

distinction of imagination and fancy. "It lapses," he says, "in Shakespeare." Coleridge wrongly devalues fancy and wit and thus reintroduces a ranking of poetic subjects, a depreciation of the witty and low in favor of the serious and sublime. It is an inheritance of the eighteenth century or rather of the neoclassical doctrine of the levels of style. Cleanth Brooks also objects to Coleridge's suspicion against the share of intellect in poetry, to his defense of inspiration and even divine madness. The view of poetry of Coleridge (and many other romantics) as "revelation of the Divine" is merely "a restatement of the didactic conception which remained to confuse critical theory." [21] The attempts of some recent commentators such as Richard Foster to derive the New Criticism from Coleridge, and hence to claim the New Critics as romantics despite their antiromantic professions, clearly fail in the case of Cleanth Brooks. He sees Coleridge through the lenses of Richards' interpretation of Coleridge: Richards expressly declared that he was writing on Coleridge "as a Materialist trying to interpret . . . the utterances of an extreme Idealist." [22] Brooks thus can accept Richards' interpretation of the comment by Coleridge on a passage from *Venus and Adonis* which reduces Coleridge's distinction between "esemplastic imagination" and "associative fancy" to a purely descriptive and even quantifiable typology of metaphors. Brooks's review of Richards' *Coleridge on Imagination* completely ignores Richards' attempt to resuscitate the Fichte-Schelling dialectic used by Coleridge. [23]

In commenting on Ralph Waldo Emerson—who could be considered *the* Neoplatonist among philosophers of art—

<hr />

21 Cleanth Brooks, *Modern Poetry and the Tradition* (Chapel Hill: University of North Carolina Press, 1939), 26, 6–7, 19, 52.

22 Richard Foster, *The New Romantics: A Reappraisal of the New Criticism* (Bloomington: Indiana University Press, 1962); I. A. Richards, *Coleridge on Imagination* (London: Routledge, 1934), 19.

23 Wimsatt and Brooks, *Literary Criticism*, 636–37; Cleanth Brooks, review of I. A. Richards' *Coleridge on Imagination*, in *New Republic*, LXXXV (November 13, 1935), 26–27.

Brooks dismisses his "coalescence of man with nature," criticizes his "symbolistic monism," and states, "There are no fixities and definites at all but only symbolic fluidity." Coleridge's terms for fancy are invoked against Emerson's imagination. "If all the cards in the deck are 'wild' and can be counted as belonging to whatever suit and constituting whatever value we care to assign to them, then the game ends," comments Brooks, apparently unaware of Emerson's own saying: "In the transmission of the heavenly waters, every hose fits every hydrant." [24] Edgar Allan Poe is grouped by Brooks with the transcendentalists and criticized for his occult and magical views. "Things and thoughts are made to lie down beside each other as if any invidious distinction between them had been obliterated." [25]

In short, Cleanth Brooks is no idealist. He inherited from Coleridge (and his sources, Kant and August Wilhelm von Schlegel) the concept of organism and with it all the difficulties raised by a view which seems to make the work of art self-enclosed and to make criticism, in Eliot's term, "autotelic." The troubles into which such a view, rigidly held, runs have been explored in Murray Krieger's *The New Apologists for Poetry* (1956) and more recently in Gerald Graff's *Poetic Statement and Critical Dogma* (1970). But Brooks never embraced the identification of a work of art with a biological organism, or even analogue to God's creation, but picked the term "organism" to mean "organization," ordering, coherent design. It is used as a defense of the inseparability of content and form, as a term implying a rejection of the reduction of a work of poetry to a disguised statement of philosophical truth or an immediate appeal to the reader's beliefs and convictions. It serves as an equivalent of

---

24 Wimsatt and Brooks, *Literary Criticism*, 586, 708; Edward Waldo Emerson (ed.), *The Complete Works of Ralph Waldo Emerson* (Boston: Houghton Mifflin, 1903), III, 34–35.
25 Wimsatt and Brooks, *Literary Criticism*, 590.

illusion, semblance, *Schein*, or generally art as distinguished from reality, but it is not and could not mean "aestheticism" or "formalism" or even an isolation of the work of art from everything outside itself. Brooks tirelessly argues that language itself carries us outside of the poem: that the very words can be understood only in the context of an inherited language and that their meaning is circumscribed by external reality. He has, on many occasions and with many examples, combated the misunderstanding that he would want to interpret poems in a historical vacuum. He has picked poems such as Marvell's "Horatian Ode" to demonstrate the relevance of understanding a specific historical situation for a proper interpretation of a poem, and he has never been a "formalist" in the sense in which the term has been used by the opponents of the New Criticism. A formalist of the Russian persuasion could rather complain that Brooks rarely discusses form apart from meaning. He does—in the textbook *Understanding Poetry* and elsewhere—pay attention to metrics, but always in order to show that prosody is not independent of meaning. Mostly, he is concerned with themes, with motifs, with tone and attitude, with what would be called "content" in older aesthetics, though Brooks of course considers themes as functioning in a whole, as cooperating even in contradiction, as working toward a unified structure which is far from being merely formal but is not merely raw, extraliterary, unshaped content.

Actually, Cleanth Brooks upholds a version of imitation, *mimesis*. Twice we are explicitly told that "the poem if it be a true poem, is a simulacrum of reality—in this sense, at least, it is an 'imitation'—by *being* an experience rather than any mere statement about experience or any mere abstraction from experience," and in the later version: "It is a portion of reality as viewed and valued by a human being. It is rendered coherent through a perspective of valuing." He recognizes that "the coherence of parts in a literary work depends upon our belief in the plausibility of certain human actions and reactions, responses and valuations." We must believe in them or "the work of art is indeed incredible and monstrous." Still, "the correspondence to reality that a poem achieves is mediated through its special kind of structure." [26] Brooks quotes W. K. Wimsatt on art as "refraction" and his statement that "the refraction itself is a kind of reality." We are back at the old problem of "verisimilitude." It sounds commonplace but is a simple recognition that literature interprets reality existing outside the mind of man. Brooks is not a critic à la Georges Poulet or Northrop Frye, who believes that "there is nothing outside the mind of man," that "literature exists in its own universe containing life and reality in a system of verbal relationships." [27] Brooks, especially in his book on Faulkner, discusses the relationship between the "truth of reference" and the "truth of coherence," which he sees as complex but real. "The reader must be able to sense what is typical and what is exceptional, what is normal and what is an aberration" in Faulkner's picture of his South. Brooks emphasizes that Faulkner is writing fiction and not sociology or history but still compares his fictional picture with reality and concludes, for instance, that it is accurate when Faulkner describes the yeoman farmer or the poor white. The historian David Potter is quoted to support Brooks's view that Faulkner in the figure of Gavin Stevens in *Intruder in the Dust* depicts actual attitudes held in life by real people. [28]

26 Cleanth Brooks, *The Well-Wrought Urn* (New York: Harcourt Brace, 1947), 194; Brooks, "Implications of an Organic Theory of Poetry," 68, 71.

27 Wimsatt and Brooks, *Literary Criticism*, 737–38; Northrop Frye, *The Educated Imagination* (Bloomington: Indiana University Press, 1964), 29; Northrop Frye, *The Anatomy of Criticism* (Princeton, N.J.: Princeton University Press, 1956), 122.

28 Cleanth Brooks, *William Faulkner: The Yoknapatawpha Country* (New Haven, Conn.: Yale University Press, 1963), 6, 13, 423.

Brooks's main theoretical interests converge on twentieth-century English and American critics: Eliot, Richards, William Empson, Ransom, and Allen Tate. Older views are sometimes rejected but rarely discussed *in extenso*. Thus A. E. Housman's lecture "The Name and Nature of Poetry" is quoted several times for saying "metaphor and simile are inessential to poetry" and for the well-known passage naming "the chill down our spine" as a criterion of good poetry.[29] Both these conceptions run counter to everything Brooks could conceive to be the essence and test of poetry. Housman's views disturb him the more because he admires Housman as a metaphorical and intellectual poet. F. L. Lucas, "a late and decadent Romantic," is dismissed for his harsh comments on Richards and Coleridge.[30] Max Eastman is chided for his crude theories about "heightened consciousness" induced by literature and for his ridicule of the cult of unintelligibility. So is John Sparrow, as an enemy of modern art for his book *Sense and Poetry* (1934).[31]

Brooks is singularly indifferent to Marxist literary theory. He dismisses it as a revival of the didactic heresy. He protests Alfred Kazin's Marxist attack on the new formalists in *On Native Grounds*.[32] In a review of Kazin's *The Inmost Leaf*, he complains of "loose opinions" and doubts that Kazin's question of what a work of art "can mean to our living" concerns anyone except an

---

29 Cleanth Brooks, review of A. E. Housman's *The Name and Nature of Poetry*, in *Southwest Review*, XIX (Autumn, 1933), 25–26. Brooks quotes Housman in the following: "Metaphor and the Function of Criticism," 133; "Metaphor, Paradox, and Stereotype in Poetic Language," *British Journal of Aesthetics*, V (October, 1965), 316; "Literary Criticism: Poet, Poem, and Reader," 113; and "The Quick and the Dead," 43.

30 Brooks, "The Poem as Organism," 26, 38.

31 Brooks, *Modern Poetry and the Tradition*, 2, 59, 66. See also Brooks, *The Well-Wrought Urn*, 70, and Brooks, "Implications of an Organic Theory of Poetry," 57.

32 Brooks, *Modern Poetry and the Tradition*, 47; Brooks, *The Well-Wrought Urn*, 179–80. See also Brooks's introduction to R. W. Stallman (ed.), *Critiques and Essays in Criticism* (New York: Ronald Press, 1949), xvii.

eastern liberal. The only close attention to a Marxist text is to
E. B. Burgum's article, "The Cult of the Complex in Poetry,"
which, Brooks shows, treats William Wordsworth's poem "She
Dwelt Among the Untrodden Ways" merely as a "document of
manners, morals, and value judgments of its age."[33] It is the
familiar charge against historical relativism, which few Marxists
could or would want to reject.

Among the modern American critics, Edmund Wilson seems
to Brooks "the most old fashioned." He talks "sensitively, intel-
ligently, and learnedly, but not too learnedly, about a wide
variety of topics." He enjoys "the great advantage of sharing not
only the positive views and values of the typical American
intellectual, but the prejudices and blind sides as well." Brooks
thinks that "Wilson has been wrong on almost all the big issues
of the past," as has the typical intellectual. He marvels at Wil-
son's new jingoistic Americanism, quoting his paean to the
American bathroom in preference to the cathedrals of Europe.[34]
But Brooks disagrees also on strictly literary matters. He rejects
the reading of *The Waste Land* as a statement of despair and
Wilson's interpretation of Faulkner's *Intruder in the Dust*.[35] The
book is a novel and not a tract as Wilson would have it. The
views expressed by the lawyer Gavin Stevens are not necessar-
ily Faulkner's. "Stevens occupies no privileged position in
Faulkner's novel: sometimes he talks sense and sometimes he
talks nonsense."[36] Earlier Brooks took issue with Wilson's dis-

33 Cleanth Brooks, review of Alfred Kazin's *The Inmost Leaf*, in *New York Times
Book Review*, VII (November 6,1955), 40; Wimsatt and Brooks, *Literary Criti-
cism*, 649. E. B. Burgum's "The Cult of the Complex in Poetry" appears in
Science and Society, XV (1951), 31–48.
34 Cleanth Brooks, "The State of Criticism: A Sampling," *Sewanee Review*, LXV
(Summer,1957), 485–86.
35 Wimsatt and Brooks, *Literary Criticism*, 166. Edmund Wilson's article is
reprinted in his *Classics and Commercials* (New York: Farrar, Straus, 1950),
460–70.
36 Brooks, "The Quick and the Dead," 45. See also Brooks, *William Faulkner*,
279, 281, 420–24.

cussion of symbolism in *Axel's Castle*. He rejects the view that symbolism is decadent romanticism. Wilson's attempt to connect classicism with science, opposing to these "the poetic-romantic," seems to him gratuitous and confusing. He argues that the symbolist's detachment, his lack of propagandist intent, and his fidelity to the subject at hand place symbolist poetry far closer to the spirit of science. Brooks also emphasizes the differences within the French symbolist groups. Tristan Corbière and Jules Laforgue are witty and ironical: they are models of the early T. S. Eliot. Wilson wrongly ascribes the serious aesthetic tradition to all of symbolism and thus manages to identify Eliot with romantic escapism.[37] The last point seems well taken though one can hardly doubt the continuity of French symbolism with romanticism. One needs only to steer away from the facile concept of decadence which Baudelaire and others touted as a hallmark of sophistication.

Ezra Pound, the immediate predecessor of Eliot (who paid homage to Pound also as a critic), does not much interest Brooks in that function. He questions whether "in any language the discrete elements could retain so much of their original integrity as Pound claimed for Chinese ideograms." Brooks would have the strong support of the late George Kennedy, the Chinese scholar who, in a little-known article, cogently demolished these fancies derived from Ernest Fenollosa.[38]

T. E. Hulme is seen by Brooks as a forerunner of Eliot, though their agreement can be largely explained by common sources in French criticism. Brooks praises him for valuing metaphor and for embracing "the doctrine of original sin." His classicism is a form of objectivism since Hulme "much more cleanly than

37 Cleanth Brooks, "A Note on Symbol and Conceit," *American Review*, III (April, 1934), 201, reprinted in Brooks, *Modern Poetry and the Tradition*, 54.
38 Wimsatt and Brooks, *Literary Criticism*, 664; George Kennedy, "Fenollosa, Pound, and the Chinese Character," *Yale Literary Magazine*, CXXVI (1958), 24–36.

Coleridge" stresses the art object. But Hulme is guilty of romantic clichés about "sincerity" and zest which go into poetic activity.[39] Brooks's sympathy with Hulme is obviously partial.

Cleanth Brooks's main admiration goes to T. S. Eliot as a poet, as a thinker on culture and religion, and as a literary critic. The experience of Eliot's poetry must have profoundly shaped Brooks's taste. He is in the company of Allen Tate rather than his teacher John Crowe Ransom, who had criticized *The Waste Land* severely when it appeared. The influence of I. A. Richards—important for Brooks's vocabulary and critical practice—came later. Brooks says himself that he "must have read *Principles of Literary Criticism* through fifteen times in the early thirties," and he read Empson's *Seven Types of Ambiguity* in 1938 (it was first published in 1930).[40] Brooks has always felt that there is no radical difference between the concepts of poetry of Eliot and Richards. Eliot, Tate, Ransom, and Richards, "employing diverse terminologies and approaches, corroborate each other emphatically," said Brooks in his first book, *Modern Poetry and the Tradition* (1939), and he repeats in 1956, "Unless one recognizes the amount of agreement between Richards and Eliot, one will find it difficult to understand the relative ease with which Richards' influence upon criticism has merged with that of Eliot." Not that Brooks did not see their differences. Especially later he recognized that "Eliot stands by his bold assertion that a poem is a *fusion* of thought and feeling." Richards, on the other hand, "from the first has endeavored to maintain a careful distinction between the emotional state produced in the reader (the balance of impulses or the state of synaesthesis) and the means to produce this emotional state."[41]

39 Brooks, "Metaphor and the Function of Criticism," 136–38; Wimsatt and Brooks, *Literary Criticism*, 661–62.
40 Cleanth Brooks, "Empson's Criticism," *Accent*, IV (Summer, 1944), 208.
41 Brooks, *Modern Poetry and the Tradition*, 70; Wimsatt and Brooks, *Literary Criticism*, 623.

In general, Eliot is invoked on central points of Brooks's concern: Brooks quotes Eliot's "Tradition and the Individual Talent" prominently and describes tradition in Eliot's terms in an article for a dictionary. Elsewhere he says, "In a time of disorder, Eliot moved toward a restoration of order."[42] He quotes him on true originality and approves of his concept of poetry as a synthesis of intellect and feeling, a fusion of opposites, with all its consequences: the recovery of the metaphysicals who combine wit and seriousness not only as a rehabilitation of neglected poets but also as a definition of the very nature of poetry.[43] It implies also the minimizing of the difference between imagination and fancy and, at least in principle, an acceptance of Eliot's basic scheme of the history of English poetry: the "dissociation of sensibility" in the seventeenth century.[44] Whereas Eliot's statements are more cautious, Brooks makes much of the "deadening" influence of Thomas Hobbes, a singling out of a figure who could not have played such a decisive role in a deep change pervading all Europe. Brooks also endorses Eliot's view of poetic language: the poet "dislocates ordinary language into meaning" or at the very least slightly alters it.[45] He also agrees with Eliot's views on poetic beliefs: the mind of the reader must be able, Eliot argued, to accept them as

---

42 Brooks, "The Poem as Organism," 27–29, 30; Cleanth Brooks, "Tradition," in Joseph T. Shipley (ed.), *Dictionary of World Literature* (New York: Philosophical Library, 1943),585–86; Cleanth Brooks, *A Shaping Joy: Studies in the Writer's Craft* (London: Methuen, 1971), 37.

43 Brooks, *Modern Poetry and the Tradition*, 70, 39; Brooks, *A Shaping Joy*, 39.

44 Brooks, *The Well-Wrought Urn*, 26. See "Notes for a Revised History of English Poetry" in Brooks, *Modern Poetry and the Tradition*, 219–44, in which Brooks does not use Eliot's term.

45 Brooks, *Modern Poetry and the Tradition*, 235; Cleanth Brooks, "The Language of Poetry: Some Problem Cases," *Archiv für das Studium der Neueren Sprachen und Literaturen*, CCIII (April, 1967), 401; Cleanth Brooks and Robert Penn Warren, *Understanding Poetry* (Rev. ed.; New York: Henry Holt, 1950), 587; Brooks, *The Well-Wrought Urn*, 192, 8.

"coherent, mature, and founded on the facts of experience."[46] Brooks shares Eliot's distaste for Shelley and in *Understanding Poetry* singles out "The Indian Serenade" as a sentimental poem, as an example of the poetry of "exclusion," ignoring his own advice to read poems with their speakers in mind.[47] "The Indian Serenade" is, after all, put into the mouth of a yearning oriental lover.

On some points Brooks has disagreements with Eliot and some misgivings about his theories. He recognizes that Eliot is sometimes inconsistent, that there is much psychologism left in Eliot's concept of synaesthesis, and he is impressed by Eliseo Vivas' destructive analysis of the concept of the "objective correlative" and even agrees with Vivas' rejection of Eliot's analysis of *Hamlet*.[48] But, in general, Brooks shares Eliot's critical doctrines: the impersonal theory, the poetry of synaesthesis, the dissociation of sensibility, the view of tradition. Brooks also, in a rather lukewarm review of *The Use of Poetry and the Use of Criticism* (1933), defends Eliot's method of careful qualification, complaining of Edmund Wilson's parody in *Axel's Castle* of Eliot's critical style.[49]

Eliot's influence merged with that of Richards. Brooks is particularly impressed by the "all-important" Chapter 32, "The

46 Brooks, *Modern Poetry and the Tradition*, 48; Brooks, *The Well-Wrought Urn*, 228; Cleanth Brooks, "Irony as a Principle of Structure," in Morton D. Zabel (ed.), *Literary Opinion in America* (Rev. ed.; New York: Harper, 1951), 732. This essay is a revision of Cleanth Brooks, "Irony and 'Ironic' Poetry," *College English*, IX (February, 1948), 231–37. Cf. T. S. Eliot, *The Use of Poetry and the Use of Criticism* (London: Faber and Faber, 1933), 96.
47 Brooks, *The Well-Wrought Urn*, 229; Cleanth Brooks and Robert Penn Warren, *Understanding Poetry* (1st ed.; New York: Henry Holt, 1938), 319.
48 Wimsatt and Brooks, *Literary Criticism*, 668–69, 623; Eliseo Vivas, *Creation and Discovery* (New York: Noonday, 1955), 175–89.
49 Cleanth Brooks, review of T. S. Eliot's *The Use of Poetry and the Use of Criticism*, in *Southwest Review*, XIX (Winter, 1934), 1–2. Cf. Edmund Wilson, *Axel's Castle* (New York: Scribner's, 1945), 124.

Imagination," in *Principles of Literary Criticism*, which distinguishes two types of poetry: a poetry which excludes the opposite and discordant qualities of experience and one which synthesizes the heterogeneity of the distinguishable impulses and thus will bear ironical contemplation.[50] Irony in this wide sense of detachment and awareness of the inclusiveness of experience became Brooks's main standard of good poetry. It hardly differs from paradox and the more limited verbal ambiguity. The terms have been often misunderstood; they are used not in the usual senses in which irony implies the opposite of the literal sense and paradox implies a proposition contrary to received opinion. Irony, in Brooks's best-known formulation, is "the *obvious* warping of a statement by the context." It is "a general term for the kind of qualification which the various elements in a context receive from a context."[51] It is simply the "interanimation of words," the "transaction between contexts," the principle which Richards expounded in *The Philosophy of Rhetoric* (1936), which Brooks singles out as one of Richards' "best books."[52] Brooks's method is an examination of the interanimation not only of words but of motifs, themes, metaphors, and symbols. Brooks does this by inspecting the poem's text, though particularly in his early work he often uses misleadingly the psychological vocabulary of Richards. Conceit, for instance, is defined as an "instrument" to bring "the counter-impulses into momentary conflict with the primary impulses." Later Brooks recognized that Richards' psychological vocabulary "evaporates when we get ready to use it," but he insists that we need not accept his "particular psychological

50 Brooks, *Modern Poetry and the Tradition*, 41. Cf. Cleanth Brooks, *The Poetry of Tension* (St. John's: Memorial University of Newfoundland Press, 1972), 3–4.
51 Brooks, "Irony as a Principle of Structure," 730; Brooks, *The Well-Wrought Urn*, 191.
52 Brooks, *A Shaping Joy*, 95. Cf. Brooks, "The Language of Poetry," 407.

theory" to agree with his theory of criticism.[53] I. A. Richards, "even while arguing that the value of a poem was to be sought, not in its makeup, but in the psychological reaction of its reader, was actually directing our attention to the subtle interconnections of the structure of poetic meaning."[54]

Brooks defends himself against the charge of denying any value to simplicity, which seems to follow from his praise of "complexity." But he does not approach it directly, deflecting attention to E. B. Burgum's idiosyncratic disposal of simplicity and suspecting defenders of simplicity of doubting that the complexities and ironies discovered in (and not merely read into) the poems discussed were not and could not have been consciously in the poets' minds. Brooks, then, argues convincingly that a bare statement such as "ripeness is all" assumes its meaning only in the context of *King Lear* and that an apparently simple lyric such as "western wind, when wilt thou blow" is not really simple at all.[55] But one can hardly deny that Brooks's taste and preference, as well as his theory, work against wide varieties of the world's poetry: folk poetry, narrative poetry, poetry of statement, romantic mood poetry, poetry with no metaphors. He must define "the principle task of criticism— perhaps *the* task of criticism—as making explicit the implicit manifold of meanings."[56] Brooks feels acutely the need of making a case for complexity to readers brought up with a taste for romantic poetry. The showpieces of Brooks's close readings are inevitably instances which allow him to reveal undervalued or unsuspected complexity. Texts which are transparent at first

53 Brooks, "A Note on Symbol and Conceit," 208; Wimsatt and Brooks, *Literary Criticism*, 620; Cleanth Brooks, "The Pernicious Effects of Bad Art," *Et Veritas* (May, 1949), 14.
54 Brooks, "Implications of an Organic Theory of Poetry," 63.
55 Wimsatt and Brooks, *Literary Criticism*, 648–50.Cf. Brooks, "Irony as a Principle of Structure," 730.
56 Wimsatt and Brooks, *Literary Criticism*, 652.

sight have not tempted him, though on occasion he grants their appeal and value.

Richards also taught Brooks to dismiss the old criterion of the visual vividness of metaphor and to see the need of metaphor for the expression of subtler states of emotion as well as the lack of poetic effect of mere sound divorced from meaning.[57] Brooks approves and quotes Richards on many issues; I have mentioned the remarks on Coleridge's comments on *Venus and Adonis* and may add Richards' discussion of "intrinsicate" in *Antony and Cleopatra* or of the telescoped conceits in John Donne.[58] Brooks praises Richards for focusing attention upon the problem of discriminating good art from bad—alluding presumably to the chapter "Badness in Poetry" in *Principles of Literary Criticism*—though a few pages before Brooks admits that Richards' distinction between defectiveness of communication and the worthlessness of experience communicated (illustrated by poems of H.D. and Ella Wheeler Wilcox) cannot be maintained.[59]

In general Cleanth Brooks approves of Richards' concept of poetry and of his defense of myth. He quotes Richards' saying, "Without mythologies man is only a cruel animal," and refers to a passage to suggest that the study of poetry "would amount to a study of metaphysics." He is, however, convinced that "a metaphysics approached from a new angle" would be more than a study of the "resourcefulness of words," Richards' new term by which he attempted to replace the "evil-sounding name 'ambiguity.'"[60] Brooks likes Richards' raising of the problem

---

57 *Ibid.*, 642, 644; Brooks and Warren, *Understanding Poetry* (1938), 230; Brooks, *The Well-Wrought Urn*, 9.
58 Brooks, "The Poem as Organism," 23–24, 25–26. Cf. Brooks and Warren, *Understanding Poetry* (1938), 230; Brooks and Warren, *Understanding Poetry* (1950), 576; Brooks, *The Well-Wrought Urn*, 22.
59 Wimsatt and Brooks, *Literary Criticism*, 632, 624.
60 Brooks, "Metaphor and the Function of Criticism," 135; Brooks, *The Well-Wrought Urn*, 236, 237. See also I. A. Richards, *Speculative Instruments* (Chicago: University of Chicago Press, 1955), 75–76.

but cannot agree with his positivistic solution: he speaks of the "debonair ruthlessness of his [Richards'] original treatment of the problem." The poet, in Richards' earlier formulations, makes pseudostatements, is not concerned with truth at all. "His task was rather to furnish therapeutic exercise for the reader's neural system and thus promote his mental health." According to Richards, "Poetry is nonsense but a valuable nonsense." Brooks professes to find "reservations and refinements" in the later Richards and sees a shift of emphasis in *The Philosophy of Rhetoric.* Here Richards, Brooks believes, "laid aside the distinction between the referential and emotive aspects of language," a change for which I do not see any evidence. Richards' lecture at Yale in 1946 was rightly called "Emotive Language Still." Cleanth Brooks is unhappy about Richards' divorce between text and criticism and the obscurity of "the alleged goings-on in the reader's neural system"[61] and at least once openly states his disagreement. Richards, says Brooks, "puts a burden on poetry as an activity which poetry does not need to assume and which it probably cannot assume."[62] We are back at Brooks's objection to Matthew Arnold.

In his public pronouncements, at least, Cleanth Brooks avoids confronting the fact that Richards is and remains a behaviorist, a positivist who considers poetry, metaphysics, and religion "nonsense," whatever social utility he might ascribe to them. There is a basic misunderstanding in Brooks's allegiance to Richards; it is due to the feeling of gratitude for the formulas and techniques of analysis he has learned from him. It conceals the gulf between Richards' scientism and Brooks's religious commitment.

Brooks, on this point, resembles William Empson, who also learned much from Richards but came to distrust his emotive

---

61 Brooks, "Implications of an Organic Theory of Poetry," 55, 56; Wimsatt and Brooks, *Literary Criticism,* 626, 641.
62 Brooks, *The Well-Wrought Urn,* 231.

theory. But Empson, of course, did not embrace a religious solution. Brooks's review of *English Pastoral Poetry* praises Empson for the light he sheds on the nature of language structure, for his conception of metaphor as functional in a context, and for the poem as dynamic structure, as the fulfillment of a total process. Brooks admires Empson's "racoon-like curiosity."[63] In other contexts, he quotes Empson approvingly on several occasions, often at length. See, for instance, the comments on Pope's "mighty maze," on John Gay's *Beggar's Opera*, and on Thomas Gray's *Elegy*.[64] *English Pastoral Poetry* is highly praised as a "sampling of the ironic mode" with wide implications for a revision of English literary history. But Brooks has serious reservations about *Seven Types of Ambiguity*. The term "ambiguity" is a concession to a rationalist prejudice: the phenomenon should be called rather "plurisignation," a term derived from Philip Wheelwright. "The seven types overlap, and at points the definitions are highly arbitrary." Empson should not have bothered about categories and simply given readings of the poems with no generalizations. Tellingly, Brooks criticizes Empson's argument that there may be a type of ambiguity which "works well if it is never discovered." Brooks objects that this would make poetry hocus-pocus, white magic. He sees also that Empson's method can be applied with equal success to bad poetry, that it does not and cannot lead to critical conclusions.[65]

A later review of Empson's *Structure of Complex Words* shows Brooks still of two minds about Empson's methods and results.

63 Brooks, "Empson's Criticism," 208–16; Wimsatt and Brooks, *Literary Criticism*, 646.
64 Brooks, "The Poem as Organism," 21–22; Brooks and Warren, *Understanding Poetry* (1950), 514–15; Brooks, *The Well-Wrought Urn*, 102–103; Brooks, *Modern Poetry and the Tradition*, 227–29.
65 Brooks, "Empson's Criticism," 214, 211; Wimsatt and Brooks, *Literary Criticism*, 638, 639–40.

He admires the analysis of the term "wit" in Alexander Pope's *Essay on Criticism* as "a fine instance of historical recovery," and he endorses Empson's solution of the problem of belief as "admirably sensible." We imagine "some other person to hold the beliefs" we do not share in reading a poet. Brooks suggests that much of *The Structure of Complex Words* could be contained in *Seven Types of Ambiguity*; Empson's new distinction between ambiguity and "equation" is untenable. Ambiguity, in Empson, assumes the willing by a single poet; equation is caused by the historically conditioned language. But surely, Brooks argues, the poet using ambiguity is exploiting the resources of the historical language. The two claims do not cancel each other. Brooks dislikes the cumbrous mathematical notations and makes many objections to individual points. Empson is often "highly impressionistic or eccentric or just plain wrong." He interprets, for instance, the first line of the fourth stanza of the "Ode on a Grecian Urn" as making the poet "see new victims approaching." Empson says that "none of them will ever go home again," though it is obvious that the only victim will be the sacrificial heifer and that the town is empty only because everybody went out to witness the ceremony of the sacrifice. Empson, Brooks concludes, works with the most diverse approaches, such as author's psychology or audience response or lexical analysis, without much sense of distinction. He never faces the problem of relevance. "He is an incorrigible amateur." *The Structure of Complex Words* is "provocative and seminal . . . but it is also, much more than the earlier books, a kind of ragbag." [66]

Brooks's relation to the other New Critics (he has always deplored the term) is far from one of simple allegiance. He admires

66 Cleanth Brooks, review of William Empson's *Structure of Complex Words*, in *Kenyon Review*, XIV (Autumn, 1952), 669–78.

his teacher John Crowe Ransom as a poet and critic. He expounds the contents of *The New Criticism* in an encyclopedia and quotes *God Without Thunder* about the conflict of poetry, of Hobbes, and of sound symbolism approvingly, and he praises Ransom specifically for considering myths the greatest radical metaphors.[67] But this praise should not hide the deep disagreements between pupil and teacher. Brooks is upset by Ransom's low view of the role of paradox, irony, and wit in poetry. He must criticize Ransom for his advocacy of a structure-texture dichotomy which he sees as "ominously like the old content-form dualism."[68] He suggests that Ransom did not really mean that "irrelevant texture" is "irrelevant." Ransom can distinguish between "irrelevance which is really irrelevant and irrelevance which is actually highly relevant to the goodness of the poem." Brooks predicts that Ransom "would return to a theory of functional metaphor. With regard to his theory of 'structure' and 'texture', even if one concedes that it is a valuable metaphor which accounts for the surprise that the practicing poet may feel at finding that his digressions from the theme (forced upon him by metaphor and meter) actually enrich the theme, still I believe that he would discover that it is only a partial metaphor after all."[69] Elsewhere, Brooks describes what he calls a "bifocal" cognitive theory. "Poetry gives us through its structure and texture, respectively, knowledge of universals, and knowledge of particulars . . . Ransom hands over the realm of universals to science, and in effect retains for poetry no more than an apprehension of particulars." Brooks draws a

67 Cleanth Brooks, "New Criticism," in Alex Preminger (ed.), *Encyclopedia of Poetry and Poetics* (Princeton, N.J.: Princeton University Press, 1965), 567; Brooks, *Modern Poetry and the Tradition*, 91, 52, 46; Brooks, "Implications of an Organic Theory of Poetry," 58; Brooks and Warren, *Understanding Poetry* (1950), 244; Brooks, "Metaphor and the Function of Criticism," 134.
68 Wimsatt and Brooks, *Literary Criticism*, 622; Brooks, "Implications of an Organic Theory of Poetry," 58.
69 Cleanth Brooks, combined review of Yvor Winters' *Anatomy of Nonsense* and books by others, in *Kenyon Review*, VI (Spring, 1944), 287.

parallel between Ransom's and Eastman's view that poetry is "heightened consciousness." Ransom, Brooks notes with some surprise, adopted Freudian psychology on this point. "Poetry ministers to the health of the mind, and Ransom's later position tends to approximate in some features the earlier position of Richards." Brooks thinks that both Richards' and Ransom's theories run into difficulties because they both begin by "slicing apart value and knowledge." [70]

Cleanth Brooks is clearly much more in sympathy with Allen Tate and repeatedly endorses his formula: "Poetry is neither religion nor social engineering." Like Tate, he argues that the poem is an object and that "specific moral problems are the subject matter of literature, but that the purpose of literature is not to point a moral." [71] Brooks emphatically agrees with Tate that "form is meaning" and that "poetry is complete knowledge," a somewhat obscure statement which Brooks interprets to mean the knowledge that science leaves out, presumably the knowledge of qualities claimed by Ransom as the special domain of poetry. Brooks defends Tate against the charge of formalism. Tate deals, Brooks says, rather with social history, with politics, and with the cultural situation. His strength is in his belief in a traditional society and a "coherent metaphysics," [72] an allusion presumably to Tate's proximity to Roman Catholicism. Tate joined the church in 1950, a year after Brooks's review.

The other New Critics, only loosely related to the southern group, have elicited less comment from Cleanth Brooks. He has written little on Kenneth Burke, though he praises the essay on

70 Wimsatt and Brooks, *Literary Criticism*, 67, 630.
71 Brooks, review of Tate's *On the Limits of Poetry*, 132; Brooks, "Metaphor and the Function of Criticism," 127–28; Brooks, "The Poem as Organism," 29. See also Cleanth Brooks, "The Formalist Critic," *Kenyon Review*, XIII (Winter, 1951), 72.
72 Brooks, "Literary Criticism: Poet, Poem, and Reader," 98; Brooks, *The Well-Wrought Urn*, 236; Brooks, review of Tate's *On the Limits of Poetry*, 132.

the "Ode on a Grecian Urn" as corroborating his own reading. Brooks is even convinced by Burke's seeing a pun on "breed" in a line by Keats: "with brede of marble men and maidens overwrought." In a theoretical context, Brooks agrees with Burke that a poem is a "mode of action" but alludes to "several rather important reservations with respect to Mr. Burke's position."[73] But Brooks does not state them. Earlier he had quoted Burke on the issue of propaganda art.[74]

R. P. Blackmur concurs with Burke's view that a poem is a mode of action. Brooks finds an area of agreement with Blackmur's concept of "gesture," the "outward and dramatic play of inward and imagined meaning." Later, in an omnibus review of recent criticism, Brooks criticizes *Anni Mirabiles* as "a series of dark sayings," "perversely whimsical," a "personal monologue" in a "congested and involved style." Brooks asks the pertinent question whether the audience of these lectures could possibly have followed them.[75]

Yvor Winters is appreciated for his "corrective value." Brooks says that he consistently overrates conscious intention. In making poetry "a moral judgment" Winters extends the meaning of "moral" to include any and all value judgments.[76] His theory reintroduces a dualism of intellect and emotion, denotation and connotation, with Winters always coming down heavily in favor of intellect and denotation, but Brooks would argue for a view of poetry that would deny any cleavage between intellect and emotion, denotation and connotation. In Brooks's most elaborate discussion of Winters, he is characterized as "not amiable, not charming, obviously very earnest." Winters

73 Brooks, *The Well-Wrought Urn*, 139n, 186n.
74 Brooks, *Modern Poetry and the Tradition*, 51.
75 Brooks, *The Well-Wrought Urn*, 186n; Brooks, "The State of Criticism," 492–94.
76 Wimsatt and Brooks, *Literary Criticism*, 673; Brooks, *The Well-Wrought Urn*, 216.

"exhibits all the rancor of a man . . . who knows that he is right. He is perhaps our most logically rigorous critic; he is certainly one of our most intelligent; and he is undoubtedly the most cantankerous." Brooks complains about his "obtuseness" toward T. S. Eliot. The charge of "romantic mysticism" is quite unjustified. Winters is something of a stoic, insisting on man's free will and thus suspicious of any concession a poet may make to his environment. "The form of the poem must confront the chaos of a world in flux: the judgment on that world must be unequivocal; the author must know precisely what he is doing, and act with firmness and decision." Brooks protests against Winters' view of Eliot's "spiritual limpness" and argues that Winters is wrong about *The Waste Land*; it does judge modern civilization rather than "yielding" to it as Winters would have it. Once Brooks, irritated by Winters' charge of "automatism" in Eliot, speaks of him as a "moral cop, in his most vindictive mood." [77] But elsewhere Brooks endorses Winters' argument for the independence of poetry from its age and praises him for proposing "the fallacy of expressive form," the mistaken view that poets have to write chaotic poetry in a chaotic age. Brooks, however, does not share Winters' extreme unhistorical indeterminism. In agreeing, for instance, with Tate's diagnosis of cultural decay and his seeing Emily Dickinson and Hart Crane reflecting the difficulties of their respective historical positions, Brooks accepts some concept of Zeitgeist, a determinism violently rejected by Winters, who considers it predestinarianism, disguised Calvinism, or simply "obscurantism." Finally, Brooks must disagree with Winters' suspicion of the dramatic and ironic, but turns the tables on him by asserting that Winters' concept of poetry really centers on "plot" and is thus "ulti-

77 Brooks, review of Winters' *Anatomy of Nonsense*, 283–86; Brooks, "Implications of an Organic Theory of Poetry," 61, 66; Brooks, *The Well-Wrought Urn*, 215–16.

mately dramatic."[78] Still, the main disagreement with the rationalism and stoicism of Winters persists.

The parallel philosophical endeavors to restate aesthetics in symbolic terms excited some rather casual comment. Brooks sees that Ernst Cassirer's theory of symbolic forms (which he knows from the *Essay on Man*) exalts science and that Cassirer is vague about the relation among the symbolic forms of language, myth, art, and philosophy. Susanne K. Langer, usually labeled a follower of Cassirer, is in Brooks's interpretation rather an advocate of the view that art is a "life of sentience." She resembles Max Eastman, and her symbolism is completely random in the manner of Emerson.[79]

Brooks is greatly impressed by Wilbur Urban's *Language and Reality.* He quotes the book on aesthetic intuition, on the symbol, on metaphor as symbol, on myth as dramatic language, on art as the revelation of man, and on art as the realm of values, but recognizes that Urban considers all poetry covert metaphysics or imperfect philosophy.[80] Urban belongs with Cassirer.

The new myth criticism derives from Carl Jung. Brooks sympathizes with Jung's general outlook, which he sees as parallel to the symbolist movement, but he accepts Jung's own disclaimer that his method was meant to be "a substitute for literary criticism." Jung, as far as I am aware, is only once used to explain a detail in Faulkner's *As I Lay Dying.*[81] But the flourishing American myth criticism was received by Brooks with less than enthusiasm. He agrees with Harry Levin's view that the new symbol-mongering is really "a cold-blooded seek-

78 Wimsatt and Brooks, *Literary Criticism,* 670, 674, 676.
79 *Ibid.,* 700–13.
80 Brooks, *The Well-Wrought Urn,* 182–83, 189n, 232–33, 235–36, 237n. See also Brooks, "Implications of an Organic Theory of Poetry," 69.
81 Wimsatt and Brooks, *Literary Criticism,* 717, 719; Brooks, *William Faulkner,* 399.

ing out of mechanical allegories." Brooks criticizes in detail the heavy-handed symbolist interpretations common in Faulkner criticism. When Leslie Fiedler advocates a concern for archetypes, he is, Brooks argues, substantially defending "a privileged poetic subject matter in disguise."[82] Equality of subject matter whether high or low is one of Brooks's basic convictions which serves to rehabilitate the metaphysical and to recommend the poetry of T. S. Eliot.

Brooks reviews Northrop Frye sympathetically as an ingenious classifier and definer of new genres. But Brooks must disapprove of his dismissal of all value judgment and all judicial criticism as it would lead to a new historicism and relativism. He sees Frye's dilemma between a scheme which would make literature autonomous and, at the same time, fruitful for the human enterprise. Frye, like Arnold, is in danger of making literature a substitute religion—a prophetic observation if we know Frye's later writings about a "myth of concern." Myth criticism, Cleanth Brooks concludes, "provides no way of circumventing the basic problems of traditional criticism."[83]

Actually, Brooks's most sympathetic accounts of myth and archetypal criticism are devoted to the two modern poets whom he admires besides T. S. Eliot: W. B. Yeats and W. H. Auden. Every one of Brooks's books, except the monograph on Faulkner, contains a chapter on Yeats. Yeats's critical and theoretical writings are constantly referred to and expounded since they serve as a commentary on and support for the interpretation of Yeats's poems and the myth behind them, which is one of Brooks's major concerns. Since Yeats's most extravagant

82 Brooks, "The State of Criticism," 490–91; Brooks, *William Faulkner*, 6–8, 377, 380, 408–10; Wimsatt and Brooks, *Literary Criticism*, 713.
83 Cleanth Brooks, review of Northrop Frye's *The Anatomy of Criticism*, in *Christian Scholar*, XLI (June, 1958), 172, 170, 171; Wimsatt and Brooks, *Literary Criticism*, 711, 714.

schemes of history and of psychological types or his most preposterous pronouncements upon occult phenomena and the transmigration of souls may serve to elucidate a poem, Brooks is extremely indulgent of their truth claims. Yeats's *Vision* is considered "one of the most remarkable books of the last hundred years," and its "framework is elaborate and complex: the concrete detail constitutes some of the finest prose and poetry of our time." Only rarely does Brooks demur at Yeats's occultism and allude to Yeats's "life-long interest in table-rapping, spirit mediums, and clair-voyants."[84] *A Vision* is later called "that rich, confused, and baffling book." Brooks feels that a poet has his privileges and tries, sometimes forcing the texts a little, to make acceptable sense out of Yeats's pronouncements, which, restated in cooler terms, often can be made to agree with much of what Brooks accepts and approves. Thus Yeats's view of history appeals to him because of its rejection of progress and of the benefits of science. Brooks can quote Yeats on "Descartes, Locke, and Newton," who "took away the world and gave us its excrement instead," as corroborating Eliot's "dissociation of sensibility" and his own view of the "deadening" influence of Hobbes. He can expound Yeats's phases of the moon as a typology of characters since the idea of the antiself supports his impersonal concept of poetry; and he can take seriously even the weird pronouncements on Christ and Christianity as Yeats "goes far to restore to Christianity its proper dimension of awe and dread." Still, Brooks arrives at the right conclusion that Yeats was not a Christian but that he "found his imagination gripped by the great Christian symbols."[85]

---

84 Brooks, *Modern Poetry and the Tradition*, 173; Wimsatt and Brooks, *Literary Criticism*, 600.
85 Cleanth Brooks, *The Hidden God: Studies in Hemingway, Faulkner, Yeats, Eliot, and Warren* (New Haven, Conn.: Yale University Press, 1963), 47, 53, 60; Brooks, *A Shaping Joy*, 111.

Brooks's interest in Yeats's theories is also focused on the literary theories and criticism proper. He expounds Yeats's early essay "The Symbolism of Poetry" (1900) and uses his example from Robert Burns also in *Understanding Poetry*. He quotes Yeats on the "one great memory" as an "anticipation of Carl Jung's doctrine of the collective unconscious,"[86] an unnecessary claim since Yeats's concept resembles rather Eduard von Hartmann's or Friedrich von Schelling's or even Emerson's and goes back to the mystic tradition (as does Jung's). In an essay "W. B. Yeats as a Literary Critic" (1963) Brooks admits at the outset that Yeats as a critic "was often cranky and perverse. His *Oxford Book of Modern Verse* is a monument to an arbitrary taste." But then Brooks collects perceptive and brilliantly phrased opinions on Walt Whitman, Keats, J. M. Synge, Byron, Pope, and Wordsworth before giving a careful account of Yeats's conception of the creative process: the recourse to the buried self. The saying, "We make out of the quarrel with others, rhetoric, but out of the quarrel with ourselves, poetry,"[87] prepares us for Yeats's concept of the true poet, distinct from the rhetorician and the sentimentalist. Brooks again expounds Yeats's scheme of the original unity of culture, the community illustrated by the Canterbury pilgrims, broken by abstraction, by Descartes' dream of a mathematical universe, and by the spinning jenny, modern physics, and technology. Brooks illustrates Yeats's concept of the rhetorician by Yeats's opinions about Bernard Shaw and discusses Yeats's attitude toward Oscar Wilde. Yeats characterized him implicitly as lacking in "true personality," as "artificial, abstract, fragmentary, and dramatic." But the dramatic is also Yeats's own concern. The poet must not be a mirror

---

86 Wimsatt and Brooks, *Literary Criticism*, 598, 599; Brooks and Warren, *Understanding Poetry* (1950), 20.
87 Brooks, *A Shaping Joy*, 102, 107. For the quotation from Yeats, see his *Mythologies* (London: Macmillan, 1958), 331.

but must meditate upon a mask. Brooks is very careful to define Yeats's rejection of both anarchic subjectivity and the naturalistic recoil from it. The poet for Yeats is a maker who "has been reborn as an idea, something intended, complete." Art is, despite Yeats's own self-dramatization, ultimately impersonal. Brooks concludes by quoting Yeats on the artist's "shaping joy" which "has kept the sorrow pure, as it had kept it were the emotion love or hate, for the nobleness of the arts is in the mingling of contraries."[88] *A Shaping Joy* serves as title for Brooks's recent collection of essays (1971). "The mingling of contraries" could be called the best definition of Brooks's own concept of poetry.

W. H. Auden deserves the same indulgence as Yeats for his opinions, though Auden spoke condescendingly of Yeats's superstitions. Auden's often whimsical views serve, as do Yeats's, as a commentary on the poetry. But Auden's criticism appeals to Brooks also for quite objective reasons. In a special essay, "W. H. Auden as a Literary Critic," Brooks describes and characterizes Auden's "zest for classification," his search for patterns of motifs when he discusses the master-servant relationship in literature, and his interest in symbolic clusters which can be regarded as a form of archetypal criticism. Brooks does not conceal some misgivings. "The Guilty Vicarage: Notes on the Detective Story, by an Addict" seems "Auden at his weakest and most absurd" and "at his most special, limited and eccentric."[89] Brooks admires the introduction to *A Selection from the Poems of Alfred Lord Tennyson* (1947). There Auden called Tennyson "the great poet of the Nursery" and compared him with Baudelaire. Baudelaire had a first-rate critical intelligence,

---

88 Brooks, *A Shaping Joy*, 124–25. For the quotation from Yeats, see his *Essays and Introductions* (New York: Macmillan, 1961), 255.
89 Brooks, *A Shaping Joy*, 133, 135. W. H. Auden's "The Guilty Vicarage" is in his *The Dyer's Hand* (New York: Random House, 1962).

but Tennyson was "a fool to try to write a poetry which would teach the Ideal." We have returned again to Brooks's central concern, the "error to make a religion of the aesthetic." Brooks shares Auden's view that art has only a limited role in history and quotes him to the effect that "if not a poem had been written, not a picture painted, not a bar of music composed, the history of man would be materially unchanged." Brooks seems even to agree with Auden's view that art is "in the profoundest sense frivolous"—frivolous apparently in the sense in which Sören Kierkegaard disparaged the aesthetic compared to the ethical and religious stage—and that art must not be misused as magic or prophecy. Brooks quotes Auden as saying that Shelley's claim that the poets are "the unacknowledged legislators of the world" is "the silliest remark ever made about poets." An endorsement of Auden's view would put Brooks into the opposite camp from that of I. A. Richards, who felt aggrieved when I argued against Shelley's grandiose phrase.[90] Auden is thus left with an aestheticism which, in an essay "Nature, History, and Poetry" (1950), he tried to rescue from frivolity or mere game playing by defining the subject matter of the poet as "a crowd of historic occasions of feeling in the past. . . . The poet accepts this crowd as real and attempts to transform it into a community." With this sociological terminology (it seems to derive from Ferdinand Tönnies' distinction between *Gesellschaft* and *Gemeinschaft*), Auden restates what Brooks usually formulated in the terminology of organic aesthetics. "Community" seems here another term for organism. The basic task of criticism, says Brooks, is "discovering whether the poem is truly unified or chaotic, whether it embodies order or is rent apart by disorder." The central poetic problem for both Brooks and Auden is "the problem of securing unity," which is inclusive in fitting the

90 Brooks, *A Shaping Joy,* 133, 135, 137. Cf. I. A. Richards, *So Much Nearer* (New York: Harcourt, Brace, 1968), 152, 179.

disparate and recalcitrant into the poem and exclusive in reject-
ing what cannot be fitted. Brooks is pleased that Auden—a
serious moralist with clear religious convictions—holds "what
amounts to a formalist conception of poetry" and states, "The
assumption that poetry must be either an escape from life or else
the blueprint for a better life is obviously oversimple."[91] Brooks
does not seem to notice the contradiction of Auden's view of a
fallen but redeemable world he had quoted before, of which the
poem provides an analogue. "Analogue" differs little from
blueprint: poetry, in Auden, does provide a plan for redemp-
tion.

Auden's difficulty runs through Brooks's criticism. Aristotle's
distinction between poetics and politics, ethics and metaphysics
links up with Auden's separation of Christian faith from
"frivolous" art. Brooks must sympathize with this view because
he distrusts the confusion of realms: the Arnoldian (and
Richardsian) view of poetry as ersatz for religion. But Brooks
cannot honestly accept the view that art is frivolous (though he
seems to do so in this essay, possibly with an undertone of
despair at the ineffectiveness of high art to provide a proper
discipline for the moral life). But actually, as all his writings
show, Brooks cannot surrender the claim that literature gives us
knowledge, "knowledge of a value-structured world." The ad-
jective goes beyond the claims for the truth of literature, for the
value of imitation, or for awareness of the world's concrete
particularity as formulated by Ransom. "Value-structured" im-
plies the task which Brooks ascribes to T. S. Eliot: "the restora-
tion of order," a recognition of an "intelligible world," an
"emblem of the kind of harmony that ought to obtain in wider
realms—in the just society and in the true community,"[92] or as
the passage about a "simulacrum of reality" quoted before says,

91 Brooks, *A Shaping Joy* , 138–40.
92 *Ibid.*, 11, 37, 51.

in more general terms, a world "rendered coherent through a perspective of valuing."[93] Though Brooks holds fast to the distinctions among poetry, politics, and religion, poetry is for him ultimately a way to truth, a way to religion. The charge of "formalism" falls flat. It would be correct only if formalism means simply a grasp of the aesthetic fact, an insight into the difference between art and statement, art and persuasion, art and propaganda. Brooks's analyses of poems show this amply. But they show also that he believes in a meaning of art which transcends hedonism, play, harmony, and joy. Poetry for Brooks is "a special kind of knowledge. Through poetry, man comes to know himself in relation to reality, and thus attains wisdom."[94] Brooks is defining the view of his favorite poet Yeats, but he could be speaking of his own.

93 Brooks, "Implications of an Organic Theory of Poetry," 51.
94 Wimsatt and Brooks, *Literary Criticism*, 601.

Monroe K. Spears Cleanth Brooks and the Responsibilities of Criticism

IN HIS LATEST BOOK *A Shaping Joy,* Brooks remarks that the New Criticism for most people "vaguely signifies an anti-historical bias and a fixation on 'close reading.' The New Critic would seem to be trapped in a cell without windows or door, staring through a reading glass at his literary text, effectually cut off from all the activities of the world outside—from history and science, from the other arts, and from nature and humanity itself" (*A Shaping Joy,* xi). In this caricature, the New Critic is responsible to no one and nothing except his own perverted obligation to be ingenious; oblivious of larger human concerns, he works his little rhetorical machine to discover—or produce—ambiguity, irony, paradox, and other such effects.

If Brooks as critic may be said to have a characteristic method, it is that of demonstrating that a formula or generalization is inadequate because it will not fit all the complex facts of the individual case. Applying this method to Brooks's own work, we observe immediately that his last three books, at least, are not limited to close reading, since one, *The Hidden God,* deals

230

explicitly with the religious implications of literature and the other two, *William Faulkner* and *A Shaping Joy*, are, in their different ways, richly historical. In the latter volume, he protests against being typed "as the rather myopic 'close reader', the indefatigable exegete," and affirms mildly, "In fact I am interested in a great many other things besides close reading" (*A Shaping Joy*, 231). It is not that Brooks has changed—"I am not conscious of any fundamental change in my critical principles and what follows is no palinode," he says—but that the stereotype that made him archetypal New Critic never did correspond to the facts. The "New Criticism" was from the beginning an unfortunate and misleading label; only insofar as it meant "the first really adequate criticism" did it ever make sense. (The phrase is W. J. Ong's; I have discussed it in *Dionysus and the City*, 197.) In *A Shaping Joy*, Brooks suggests "structural or formal" to designate his emphasis on the work rather than on the reader or the writer. These labels are unquestionably better than New Criticism, but have their own misleading associations: Brooks's "structuralism" has little in common with that of recent anthropologists and linguists, and his "formalism" is neither that of the Czech or Russian schools nor that Aristotelian version once copyrighted by the University of Chicago. At any rate, though Brooks continues to maintain that close reading is the critic's primary obligation, in these later books he deals more explicitly and at greater length with the other facets he is interested in.

Far from being the irresponsible aesthete or technician that his opponents have represented him as (in the polemics of literary journals and seminar rooms), Brooks is, I propose to argue, distinguished among critics precisely by his strong sense of responsibility. This is not his only distinction; aside from such obvious gifts as perceptiveness, imagination, and intelligence, his critical integrity, his sense of proportion, and his instinct for the centrally human are rare qualities indeed. But responsibility is primary.

To whom, as Brooks sees it, is the critic responsible? I suggest that, judging from his practice, we might put the priorities in this order of ascending importance: to his readers or other audience; to his authors, whether living or dead; and to whatever standards of truth he believes in. For Brooks, the kinds of truth invoked most often are those of fact, especially linguistic and historical, and of religion in the basic ontological sense of the awareness of human nature and experience as being complex, contradictory, and mysterious.

With respect to his audience (and both meanings of "respect" are appropriate), Brooks has always seemed to think of his criticism as simply an extension of his teaching, exactly the same in nature and purpose. All the pieces in *The Hidden God* and most of those in *A Shaping Joy* were originally lectures; they differ from those written first as essays only in having a slightly more open texture. It appears never to have occurred to him to think of his criticism as autotelic; assuming its role to be obviously ancillary to that of literature itself but nevertheless vitally important, he has been concerned chiefly with its practical effectiveness upon its audience—mostly students and teachers, with some general readers. Through collaborative textbooks and editing, as well as through reviewing, lecturing, and criticism proper, Brooks has devoted himself single-mindedly to the aim of improving this audience's understanding of literature and hence its powers of discrimination. Teaching is more conducive than most professions to vanity and petty tyranny; the analyst has his analyst, the preacher has his God, but the teacher has only his students to keep him humble, and students are not often in a position to be as effective as the other agencies mentioned. An excessive confidence in one's own righteousness is also one of the occupational hazards of criticism; from

Thomas Rymer down to F. R. Leavis, Yvor Winters, and (descending steeply) John Simon, there have been some critics who have seemed to writers to stare, "Tremendous! with a threatning Eye" like fierce tyrants in tapestry. In the face of these combined temptations, Brooks's modesty is conspicuous and unusual. The myth one sometimes encounters of him presiding with self-satisfaction over an age of criticism which he has helped to create could hardly be more remote from reality.

True collaboration—the kind that produces something different from what either collaborator could do separately—requires a difficult self-abnegation and openness. Few manage it successfully even once. But Brooks has collaborated brilliantly not only with Robert Penn Warren, in their great series of pioneering textbooks, but with numerous others; *Understanding Drama*, with R. B. Heilman, and *Literary Criticism*, with W. K. Wimsatt, may be singled out as especially impressive. In giving his time to these collaborative textbooks, Brooks has been willing to be almost anonymous in order to achieve his purpose. His work as editor of periodicals and various other books, his tireless lecturing and reviewing, and his service as U.S. cultural attaché in England (by common consent, I understand, the best one ever), all show the same self-effacing concern for the good health of the literary audience.

The personal qualities of courtesy and tact (in addition to modesty) are, I would suggest, what has enabled Brooks to establish the relation to his audience that has made him so effective as teacher-critic. Like W. H. Auden, another natural teacher, he has also the gift of simplification, of reducing complex problems to their essentials. This gift, together with Brooks's unpretentiousness, is probably responsible for the illusion encountered now and then that his kind of criticism is easy to practice. His devotion to literature is, in a sense, purer than Auden's; though Auden's mind is often willingly violated by ideas, Brooks always rigorously brings the reader back to the complexity of the literary work itself and leaves him confronting its inexhaustible richness. Let us return, however, from this tempting bypath to the quality of tact. In this context, tact means primarily knowing when to stop—a talent notoriously lacking in many of Brooks's imitators—but also being able to provide information and direction without condescending. Like courtesy (which, in this context, has the full, traditional, Christian meaning it has in Chaucer and Spenser and in more recent interpretations by such writers as Charles Williams and C. S. Lewis), tact is based on respect for other persons—for their dignity, integrity, and value. Whether these qualities are inborn or infused by grace, they require also an inner discipline. They are, obviously, humane qualities, the very opposite of the kind of bloodless formalism or mechanical ingenuity attributed to the New Critic by popular mythology.

The same personal qualities lie behind the second kind of responsibility demonstrated by Brooks, that toward his authors. Some critics do not hesitate to instruct their authors (living or dead) and show them the error of their ways. F. R. Leavis, for example, at his best excels in discriminating between the good and the less good; at his worst he seems to take special satisfaction in showing where authors went wrong and why their later careers were so much inferior to their early work (Henry James, T. S. Eliot, Auden). Brooks seems to feel that this would be presumptuous. The critic's function, as he sees it, is to improve the reader, not the author, though the aspiring author may well be also an educable reader. Thus Brooks usually begins his analysis with the tacit assumption that whatever the author has done is right; if it seems wrong, the probable fault is in the reader's understanding, which is enlightened and corrected through Brooks's patient analysis and interpretation. It is not that Brooks is uninterested in evaluation; if his hypothesis that the work is good will not stand up under analysis, he abandons it, and he can both demolish bad work with gusto and make fine discriminations between degrees and kinds of goodness. But his primary dedication is to helping the reader to understand as fully as possible why good literature is good.

If it is not part of the critic's responsibility to correct or guide his author, or to cut him down to size, then for what is the critic responsible to the author? He is responsible primarily, as Brooks sees it, for respecting the integrity of the author's works and defending them against violation and for reading these works in the right way and thus helping to provide him with the right kind of audience. John Crowe Ransom long ago remarked that Brooks was our best living "reader," and this distinction seems to be generally conceded even by opponents. The essential secret is to be found, I think, in his personal attitude. To revert to previous terms, this attitude may be described as exhibiting a kind of metaphysical tact. One feels that Brooks never claims to pluck out the heart of the mystery of art. He does his best to explain, and he is in no doubt about the legitimacy and importance of his enterprise; but the reader never feels that Brooks is inclined to set up his version as exclusive and complete truth or to substitute it for the original work. The poem, he always remembers, is more complex and more permanent than the critic; and life is larger and more mysterious than either. Hence Brooks always appeals finally to a standard beyond literature: truth to experience. His firm sense of limitations, of an order of priorities and significances, of man's creatureliness and mortality, is (I suppose) ultimately religious. In this respect, as in many others, Brooks stands in strong contrast to his only serious rival as "reader," F. R. Leavis. Leavis is like Brooks in seeing criticism as simply an extension of teaching, in feeling antipathy toward the dominant culture, and in advocating a humane critical discipline as remedy. But Leavis' rigid insistence on exclusive possession of the total truth, with consequent feelings of persecution and tendencies to the messianic, is utterly unlike Brooks's philosophy. Perhaps it is not without significance that Auden, Eliot, and Allen Tate, who share Brooks's freedom from such attitudes, have similar religious allegiances; the religious convictions appear to restrain any hubristic or dogmatic inclinations.

Insofar as "close reading" is a method, it has been well learned; reasonable competence in it seems fairly common. True excellence is, however, extremely rare. Brooks's academic epigones often seem like the sorcerer's apprentices; they know how to work the machine but do not fully understand it, so that finally the machine takes over. It was Brooks's distinction that he, not the machine, was always master. In adapting and synthesizing the theories of other critics for pedagogical purposes and reducing them to a practical method, he never forgot that the method was a dynamic one of balances and tensions between opposing qualities and that it had to be operated by a responsible human being. There is a similar contrast in style. Brooks's writing is always alive, sensitive, and lucid; he seeks no meretricious charms and maintains a proper decorum; but he is without a trace of the pomposity, oversolemnity, and excessive display of method that mar the writing of many of his imitators.

It is clear in retrospect that the "autonomy of the poem" was primarily a *machine de guerre*: a battering ram with which to shatter the excessive historical emphasis then prevailing. It is obvious enough that Brooks did not really mean to insulate the poem permanently from history and other contexts. But, insofar as it inculcates respect for the integrity of the literary work, the slogan is still useful and far from obsolete. It is amusing to see Brooks, in *A Shaping Joy*, having to reprove critics of James Joyce (who pride themselves on their sophistication and extreme modernity) for practicing old-fashioned biographical interpretation.

If there is one author for whose work the critic shows a special affinity and deep affection, and particularly if it seems to be a case of literary first love, then the critic is likely to feel a very powerful kind of responsibility to him. For Brooks, this first and best-loved poet, without much question, is William Butler Yeats. There are many other favorites. Eliot, Ransom, Auden, and, especially of late years, Joyce always produce a response of particular warmth. Warren obviously holds a very special place in Brooks's admirations and affections, and both his poems and his novels have been discussed with exceptional flair and conviction. Faulkner, too, has been increasingly a favorite; the book on him is a labor of love as well as intelligence. But I feel little hesitation in suggesting that, early and late, the greatest master of all has been Yeats.

Is it not true that the critic tries (consciously or not) to make himself into the ideal reader of this best-loved author? Perhaps this whole notion is mere romanticizing on my part, but it seems to me that it applies to Brooks and Yeats. Setting aside as irrelevant the uncorrupted but illiterate "The Fisherman" and the beauties whose ignorant ears are flattered in other poems, "A Prayer for My Daughter" gives what may be the best picture of Yeats's ideal reader. How does Brooks square with the picture? Well, he is, as we have seen, notably learned in courtesy and, in the Yeatsian sense, he thinks "opinions are accursed"; he is without intellectual hatred and has a "radical innocence" rooted in the interior discipline of custom and ceremony.

The title *A Shaping Joy* comes from an essay in which Yeats describes the joy the hands and the tongue of the artist feel in the exercise of his craft, while "with his eyes he enters upon a submissive, sorrowful contemplation of the great irremediable things." He continues, "That shaping joy has kept the sorrow pure, as it had kept it were the emotion love or hate, for the nobleness of the arts is in the mingling of contraries, the extremity of sorrow, the extremity of joy." Brooks's subtitle is *Studies in the Writer's Craft*, and the "mingling of contraries" to which Yeats refers is central to Brooks's conception of literature. The first essay, "The Uses of Literature," puts it briefly and explicitly. In answer to Randall Jarrell's complaint that the New Criticism made readers too self-conscious and his advice that they should instead read naturally, for pleasure, Brooks points out that most people don't know how to read, that intensity and effort are not opposed to pleasure, and that literature is concerned primarily not with pleasure but with a kind of knowledge.

In a time when many hanker after newer and fancier critical models, when textbooks are full of "relevant" propaganda against pollution and for minorities, of new journalism, science fiction, and rock and pop lyrics, it is salutary to come back to the integrity of Brooks's position, with its utter unconcern for fashion and the topical. He has kept faith, in Yeatsian terms, with "the Muses' sterner laws." Literature, he says, is "not generalizations about life, but dramatizations of concrete problems—not remedies designed to solve these problems but rather diagnoses in which the problems are defined and realized for what they are. A formula can be learned and applied, but the full, concrete, appropriate response to a situation can only be experienced. Literature is thus incurably concrete—not abstract" (*A Shaping Joy*, 6). Those who demand relevance—and hence ultimately demand that literature be propaganda—assume "that the themes of literature are generalizations to be affirmed rather than situations to be explored." But the knowledge to be gained from literature is self-knowledge and knowledge of the world conceived in human terms: that is, dramatically.

This discussion has taken us imperceptibly across the threshold of our third kind of responsibility, that to ultimate standards of truth. The qualities we have stressed so far are humane and personal: courtesy, tact, integrity, innocence (in the etymological sense). Brooks has also an eighteenth-century sense of human limitations and respect for tradition, as well as an old-fashioned reticence about himself that makes it a little embarrassing to spell out these personal attributes. Nevertheless, we must go so far as to designate him scholar and gentleman, a phrase hardly to be used nowadays without irony, but applying to Brooks so precisely that it cannot be avoided. Gentleness and mildness (sometimes deceptive) are conspicuous characteristics of the man, as is respect for his opponents even in vigorous controversy. While exposing the errors and pretensions of individual scholars, he has demonstrated his faith in scholarship by his own excellent practice, especially in his Faulkner book and his collaborative editions of Milton's early poems and the Percy letters.

As has often been pointed out, moral and religious assumptions were implicit in *Understanding Poetry* and *Understanding Fiction*, as well as in *Modern Poetry and the Tradition* and *The Well-Wrought Urn*: questions that seemed to be aesthetic or rhetorical turned out to be at bottom moral. It has also been observed that much of the history and other matters that were theoretically excluded from these books was in fact smuggled in and taken account of, at least tacitly. But what was handed out under the counter was not (as some said) crypto-fascism, snobbery, or other vicious doctrine, but a traditional respect for facts (especially linguistic and historical) and for the complexity of human nature and experience, as against simplifiers of all varieties. Brooks's most frequent critical "strategy," as we noted earlier, is that of showing that a stereotyped or partial response to the literary work is inadequate. It is true that the implications go beyond literature; when the reader is shown that simple and abstract interpretations do not do justice to the literary work, he is likely to be suspicious of simplistic and abstract explanations of human experience in other realms—in politics or religion, for example. But Brooks's concern is with the nature of truth, and his conviction is that truth—at least that most important kind with which literature deals—is never simple or easy and that to learn the truth about himself and his world is man's basic need. Human experience is seen as complex and contradictory, involving the recognition of evil and hence of duality (indicated by such rhetorical devices as ambiguity, irony, and paradox); the point of view is not explicitly or specifically religious, but grounded in the tradition of Christian humanism. Man is seen as weak and limited, guided by inherited patterns and by instinct and emotion far more than by reason. Truth is seen as real and absolute, though forever exceeding the comprehension of the individual, and as multiform and perceived by other faculties as well as by reason. This credo is not set forth positively, but becomes apparent by implication as the converse is held up for doubtful scrutiny: that man is naturally good and rational, perfectible and progressing, needing only such external aids as political and social planning can provide to remove the evil that comes entirely from outside himself; and that man is completely in charge of his own destiny. Brooks is not, however, concerned with the writer's beliefs or philosophy as such, but rather with the nature of the world he presents, and not with what the poem says, but with what it is. Nevertheless, such qualities as wit, ambiguity, irony, paradox, complexity, and tension are valued for more than aesthetic reasons; they are indexes to the view of reality—of man and truth—in the work. They are, therefore, not really aesthetic or rhetorical but, since they are modes of apprehending reality, ontological or, in the broad sense, religious. If students now seem less impressed than they used to be by the goal of maturity of insight as opposed to sentimentality, this may reveal more about the students than about the doctrine.

The notion of Brooks as pure aesthete has never been plausible to anyone with even a slight acquaintance with his career. His profound respect for and deep concern with history, especially in its relation to literature, are increasingly apparent in the third edition of *Understanding Poetry*, in *William Faulkner*, and in *A Shaping Joy*; he has also practiced the more "scientific" varieties of literary scholarship in his early linguistic treatise (to be discussed shortly) and in his editing, still in progress, of the Percy letters. But he has always insisted on a firm distinction between the literary work considered as art and its use as historical document, case history, sermon, or sociological or moral tract.

Important among the third category of critical responsibilities—fundamental, in fact—is the English language itself. This Brooks seems to think of as a tradition in the literal sense, a heritage passed into his stewardship to be cherished and improved if possible (if not, preserved) and handed on to succeeding generations. This attitude is the opposite of the apocalyptic one now so fashionable; Brooks is, in this respect as in others, concerned not only with the present, but with the past and future; and his sense of the present is thereby greatly enriched. His attitude toward the language is similar to Eliot's, for which the *locus classicus* is the famous passage in "Little Gidding" in which the "dead master," echoing Stéphane Mallarmé, states the poet's function as "to purify the dialect of the tribe." A more recent parallel is the letter of the Russian poet Iosif Brodsky asking for readmission to the Soviet Union: "Language is a thing far older and more inescapable than the state. I belong to the Russian language. As regards the state, the measure of a writer's patriotism is not, I think, a loyalty oath pronounced upon some high public platform, but the way in which he writes the language of the people among whom he lives" (Quoted by Heinrich Böll in *Intellectual Digest* [May, 1973], 65). The notion of the critic as owing a similar allegiance to the language itself, and as helping the author and the reader to keep faith with it, is fundamental to Brooks's criticism.

Brooks's concern with language was shown early in his one linguistic publication, *The Relation of the Alabama-Georgia Dialect to the Provincial Dialects of Great Britain* (1935). This treatise has recently enjoyed a curious revival, figuring as one of the *bêtes noires* in J. L. Dillard's important book, *Black English*. (Brooks thus reappears as culture villain, a role he used often to play when the New Criticism was being attacked. Perhaps it is his clarity and definiteness that make one so inoffensive a tempting target.) Brooks holds, to put it very briefly, that both black and white English are the same in the dialect he is studying and derive from the provincial dialects of southwestern England. Dillard attacks him for failing to recognize the uniqueness of black English and its true derivation from Africa and, by implication, for racial prejudice. Actually, Brooks is admirably scientific in this study, very clear about his sources and methods. Insofar as any motive is apparent, it would seem to be to remove the southerners' sense of inferiority about their language by showing that it is not a corrupt or slovenly version of standard English, but derives from older or regional forms that are equally legitimate. Presumably he saw the conclusion that black and white speech are identical as favorable to black self-respect; in any case, it was decreed by his sources. There are additional sources for Dillard to use, and Brooks's work may now be partly superseded; but it is not racism that prevents him from anticipating Dillard's thesis that the black forms derive from Africa and the white from the black. At any rate, the treatise is evidence of Brooks's deep interest in language and his technical competence (within self-imposed limits) in linguistic study.

In *A Shaping Joy* Brooks stresses the fundamental importance of language. He draws an audacious parallel between James Joyce's use of cliché in the Nausicaa episode of *Ulysses* and Adolf Eichmann's banality (as observed by Hannah Arendt); in both cases, debasement of language makes possible dehumanization. "When the very means for registering value are as coarsened and corrupted as Gerty's, how can one hope for honesty, decency, charity, or any of the other virtues on which any healthy civilization is founded?" Brooks asks (*A Shaping Joy*, 14). And he suggests that Joyce's parody may be therapeutic: "to peel off the dead skin and callosities from the language—even if this seems to be done simply for the fun in it—is not merely to remove dead tissue. It could mean exposing once more the living fibres of the imagination so that men might once again see who they are and where they are." For the Nazis, evil became banal: "People who are sensitive and fully aware of what they are doing and whose responses to the world about them, including their responses to other human beings, are fresh and individual, are simply incapable of this kind of wickedness" (*A Shaping Joy*, 15). The death of language, he argues, is a serious matter indeed. "One of the uses of literature is to keep our language alive—to keep the blood circulating through the tissues of the body politic. There can scarcely be a more vital function"(*A Shaping Joy*, 16). Discussing Eliot, he remarks that "a poetry that can deal with the clutter of language in an age of advertising and propaganda restores to that degree the health of language"(*A Shaping Joy*, 50). Brooks's most extensive treatment of this theme, however, is in the essay "Telling It Like It Is in the Tower of Babel" (*Sewanee Review*, LXXIX [Winter, 1971], 136–55). Ours is a time, he says, "in which language is systematically manipulated by politicians, advertisers, and publicity men as it has probably never before been manipulated. I am concerned with what is happening to our language. But I am, of course, even more deeply concerned with what is happening to ourselves. The two concerns cannot, in fact, be separated. If you debauch a language, you run a grave risk of debauching the minds of the people who use it." Ranging widely over contemporary examples, from the verbal smog poured over us by the media to the religious press, Brooks comments: "Language is important, and debased and corrupted language accounts for the currently lamented failure in communication. More even than that—for the failure in self-knowledge. We shall have difficulty in identifying our true selves if we lack the language of meditation and self-analysis."

But let us return to *A Shaping Joy* for additional examples of the importance of language and of fact in Brooks's criticism. As Brooks recurrently distinguishes close reading from its perversion, symbol-mongering, it becomes clear that irresponsibility with regard to language and fact is one of the distinguishing characteristics of the latter. Thus he observes that blind trust in even so great an author as Faulkner is misplaced and shows that Faulkner misuses the word *equinox* in one passage. Symbol-mongering "magnifies details quite irresponsibly; it feverishly prospects for possible symbolic meanings and then forces them beyond the needs of the story" (*A Shaping Joy*, 144). Courteously but firmly, Brooks demonstrates the foolishness of some such readings. The view of André Gide, Jean-Paul Sartre, and others that "Faulkner's characters make no decisions at all and are merely driven and determined creatures" Brooks characterizes as "nonsensical," the result of not reading closely enough. In fact, as he shows, though Faulkner does not often dramatize "the agony of choice—the process by which the character actually arrives at his decision"—he does dramatize the character's "sustaining of a choice," as when Bayard, in "An Odor of Verbena," maintains his decision against every pressure. Brooks's analysis of Joyce's "Clay" is especially helpful because the story has been a favorite of symbol-mongers who have nevertheless often missed the point, not through reading too closely, but through not reading closely enough or with enough responsibility to the integrity—the total meaning—of the story. It is the "ruthlessness" of the dedicated symbol-monger that Brooks finds horrifying: his determination, for instance, to find significance in Maria's name or in her witchlike profile, though unable to show how such significance would contribute to the total meaning of the story. Brooks himself reads the story in basic human terms, stressing the pathos of Maria's situation (though it is presented unsentimentally) and refusing to be drawn into speculation about the significance of every detail.

Brooks's discussion of *Ulysses* provides the same contrast between symbol-mongering and close reading that is informed by his kinds of responsibility. He agrees with the general thesis of R. M. Adams (in *Surface and Symbol*) that "some parts of *Ulysses* are merely surface and have no symbolic reference" (*A Shaping Joy*, 68). But Brooks proceeds to show, with courtesy, that Adams has failed to see many symbolic patterns that are really there. He finds, characteristically, that part of the trouble is linguistic, part is religious, and part is characterological or dramatic: in all these areas, previous critics have not known enough (about *dogsbody*, for instance) and have failed to see the intricate patterns that Brooks is able to clarify. With erudition controlled by tact and his usual instinct for centrality, Brooks elucidates the way the dog symbolism expresses the central meaning of the book. Reading closely, he argues against many a facile symbol-monger that Bloom and Stephen do not communicate. "To argue that since an atonement is desirable it must occur takes the intent for the deed. In fact, it does more: it makes an assumption about the author's intent that cannot be supported by the author's text"(*A Shaping Joy*, 83). And Brooks concludes that even though *Ulysses* is, as Adams has shown, many other things, it is still primarily a novel. It is refreshing to see him insist, quite properly, that Joycean interpreters, who think of themselves as the very tip of the avant-garde, really must not commit the nineteenth-century error of interpreting the novel in terms of the author's biography.

How does Brooks relate literature to religion? Though his position is clearly that of orthodox Christianity, he is scrupulous not to suggest that Christian writers are likely to be better than the unblessed. As in so many other matters, he takes his basic text from Yeats in this case: the necessity of the vision of evil to the poet. Yeats was "no utopian activist" and "expressed rather caustically his lack of belief in progress, which he called the sole religious myth of modern man"(*A Shaping Joy*, 100). Brooks observes that "up to our time at least all great poetry reflects a mixed world, a world of good and evil, and that the good which it celebrates can be seen full perspective only by means of the shadows that the good itself casts. Though as decent men we are committed to try as hard as we can to make this a better world, some of us are disposed to think that the struggle with evil, in one form or another, is probably destined to go on for a very long time" (*A Shaping Joy*, 100). The basic attitude is that made familiar to us by Eliot and T. E. Hulme (and J. H. Newman and Baudelaire before them); but it is very much Brooks's own. He is especially good on Milton, remarkable among critics in keeping his humane central focus, without wandering off into history of ideas or amateur theology on the one side or purely aesthetic analysis on the other. He is as unaffected by Eliot's hostility to Milton's verse and personality as by William Empson's hostility to Milton's God. Interpreting the Fall in *Paradise Lost*, Brooks is much less interested in playing with theological paradoxes of the *culpa felix* than in working out in human and dramatic terms the consequences: these are unpleasant and very real, however hard prelapsarian life may be to imagine. What Brooks stresses is the fact that evil is not just a concept to be glibly manipulated by theologians, but a dreadful and ugly reality, and that its entrance into human life (in Milton's archetypal situation) is tragic. The modern reader is too ready to assume "that Milton as a renaissance humanist couldn't really have believed that Adam could have been happy to continue in paradise, that Adam's moral development required his sowing his wild oats, and that Milton was really on Lucifer's side unconsciously if not consciously. The real remedy for these misconceptions is to read the poem itself" (*A Shaping Joy*, 365).

Brooks is also especially good on Marlowe's *Dr. Faustus*. He compares it to Eliot's *Murder in the Cathedral* and Milton's *Samson Agonistes*; in all three, the question is whether the middle functions viably to unite the beginning and the end—a question primarily aesthetic but also religious. The essay is too complex for summary (brief but illuminating comparisons are made also to *The Countess Cathleen*, *The Hamlet*, and *Heart of Darkness*); the conclusion is that *Faustus* does constitute a unity and that its protagonist, though fallen and damned, retains admirable qualities: "Faustus at the end is still a man, not a cringing wretch. The poetry saves him from abjectness. If he wishes to escape from himself, to be changed into little water drops, to be swallowed up in the great ocean of being, he maintains to the end . . . his individuality of mind, the special quality of the restless spirit that aspired. This retention of his individuality is at once his glory and his damnation" (*A Shaping Joy*, 380). He remains similarly humane and undogmatic in discussing so mundane a topic as the southern temper, though the religious implications are clear. With Peter Taylor's "Miss Leonora When Last Seen" as principal text, he concludes that the southern writer "respects a mystery lying at the heart of things, a mystery that at some level always evades the rational explanation, a reality that can be counted on to unpredict prediction. . . . He finds human beings wonderful in their courage and generosity, but also wonderful in their 'orneriness' and folly. He is continually fascinated by the teasing mixture of elements that is man" (*A Shaping Joy*, 214).

The Hidden God is Brooks's most extended discussion of the religious significance of literature. Of the five writers considered, only one, Eliot, is explicitly Christian; on the other hand, he and all the others except Ernest Hemingway (Yeats, Faulkner, and Warren) are among those we listed earlier as special favorites of Brooks's. Clearly, then, Brooks chose for discussion (as, indeed, his title suggests) not writers who profess adherence to Christian doctrine, but writers who are among our greatest and with whom he feels a special affinity. He begins his lecture on Faulkner by disagreeing with a critic who calls the writer "profoundly Christian" and by terming him rather "profoundly religious"; Faulkner is Christian only in the sense "that his characters come out of a Christian environment, and represent, whatever their shortcomings and whatever their theological heresies, Christian concerns; and that they are finally to be understood only by reference to the Christian premises" (*The Hidden God*, 22–23). Faulkner's criticism of secularism and rationalism is considered through his treatment of the theme of discovery of evil as initiation into the nature of reality. "That brilliant and horrifying early novel *Sanctuary* is, it seems to me, to be understood primarily in terms of such an initiation. Horace Benbow is the sentimental idealist, the man of academic temper, who finds out that the world is not a place of moral tidiness or even of justice. He discovers with increasing horror that evil is rooted in the very nature of things" (*The Hidden God*, 25). It is not the sensational corncob rape or the murder that most disturb him. "What crumples him up is the moral corruption of the girl, which follows on her rape: she actually accepts her life in the brothel and testifies at the trial in favor of the man who had abducted her. What Horace also discovers is that the forces of law and order are also corruptible." And Brooks sums up Faulkner's attitude thus:

Man is capable of evil, and this means that goodness has to be achieved by struggle and discipline and effort. Like T. S. Eliot, Faulkner has small faith in social arrangements so perfectly organized that nobody has to take the trouble to be good. Finally Faulkner's noblest characters are willing to face the fact that most men can learn the deepest truths about themselves and about reality only through suffering. Hurt and pain and loss are not mere accidents to which the human being is subject; nor are they mere punishments incurred by human error; they can be the means to the deeper knowledge and to the more abundant life. (*The Hidden God*, 43)

If asked which is his best single book, I should vote (not without hesitation, since each book attempts something quite different from the others, and all of them will endure) for the *William Faulkner* as exhibiting most fully all of Brooks's mature virtues and as being most helpful to the greatest number and variety of readers. Brooks has here quietly and unobtrusively managed to do what others have debated endlessly about: bring about a happy marriage of the historical with the aesthetic approach. He knows the life Faulkner writes about intimately, but he buttresses his personal impressions by meticulous scholarship. Similarly, he uses the writings of psychiatrists to check his own interpretations of Faulkner's more peculiar characters (Vardaman, Addie, Benjy, for instance). He finds Faulkner, as man and artist, extremely sympathetic; but Brooks maintains a firm distinction between the man and the artist, and he manages never to use either as stalking-horse for his own opinions. The book is a marvel of conciseness and imaginative tact—both a handbook to Faulkner and the most profound and comprehensive interpretation.

What is immediately impressive is the precision and

thoroughness of his reading; again and again he corrects the errors, distortions, or partial interpretations of other critics, though with his usual courtesy he relegates most of these corrections to the notes. In discussing *Light in August*, for example, he shows how inaccurate it is to say, as many commentators do, that Joe Christmas is lynched. The point is important because it distorts the role of the community (which Brooks properly emphasizes in this novel as throughout Faulkner) and relates to that favorite theme of the symbol-mongers, Joe as Christ symbol—a theme which Brooks finds of little interest or significance. Brooks is in general vastly better than anyone else on Faulkner's treatment of religion, his attitude toward nature, and his representation of the Negroes—all vitally important to *Light in August*.

His discussion of *The Sound and the Fury* is notable because, instead of focusing on the matter of technique, as he would if he were a stereotypical New Critic, Brooks stresses the different conceptions of love implied by the four sections and the different kinds of time as related to them. "Benjy's idiocy and Quentin's quixotic madness are finally less inhuman than Jason's sanity. To be truly human one must transcend one's mere intellect with some overflow of generosity and love" (*William Faulkner*, 338). "Benjy represents love in its most simple and childlike form. . . . Quentin is really, as his sister knows, in love with death itself. In contrast with this incestuously Platonic lover, Jason has no love for Caddy at all, and no love for anyone else" (*William Faulkner*, 327). In contrast to the popular reading of this novel and others as quasi-allegorical—a legend of the South—Brooks reads it in basic human terms: "The basic cause of the breakup of the Compson family—let the more general cultural causes be what they may—is the cold and self-centered mother who is sensitive about the social status of her own family . . . who feels the birth of an idiot son as a kind of personal affront, who spoils and corrupts her favorite son, and who withholds any real love and affection from her other children and her husband" (*William Faulkner,* 334). As this quotation suggests, Brooks's explanations are often psychological, in a sensible and undogmatic way, and he buttresses them by citing psychologists from Carl Jung to Rollo May. Whether one calls it psychological or dramatic or merely humane, his approach makes more sense than any other, finally, of the technique too, but the technique comes last. Sociologizing and symbol-mongering are different ways, Brooks says in his first chapter, of "evading the central critical task: to determine and evaluate the meaning of the work in the fullness of its depth and amplitude." It is a task that Brooks does not evade, but carries through magnificently.

In discussing *Absalom, Absalom!*—which he considers the greatest of all the novels—Brooks focuses on the theme of innocence: Sutpen's tragic innocence about the nature of reality. This is not shared by the community, but is "peculiarly the innocence of modern man," rationalistic, cut off from the past, believing that hard work and planning can accomplish anything. "The only people in Faulkner who are 'innocent' are adult males; and their innocence amounts finally to a trust in rationality—an overweening confidence that plans work out, that life is simpler than it is" (*William Faulkner,* 308). In one of the most brilliant essays in *A Shaping Joy,* Brooks compares Faulkner's treatment of American innocence in this novel with those of Henry James in *The American* and F. Scott Fitzgerald in *The Great Gatsby* (Chap. 11).

Brooks understands Faulkner's appreciation of the homely mule, as well as the chivalric horse, and of the virtues associated with each; he understands the nature and dominance of southern puritanism as against the cavalier myth and the importance of the plain folk or yeomen as against either planters or white trash. One feels, in fact, that he understands almost everything about Faulkner and that much of the time he is the first critic to do so. But I must include his masterly characterization of Faulkner's world: "Its very disorders are eloquent of the possibilities of order: Joe Christmas's alienation points to the necessity for a true community, and the author's dramatically sympathetic delineation of Joe's plight may be said to point to the possibility of that true community. It is difficult to think of an author whose basic assumptions are farther from the currently fashionable world of the absurd. For Faulkner's work speaks ultimately of the possibilities and capacities of the human spirit for finding and embodying meaning" (*William Faulkner*, 368).

To conclude, let me repeat my paradigm of the critic's responsibilities as I think Brooks sees them; or, to put it another way, let me describe Brooks's work as a model of responsible criticism. First, he is responsible to the reader for treating him tactfully and courteously. But, since Brooks takes him seriously as a human being, he also treats him with a certain rigor and strictness: he insists that the reader confront *all* of the literary work and will not allow any evasion or easy out. He enforces the Muses' sterner laws after he has made these ladies as seductive as possible. Second, he takes his authors as serious artists and respects the complexity and integrity of their works. Moreover, he responds to these works not only through "the fascination of what's difficult," but as a human being, with love. (As Auden once remarked, love is another name for intensity of attention.) Finally, his criticism respects language and historical fact, elucidating them and preserving them against distortion, and it deals responsibly with the full complexity of human nature and experience as they are manifest in the work of art. Political, moral, and religious issues are recognized and explored; but no abstraction or simplification is allowed to be a shortcut or escape route from the contemplation of the whole work. Brooks's criticism embodies a high, noble, and strenuous view of art and of human nature. It will remain useful and inspiring (to use a word that might make Brooks wince) for a very long time.

Notes on Contributors

CLEANTH BROOKS, the distinguished subject of this book and a contributor to it through his conversation with Robert Penn Warren, is Gray Professor of Rhetoric Emeritus, Yale University. He has held many posts, among them that of cultural attaché to the American embassy in London (1964–1966).

ROBERT B. HEILMAN, Professor of English at the University of Washington, served as chairman of his department from 1948 to 1971. He has written a number of well-known studies of the drama, including *This Great Stage: Image and Structure in King Lear* and *Tragedy and Melodrama: Versions of Experience.*

WALTER J. ONG, S.J., is Professor of English and Professor of Humanities in Psychiatry at St. Louis University and in 1973–1974 was a Fellow at the Center for Advanced Study in the Behavioral Sciences in Stanford, California. His books include *The Presence of the Word*, now translated into several languages, *In the Human Grain*, and *Rhetoric, Romance, and Technology.*

LEWIS P. SIMPSON is William A. Read Professor of English Literature and coeditor of the *Southern Review* at Louisiana State University, Baton Rouge. He has written *The Man of Letters in New England and the South* and *The Dispossessed Garden: Pastoral and History in Southern Literature.*

MONROE K. SPEARS is Libbie Shearn Moody Professor of English at Rice University. Editor of the *Sewanee Review* from 1952 to 1961, he is the author of *The Poetry of W. H. Auden: The Disenchanted Island* and *Dionysus and the City: Modernism in Twentieth-Century Poetry*. His *The Levitator and Other Poems* appeared in 1975.

ALLEN TATE, poet, critic, and novelist, is Regents' Professor Emeritus, University of Minnesota. His *Memoirs and Opinions* was published in 1975. *The Swimmers and Other Selected Poems* appeared in 1970 and his *Essays of Four Decades* in 1969.

ROBERT PENN WARREN, novelist, poet, critic, and historian, has received the Pulitzer Prize for both fiction and poetry. His *Democracy and Poetry* appeared in 1975.

RENÉ WELLEK is Sterling Professor of Comparative Literature Emeritus, Yale University. He is the author of *The Rise of English Literary History*, *Theory of Literature* (with Austin Warren), and the monumental *History of Modern Criticism*.

THOMAS DANIEL YOUNG, Gertrude Conway Vanderbilt Professor of English, Vanderbilt University, is the editor of *John Crowe Ransom: Critical Essays and a Bibliography* and the author of a forthcoming biography of Ransom.